At-Tuwani
Journal

Christian Peacemaker Teams Titles

At-Tuwani Journal

Hope & Nonviolent Action in a Palestinian Village

[signature]

ARTHUR G. GISH

Foreword by Mike Daly

Herald Press
Scottdale, Pennsylvania
Waterloo, Ontario

Library of Congress Cataloging-in-Publication Data

Gish, Arthur G., 1939-
    At-Tuwani journal : hope and nonviolent action in a
Palestinian village / by Arthur G. Gish.
        p. cm.
    Includes bibliographical references.
    ISBN 978-0-8361-9406-7 (pbk. : alk. paper)
    1. Palestinian Arabs—West Bank—At-Tuwani—Social condi-
tions. 2. Arab-Israeli conflict—1993—West Bank—At-Tuwani—
Influence. 3. Christian Peacemaker Teams. 4. Gish, Arthur G.,
1939- I. Title.
    DS113.7.G57 2008
    956.95'1—dc22
                                                    2008023776

AT-TUWANI JOURNAL
Copyright © 2008 by Herald Press, Scottdale, Pa. 15683
    Released simultaneously in Canada by Herald Press,
    Waterloo, Ont. N2L 6H7. All rights reserved
International Standard Book Number: 978-0-8361-9406-7
Library of Congress Catalog Card Number: 2008023776
Printed in the United States of America
Cover photo: Susiya woman near At-Tuwani; cover and inside
photos provided by the author
Cover design by Cathleen Benberg

14 13 12 11 10 09 08   10 9 8 7 6 5 4 3 2 1

To order or request information please call 1-800-245-7894 or
visit www.heraldpress.com.

In memory of my parents, Paul and Ruth Gish, who feared for me, but prayed for me every day

Contents

The ultimate weakness of violence is that it is a descending spiral, begetting the very thing it seeks to destroy. Instead of diminishing evil, it multiplies it.

Through violence you may murder the liar, but we cannot murder the lie, nor establish the truth.

Through violence you murder the hater, but you do not murder hate. In fact, violence merely increases hate.

Returning violence for violence multiplies violence, adding deeper darkness to a night already devoid of stars.

Darkness cannot drive out darkness; only light can do that. Hate cannot drive out hate; only love can do that.

—Martin Luther King Jr.

Foreword

In this book Art Gish provides an important snapshot of life in and around the South Hebron hills over the last few years. His account exposes the detail of everyday life in a Palestinian culture under attack from all sides while also revealing the larger polices and issues that structure this reality. The author knows his subject well—his reflections and observations come from many years of on-the-ground experience of "getting in the way" and wrestling with his role as an international interested in helping to foster peace with justice in Israel/Palestine.

Art's experience as a witness for peace is one that I share; many of his experiences remind me of my own in Israel/Palestine and help to frame the work that I and many others are doing to build movements for peace and justice in North America. I work with Christian Peacemaker Teams (CPT) and introduce many North Americans to their work through delegations that Interfaith Peace-Builders sends to the region. I offer a few comments in the hope that they'll encourage you to keep turning these pages, to consider the realities that Art discovered in At-Tuwani, and to open yourself to the stories of the individuals and communities that Art encountered in the many months from 2004 to 2008.

In the summer of 2000 I moved to the West Bank to begin a new job in Ramallah. Weeks after my arrival, a routine staff meeting was interrupted by one of the first large "clashes" between rock-throwing Palestinians and the fully-equipped Israeli army in what would become the second, or *Al Aqsa*, intifada. Then Israeli opposition leader Ariel Sharon had made a provocative visit to the holiest Muslim site in Jerusalem, the *Haram As-Sharif*, and

demonstrations and protests soon spread throughout the West
Bank and Gaza. In the coming days, Palestinian demonstrators
and rock throwers were met with overpowering—and very often
lethal—Israeli force.

At this time, in the tea room of Jerusalem's Faisal Hostel, I
first learned of the important and courageous work of CPT. As we
all tried to make sense of the beginnings of the intifada and the situation around us, internationals would gather in the hostel and
tell stories of things seen and witnessed—of conflict, of demonstrations, of checkpoint abuse, of bus bombings, army incursions,
and settler violence. CPT members and volunteers often passed
through Jerusalem and the Faisal on their way to other parts of
the West Bank or for a few days' break. In conversations with
them, I learned of CPT's mission, history, and current work in
Hebron and beyond during those first months of the intifada.
Reading this book reminded me of our community in Jerusalem
in 2000 and sharing of everyday experiences in a sort of continuing education for one another.

Employing the same informal style of daily chronicles inter-
spersed with more personal reflections, Art's account here of the
realities in the South Hebron hills during this critical period
addresses the larger issues of the nature of the Israeli occupation,
the very real threats facing Palestinians and traditional Palestinian culture, the role of internationals in advocating justice, and
the prospects for reconciliation. As such, it should find a wide
audience among those committed to learning more about
Israel/Palestine and those interested in working for peace with
justice in the Middle East.

As you'll find within, all facets of daily life for Palestinians in
the South Hebron hills revolve around the occupation. Many of
Art's stories challenge our preconceptions of the Israeli/Palestinian
conflict. Indeed the reality that Art discovers in and around At-
Tuwani may be so far removed from mainstream coverage of the
conflict that the reader has trouble at first believing documenta-
tion of abuse piled upon abuse. All the more important to read on.

Israeli settlers, already living on Palestinian villagers' land, attack and intimidate Palestinian school children. Roads are closed to Palestinians, but not Israelis; areas are declared closed military zones. Informal agreements delimiting which part of *their own* land Palestinian farmers may tend require coordination with the Israeli army and settlers.

Even amid the violent abuse, *At-Tuwani Journal* reveals the warm and welcoming culture of Palestinian society in At-Tuwani and beyond. Invited to mosque services, called over for cups of tea by shepherds, and playing with the school children, Art is over-whelmed with the hospitality, generosity, and openness of the Palestinians among whom he and other CPT members are living. These stories—of a Muslim Palestinian welcoming a U.S. citizen, of a feminist woman in a traditional village—not only challenge our preconceived notions of Palestinians, but also of Arabs and Muslims in general.

As we read on, Art confronts larger issues that are impor-tant for North Americans to grasp if we are to understand the conflict. The challenges that Palestinians face in the Hebron area are part and parcel of a long-term drive to cleanse the land of indigenous Palestinians. The separation of communities along Jewish and non-Jewish lines parallels many facets of apartheid. Debates and discussions around these issues often are rare, and sometimes even silenced in the United States, but for those living in Israel/Palestine they are unavoidable and common. In many ways, this book opens a window for North American audiences to understand what are often seen as taboo analogies here.

Ultimately, Art works for, and genuinely seeks, reconcilia-tion between Palestinians and Israelis. He relays stories that show—despite the many abuses he witnesses—that he is com-mitted to finding and drawing out the shared humanity of every-one he meets, soldier, settler, or shepherd, Israeli or Palestinian. In journal entries spanning several years, Art attempts to engage in real and meaningful conversation with one of the most extreme Israeli settlers near At-Tuwani. Direct action and the commitment to nonviolence that the villagers engage in even begin to bear fruit; soldiers sometimes seem to begin to *hear* villagers they've previously not even feigned listening to.

Art challenges himself, and by extension, us, to "build the answer," to build on the courageous work of Palestinians and Israelis who fight injustice, organize nonviolently, and envision a better future for all people in the Middle East. He encourages and inspires us to transcend religious differences, to look for the humanity in all, to support the work of local Israeli and Palestinian organizers, and to educate others in North America.

This last point is most important for all of us as we move forward to create and strengthen networks of peace and justice in our home communities. Near the end of the book, Art suggests that his work in the United States to educate others about Israel/Palestine and inspire action for peace may be more important than his work on the ground in At-Tuwani. I agree. This too is the work of Interfaith Peace-Builders: send ordinary people to Israel/Palestine to get a glimpse of the realities, and then give them the skills and support for their efforts at media advocacy, public speaking, and engagement with elected officials. Being open to firsthand experience, whether we're able to travel ourselves or whether we glean it from courageous activists and writers like Art Gish, is the first step. Making a commitment to share this information with others, to organize for change using our skills and contacts, and to lift up the voices of Israeli and Palestinian peacemakers is the next step. The stories and reflections you'll find here should make clear the urgency of our task.

Mike Daly
Program Coordinator
Interfaith Peace-Builders
August 2008

Acknowledgments

This book obviously was not written alone. Every page, every line is dependent on the contribution of others. I immediately think of my CPT teammates who daily inspire, inform, and correct me, and also members of Operation Dove whom I have learned to love and respect as I worked with them in At-Tuwani. Without the inspiration of my teammates, I would have little to contribute. Each of my teammates has many important stories of their own not included in this book. Some may interpret events differently than I do.

A special thank you to John Lynes for making the map of the South Hebron Hills.

I think of those who have gone before me: my parents and grandparents, my teachers, church leaders who inspired me, innumerable people who took the time to support and encourage me over the years since my childhood.

My wife, Peggy, has been a constant support. Although we are often separated because of our CPT work, we share a common commitment to stand both with the oppressed and the oppressors, and struggle for a new spirit of justice and love.

Many people have taken time to read various editions of this manuscript. Their criticisms and suggestions have been invaluable. I thank Peggy, Chabella Graziani, Jonathan Maffay, Matt Chandler, Ivars Balkits, Diana Zimmerman, Levi Miller, Rich Meyer, Michelle Ajamian, Trisha Lachman, Sally Hunsberger, John Funk, Hafez Hereni, Neil Bernstein, and James Odom. Any flaws in this final manuscript are my responsibility.

I deeply value my relationships with the people of Palestine/

Israel, the Israeli activists who put their vision for peace above narrow nationalistic interests, the Palestinians who have not given up, and for my special relationship with the people of At-Tuwani, the South Hebron Hills, and Hebron. A special thank you to the Adara family, who have taken me in as one of their own, especially Kiefah and Nasser. I also have a special place in my heart for the Israeli settlers and soldiers with whom I have had such an intense relationship.

Finally, my thanks to the One we call God, Adonai, or Allah, that ultimate reality that sustains all that is.

Author's Preface

After centuries of trial and error, the evidence is clear: violent armed intervention in conflicts does not solve problems. War is not the answer. Is there, however, a better answer? Can nonviolent action make a difference? We in Christian Peacemaker Teams (CPT) believe the answer is yes. CPT is an experiment, a test of whether it is possible to send teams of people, trained in nonviolence, into violent situations and make a difference. We believe our presence in Haiti, Chiapas, Mexico, Colombia, Iraq, Israel/Palestine and our presence in Native American communities in North America has reduced the violence in those communities. Our presence on the volatile border between Arizona and Mexico raised the issue of the deaths of so many people seeking economic survival.

The roots of CPT are in the Peace Churches, the Quakers, the Mennonites, and the Church of the Brethren. These churches have always rejected the use of violence and taught that Jesus showed a better way to deal with evil. The work of CPT was started in 1986, based on the idea that people who believe in nonviolence should be willing to take the same risks as soldiers take, to go into violent situations, and to be a nonviolent presence in situations of extreme violence. After sending short-term delegations to Haiti, Iraq, and the West Bank in the late 1980s and early 1990s, CPT began to see the need for a trained, full-time corps of peacemakers to form more permanent teams in places of conflict.

In June 1995, CPT began a team in Hebron, West Bank, where my involvement with CPT began in December 1995. I have told some of that story in my previous book, *Hebron Journal: Stories of Nonviolent Peacemaking* (Herald Press, 2003). This book, *At-Tuwani Journal*, continues the telling of that story. Although the focus of this book is the Palestinian village of At-Tuwani, it also tells more of the story of CPT work in Hebron and gives a picture of life in the West Bank. At-Tuwani, like Hebron, is a microcosm of what is happening throughout the West Bank under occupation.

CPTers live with people in the middle of oppression and violence, spending lots of time listening to all factions on every side of the conflict, and engaging in nonviolent actions aimed at exposing the oppression while pointing to possibilities for transforming the underlying conflict. We stand in the middle of tense situations in the hope not only of preventing or reducing violence, but also of exposing and confronting the injustices that are at the root of the violence. We seek to work with creative people on all sides of the conflict, peacemakers who are willing and able to think outside the box, outside mainstream modes of thinking. We work to support nonviolent movements for social change and ending the Israeli Occupation. In the West Bank, this effort has resulted in many experiences of Israelis and Palestinians coming together to work for a different future than continual oppression, domination, and control. This book tells some of these exciting stories.

One of the distinctive aspects of CPT work is that instead of being a solidarity group that works to support one side of a conflict, we stand in the middle, a precarious position because at different times we can expect to receive either praise or opposition from any faction in the conflict. One of our slogans is, "We stand on whichever side the gun is pointed at." In Hebron we have taken actions to protect both Israelis and Palestinians. As outsiders, it is not for us to take sides in the larger conflict, to affiliate ourselves with any particular political group or political agenda, or even to act as negotiators of the conflict. On the other hand, we are not neutral since we stand for justice. Working with that creative tension, although difficult at times, is one of the challenging aspects of CPT work.

Our ability to work for peace and end the Occupation will be greatly reduced if we stand only with one side in the conflict. To bridge the gap is a great need, to stand with people on both sides, to understand and interpret the pain of both sides. Many people stand on each side, but few people can relate to people on all sides of the conflict. It is intellectually dishonest, however, to oppose human rights abuses and not to also expose the basis and roots of those abuses. Why are those abuses occurring? What are the motives, values, and goals of those perpetrating the abuses? Human rights abuses occur when economic, political, or religious programs are imposed on people against their will. There is no humane way to oppress people. For more on this theme, see Naomi Klein, *The Shock Doctrine* (New York, Metropolitan Books, 2007, pp. 118-28).

Our struggle against injustice in Palestine/Israel is bigger than opposing the Israeli Occupation. Our struggle is part of a larger nonviolent resistance to U.S. imperial interests that not only support the Israeli Occupation, but also U.S. domination around the world. On an even deeper level, we also are struggling against the whole philosophy, the whole worldview, the whole system of domination and control, be it rooted in race, gender, class, or national self-interest.

The state of Israel was created partly by idealistic Zionists who believed that they could not only create a homeland for Jews, but also create a new society that would be a beacon of light to the whole world, a society of justice and equality for all. Jews had just experienced the horrors of the Holocaust, in addition to over a thousand years of persecution and pogroms from the so-called Christian world. It was hoped that the state of Israel would bring peace and security to the Jewish people. That vision was obscured.

There was one big glitch to that vision: the Palestinian people. Palestine was not a land without people waiting for a people without land. Palestinians were there and have not gone away. The creation of the state of Israel in 1948, and the Occupation of the West Bank and Gaza in 1967, brought not peace and security, but a nightmare. Both Israelis and Palestinians now live in fear of each other. Two beautiful cultures have been brutalized. Both Palestinians and Israelis have become victims. The blowback of the Occupation has affected everyone in the region, and the whole world.

Not all Israelis and Palestinians have accepted the victim role, however. Some Palestinians and some Israelis have dared to step out of the victim role, have risen above their fears, and have reached out to the other side in hopes for peace and reconciliation. This book is an attempt to tell some of their stories. We need more stories of nonviolent resistance to evil, stories that can enlighten, inspire, and empower us to continue the struggle for what is good and true and noble.

At-Tuwani: A Short History

The Bible tells the story of strife in ancient Israel between King Saul and the up-and-coming future king, David. At one point in the story, after learning that Saul is seeking to kill him, David flees to the South Hebron Hills around Ma'on and Carmel (1 Samuel 23, 24). Saul takes 3,000 soldiers to capture David and enters a cave at Ma'on in which David is hiding. Saul falls asleep and David forgoes the opportunity to kill the sleeping king. During this time David meets Abigail, a woman from Carmel, whom he later marries (1 Samuel 25).

Today, the biblical villages of Ma'on and Carmel are the Palestinian villages of Ma'in and Karmil. Just a few miles east of these villages are the modern Israeli settlements of Ma'on and Karmel. Between these Palestinian villages and the Israeli settlements one finds the ancient Palestinian village, At-Tuwani. The village is sometimes referred to as Twaneh. This area, known as the South Hebron Hills or Masafer Yatta, is ten to fifteen miles south of Hebron in the southern part of the West Bank, and southeast of the Palestinian city, Yatta. The area is on the edge of the Negev Desert to the south and east.

We have no historical records of At-Tuwani, except for archaeological remains. Little is known about the ancient history of At-Tuwani, but we do know that the area was populated by ancient Hebrews, Greeks, and Romans. Villagers find Jewish, Greek, and Roman coins in the soil around the village. Lots of pottery shards remain in the ground, dating back as far as the Early and Middle Bronze Ages. There are remains of a Byzantine church building in the village.

Village of At-Tuwani

The Roman presence in At-Tuwani was very important. The old Roman road from Jinba north to Hebron is still visible in At-Tuwani. There are Roman tombs in the area, and across the street from our team house in At-Tuwani are about six adjoining caves dating back at least to Roman times. A tunnel at the back of the caves connects the caves to a cistern. In times of war, invasions, or other dangers, the people could close their caves and hide for months with their animals in that network of caves.

The people in the South Hebron Hills, as other Palestinians, are not simply Arabs. Since this area was a crossroads for thousands of years, many different peoples left behind a lot of cultural and genetic information, including the ancient Canaanite tribes, Philistines, Egyptians, Jews, Greeks, Romans, European crusaders, Bedouins, and Arabs from the south and east. The Bible records some of the many ethnic groups living in Jerusalem at the time of Jesus (Acts 2:9-11). All this is part of Palestinian identity. The people in the South Hebron Hills are descendants of these people, including Jews and Christians, who have lived there for thousands of years. They have developed a unique culture and lifestyle of cave dwelling, shepherding, seasonal farming, and simple living.

The biblical descriptions of shepherds living in caves in the area come alive as one learns to know the cave-dwelling shepherds who continue to live in those caves and rugged mountains. Although not Bedouins, their lifestyle and culture has been influenced by their Bedouin neighbors to the south and east.

Today, four extended families (Rabai, Adara, Hereni, and Amor), about 150 people, live in the village. Unlike other villages in the area, only one family in At-Tuwani continues to live in a cave. Most of the caves in At-Tuwani are now used for animals. The buildings are a mixture of more modern concrete houses and ancient stone houses that remind me of Sunday school pictures of village life in ancient Palestine.

✻

Israel's capture of the West Bank in 1967 dramatically changed life for the people of the South Hebron Hills. The coming of Israeli soldiers and the beginning of the Occupation in 1967 was a frightening time for the people of At-Tuwani. Everyone hid in their caves. They remembered the massacres and destruction some of their families had experienced just across the Green Line in 1948 when the Israeli military drove everyone out of their homes and leveled village after village, town after town, in a major campaign of ethnic cleansing begun in 1947 and continued throughout 1948. For a detailed history of this program of ethnic cleansing, see the ground-breaking book by Israeli historian, Ilan Pappe, *The Ethnic Cleansing of Palestine* (Oxford: Oneworld Publications Limited, 2006). Pappe argues that the program of ethnic cleansing (tihur and bi'ur hametz, Hebrew words used in the program) was planned years in advance and started long before the beginning of any hostilities in 1948.

Villagers describe the Occupation as being brutal from the beginning. Palestinians were randomly killed by Israeli soldiers. No one knew who would be next. It wasn't long before the Israelis ordered the school in At-Tuwani to be closed. Villagers' freedoms were curtailed. Nothing would again be the same. This time, however, the Palestinians did not flee. Instead, they survived a campaign of terror, both official and unofficial, and continue to resist the theft of their lands and the loss of their freedom.

Already in the 1970s, the Israeli government began making momentous decisions regarding the future of the Palestinian people. One significant decision was to declare a large portion of the South Hebron Hills a "closed military area," with the intention of eventually expelling the more than one thousand residents of the area. Since the 1970s, every decision and action of the Israeli government and military affecting the South Hebron Hills must be understood in light of the Israeli determination to cleanse this area of all its Palestinian residents. It must be noted here that Article 49 of the Fourth Geneva Convention expressly forbids the forced removal of people from occupied territories, regardless of the motive.

A period of intense oppression of the people in the South Hebron Hills began in the 1980s when the Israeli government decided to implement their goal of creating an all-Israeli corridor from the southern part of Israel north to Hebron. This resulted in a concerted effort to remove the people by making life extremely difficult for them. Even Prime Minister Ehud Barak's so-called generous offer preserved Israeli control over this corridor to Hebron from the south. Both Labor and Likud governments have worked to remove the people from the South Hebron Hills.

One major part of the strategy of the Israeli government and military for achieving their goal of creating this corridor north to Hebron and driving out the Palestinians was to build a line of settlements from the Green Line in the south the whole way north to Hebron. The village of At-Tuwani lies in this corridor, between the Ma'on settlement to the northeast and the Avi Gail outpost to the southwest. In 1979, Mattiyahu Drobles, co-chairman of the Jewish Agency's Settlement Department, publicly argued not only for moving enough Jews into the West

Bank to create a Jewish majority, but also for strategically locating settlements so that the Palestinians "will find it difficult to form a territorial and political continuity."[1]

The presence of these settlements has been a source of many of the problems facing the residents of the South Hebron Hills. The invaders have stolen much of the land, demolished many of the homes, destroyed many of the fruit and olive trees, burned the crops, decimated the shepherds' flocks and herds, poisoned their water and land, and made life miserable for the indigenous Palestinians. Up until 1980, around 500 people lived in At-Tuwani. Every cave and ancient stone house was occupied. Because of oppression and economic strangulation, many families moved from the village to Yatta. Many of these families still own land in the area and regularly come back to visit relatives.

The same story can be told of every village in the area. Settler activity in the At-Tuwani area began in 1980 when a group of Israelis from Karem Kayemet le Israel planted pine trees on Tel abu Jundeeya, the mountain just southeast of At-Tuwani, what Israelis call Hill 833. In 1982, Israeli settlers brought in mobile homes and started the Ma'on settlement, which now is a town of approximately forty houses, most of which are empty.

At first the Palestinians had few concerns about Israelis moving into their area. They were told the mobile homes had something to do with the military. The settlers built a fence around their small settlement and the Palestinians thought that was the boundary. The villagers were not happy about their loss of land but were resigned to peaceful coexistence with the settlers. A few years later, however, settlers began expanding the fence. After repeated expansions, the settlement now includes over 400 acres, with the settlers claiming the whole surrounding area to be theirs. In addition to the land taken to build the settlement, settlers are now farming much of the Palestinian farmland in the area.

It wasn't long before the people of At-Tuwani were experiencing problems from the settlers. As early as 1984, settlers began attacking shepherds with clubs. In 1986, settlers uprooted twenty-five At-Tuwani olive trees and stole a flock of about fifty sheep. Problems have also come from the Israeli military, which has been ever-present "to protect the settlers." B'Tselem, the Israeli human rights organization, states that "In many cases, soldiers do nothing to protect Palestinians and at times even join in the settlers' acts of violence."[2] Most of the residents of the South Hebron Hills tell stories of physical abuse from Israeli soldiers. In many cases, team members have observed Israeli soldiers abusing Palestinians. A major part of military abuse includes demolitions of houses, caves, wells, cisterns, roads, and trees. In 1987, Israeli soldiers demolished the mosque in At-Tuwani because it had no building permit. In 1993, Israeli soldiers demolished two houses in the village. The present school building, built in 1998, was built without permission from the Israeli government and has a demolition order, as does practically every home in At-Tuwani.

The period between 1993 and 1997 was relatively quiet, as by then settlers had confiscated a large amount of land and were consolidating their gains. In 1997, settler attacks on people in the wider area became more persistent. The Israeli military also increased its pressure on the people to abandon their homes. In 1997, because of settler harassment, the nearby villages of Khoruba and Sarura were abandoned. On April 7, 1998, the Israeli military issued orders to 100 families to evacuate the area by April 12, Easter Sunday. The Palestinian cave dwellers believed the real purpose of the order was the confiscation of their lands and decided to not give in. Israeli soldiers in a number of cases confiscated the meager belongings in the caves and offered to return the belongings if the owners agreed to forfeit their land.

In 1997, Dov Driven moved to the Ma'on settlement, and Palestinians say everything was downhill from then. Driven started out very friendly and tried to establish relationships with

Palestinians in the area. He seemed to be trying to get information and was seen as a spy. After a year he started attacking villagers and their crops. On April 18, 1998, CPTers went with Abdel Hadi Hantash of the Land Defense Committee in Hebron to At-Tuwani. While there, they saw Dov Driven release his three horses to graze in Palestinian wheat fields. Local Palestinians told the CPTers that day that Dov had terrorized people in the area.

In May 1999, Dov Driven got into a confrontation with farmer Musa Abu Lan Bii, as Musa and his brothers were harvesting wheat in their field south of the Ma'on settlement. Another settler shot and wounded Musa. In the confusion that followed, Musa's brother, Issa, got hold of Dov's gun and killed Dov. A Palestinian version of the story is that Dov's friend tried to shoot the Palestinian who was struggling with Dov and accidentally shot Dov. In July, Ma'on settlers started Havot Ma'on, an "illegal" outpost settlement south of the Ma'on settlement. This outpost and Dov's house were demolished by the Israeli military in September. The outpost was rebuilt the next year on Hill 833 in the trees that were planted there in 1980. Dov's house has not been rebuilt.

The next step in the campaign to rid the area of Palestin-

Ma'on settlement with wooded hill on right.

ians came on November 16, 1999, when the Israeli military forcibly removed over 700 cave dwellers, eighty-three families, from their caves in the South Hebron Hills, because the Israeli military said they needed the area for a military firing range. In fact, the military refers to the area as "Firing area 918." The soldiers confiscated and put the belongings of the Palestinians into military vans. They demolished scores of caves, cave entrances, and wells. Flocks of sheep were scattered. Sadly, the people and their flocks had to spend the cold winter away from their caves.

The people resisted with press conferences, contacting foreign consulates and going to the Israeli High Court. The people received help in these actions from Israeli peace activists. On March 29, 2000, the villagers won a partial, temporary victory when the Israeli High Court ruled that they could return to their cave homes and land, pending a decision in the case. The families immediately returned to their homes. The residents of Khoruba and Sarura returned for a short time, but because of repeated settler attacks, they once more abandoned their homes. The Israeli military responded by trying to keep out all residents who had not signed on to the lawsuit in the Israeli High Court. The Israeli government then tried to argue that these people are not permanent residents and may be expelled. The High Court also rejected this argument. After further legal wrangling, the High Court decided that all residents could return.

✳

Israeli peace groups had been coming to the South Hebron Hills since the late 1980s, including Rabbis for Human Rights and Ta'ayush, and helped introduce CPT to the area by inviting CPTers to join actions the Israelis had initiated there. Ezra Nawi, an important Ta'ayush activist, has been visiting At-Tuwani and the area since 2001. Ezra, an Iraqi Jew, has developed a deep love for the Palestinian people. It is he and his friends in Ta'ayush that are responsible for bringing our team to At-Tuwani. Ta'ayush is an Arabic word for "living together."

By 1997, CPTers in Hebron were making visits to the Yatta area, documenting demolitions of homes, cave dwellings, and wells. They began accompanying farmers during harvest to protect them against attacks from settlers. On January 21, 2000, I joined other CPTers in At-Tuwani for a tree planting. Three busloads of Israeli activists came with olive trees. After a long standoff with Israeli soldiers, the soldiers allowed the buses to enter At-Tuwani, but not the olive trees, which supposedly represented a security threat. Actually, the olive trees represented peace and Palestinian commitment to and ownership of the land, which contradicted Israeli intentions of removing the Palestinians from the South Hebron Hills, a story which I told in *Hebron Journal* (pp. 226-29). This was just one of repeated experiences over the years of the Israeli military prohibiting the planting of olive trees.

On March 29, 2000, CPTers were present in the courtroom when the Israeli High Court announced their decision to allow families to return to their homes in the South Hebron Hills. On April 9, 2000, team members traveled to Yatta to join Palestinians and Israeli peace activists in celebrating the return of the eighty-three evicted families. On April 18, two team members spent a night with a family that had returned to its cave in Tuba. On February 1, 2002, a group of us went to the South Hebron Hills to join Rabbis for Human Rights in planting olive trees at Susiya. We never met the Israeli group because Israeli soldiers stopped them and would not allow them into the South Hebron Hills.

On January 18, 2003, CPTers Greg Rollins, Loren Friesen, and Dianne Roe joined fifteen people from Ta'ayush to accompany At-Tuwani farmers while they plowed their land. As the farmers began to plow, settlers started to shoot from the outpost above the fields. Around twelve settlers charged down the hill, shooting their guns and hurling rocks with slingshots. The settlers knocked Loren down and smashed his camera. A settler hit Greg on the side of his head, knocked off his glasses, and broke them. Settlers chased an Israeli woman. The Palestinians on tractors quickly retreated as settlers chased them, threw stones at them, and shot at them. Soldiers came and arrested a Palestinian who had thrown stones at the settlers.

Settlers put a farmer's tractor into neutral and pushed it down the hill where it flipped over. CPTers helped push the tractor up onto its wheels. For an Israeli description of the day, see David Shulman's *Dark Hope: Working for Peace in Israel and Palestine* (Chicago: The University of Chicago Press, 2007, pp. 30-36). This book is a moving, insightful, personal description of Ta'ayush activists going into the West Bank and standing with their Palestinian cousins. The first part of the book focuses on the South Hebron Hills. David is a regular visitor to At-Tuwani. On April 11, 2003, CPT members and members of Ta'ayush spent a weekend in At-Tuwani. Team members went to Jinba on January 21, 2004, to document fields of wheat and barley that the Israeli military had sprayed with herbicide from an airplane. The fields had started to turn yellow.

✱

During June and July of 2004, Operation Dove, an Italian group similar to CPT, began exploring the possibility of starting a project in the South Hebron Hills. Operation Dove is an outgrowth of the Catholic Community of Pope John XXIII in Italy. The religious order began in 1968 with a vision of members living in communal households, sharing and living with homeless and handicapped people, and serving the poor. They have similarities to Catholic Worker houses or Le Arche communities. The community now has almost two thousand members living in communities around the world.

From the beginning, the religious order had a commitment to nonviolence and to sharing life with victims on both sides of conflicts. In 1992, Italian conscientious objectors in the movement decided to take their vision to Croatia, to be a peaceful presence there. They called their group Operation Dove, which is a mission project of the Community of Pope John XXIII. Since then, Operation Dove has had a presence in Sierra Leone, Congo, Chiapas, East Timor, Chechnya, Kosovo, Uganda, and Palestine. Over one thousand people have participated in Operation Dove Projects.

Operation Dove began its work in the South Hebron Hills in the summer of 2004 by spending a week in each of the neighboring villages of Jinba and Susiya. The Doves then invited CPT to help because the work seemed to be more than they could handle. Originally, it was thought that Operation Dove and CPT would begin working in Susiya or Jinba.

Instead, the project began in At-Tuwani with CPT joining Operation Dove for the purpose of accompanying the building of a clinic. Some time was spent in the village in August. On Saturday, September 20, 2004, Operation Dove and CPT members moved into the village and have maintained a joint team since then. The plan was to have at least four international volunteers living in the village at all times.

Within a few days the team realized that a big problem involved the school children from the neighboring village of Tuba when they walked past the Ma'on settlement on their way to and from the school in At-Tuwani. Settlers repeatedly attacked the Tuba children. The parents of the Tuba children requested that there be daily international accompaniment for their children. In response, the team began accompanying the children to and from school each day, which became regular work for the team.

Soon trouble increased. On September 29, at about quarter after seven in the morning, five hooded settlers, armed with chains and bats, attacked CPTers Kim Lamberty and Chris Brown. In addition to leaving Kim with a broken arm and injured kneecap, they stole her money, passport, and cell phone. Chris had multiple bruises all over his body and a punctured lung, which required surgery. Both were treated at Soroka Hospital in Be'er Sheva.

On the day after the attack, soldiers came to the village and warned the villagers that the coming Wednesday was the Jewish harvest festival (Sukkot) and that it could be an especially dangerous time for the children. The soldiers also said that the whole problem was caused by the presence of internationals in the village, that the peacemakers were "putting the Palestinian children in danger." The soldiers did not mention the repeated attacks that occurred before the arrival of the Doves and CPT. No one knew what to expect next.

In the following days numerous Israeli peace activists came to At-Tuwani to help accompany the children. The Israeli police agreed to be present each morning and afternoon as the children walked past the Ma'on outpost. In fact, the police requested that the children wait until police arrived. The children expressed a lot of fear about walking past the settlement. The military then declared the area a closed military zone and, at the request of the settlers, declared the road to Tuba to be part of the Ma'on settlement, so that Palestinians could no longer walk on that road. The children then began using the long way, a donkey path that winds around and over the mountains for four or more miles, a hike of more than one and a half hours instead of the fifteen minute walk on the road. This path could also possibly be a more dangerous way since the children on that path would be more isolated in case of attacks from settlers.

On October 3, there was a confrontation when police and soldiers would not allow the children to go to school. Team members called Anat Vardi, a Ta'ayush activist, who contacted a member of the Knesset, who in turn contacted a general of the army to get the situation changed. As the accompaniers waited between the settlement and Tuba to hear from the general, the police offered to escort the children past the settlement if they were not accompanied by internationals. That offer was accepted and the children went to school. The children took the long path home in the afternoon. After this, Israeli activists did some of the walking with the children, or the children walked the long path.

This uncertain tug of war continued until October 9, when, at around three o'clock in the afternoon, eight masked settlers, armed with clubs and sling shots, attacked CPTers Diana Zimmerman and Diane Janzen, a Dove, one person from At-Tuwani, two people from Tuba, and two British members of Amnesty International. They were walking back from Tuba after accompanying the children to their homes. The Operation Dove member was diagnosed as having a ruptured kidney.

After this beating, the soldiers again said that the whole problem was caused by internationals, that if the internationals would leave, there would be no problem. Instead of holding the settlers accountable and taking steps to prevent these attacks, the response of the Israeli military was to declare the area a closed military zone for both internationals and Palestinians, and prohibit internationals from accompanying the school children, a victory for the settlers. Reluctantly the villagers accepted not having internationals accompany their children but insisted that we internationals continue living in At-Tuwani.

In the following days, the children used the long path or the middle road when accompanied by Israeli soldiers or police. Instead of going between the settlement and the outpost, the middle road went around the south and west sides of the outpost to the At-Tuwani village. The children expressed a lot of fear and said they didn't want to go to school any more. But they kept going, in spite of continued attacks even when soldiers were present. The attacks from Israeli settlers included verbal threats, stone throwing, and even attacks on soldiers. The settlers were often masked. On October 12, Ma'on settlers again harassed the children. Israeli soldiers were present but did nothing. On October 17, settlers threw stones at the children.

Work quietly continued on the clinic, but on October 23, soldiers came to the clinic and threatened to arrest the Palestinians for working on the clinic building. The soldiers also threatened arrest and deportation for any team members working on the "illegal" clinic.

On October 30, the head of the Israeli Civil Administration (actually part of the military) for the southern West Bank came and met with village leaders. Team members were present. Villagers expressed their concerns about lack of water and electricity, safety for school children, and closed and poor roads. When the Israeli officer tried to pressure the villagers to remove all internationals because they "were the cause of the problems here," the At-Tuwani leaders told him that the attacks from settlers and harassment from the military had been happening long before internationals arrived. However, now that internationals were present in At-Tuwani and that there had been media attention, now finally the people of At-Tuwani were getting some response from Israeli authorities. After the meeting, villagers said that it was quite unusual for ranking military officers to come to At-Tuwani.

Armed settlers attacked At-Tuwani farmers on October 15. The response of the Israeli military was to order the Palestinian farmers to leave their land. The team began to accompany farmers as they plowed their fields. A number of times soldiers came by and told the farmers they could not work in their fields without special permission. The farmers told the soldiers it was their land and they didn't need permission to go on their own land. The farmers continued working their land, often being observed by settlers on the hills above them.

Olive picking is an important time each year because of settler harassment of Palestinians as they try to pick their olives, and because soldiers often prevent Palestinians from entering their olive groves. Each fall, many Israelis travel to the West Bank to accompany Palestinians and help in the olive harvest.

From 2002 until 2004, settlers basically controlled the whole Humra valley of olive trees that goes up the hill to the south of the village, just to the west of and below the wooded outpost. For two years the settlers harvested most of the olives with the support of the Israeli military. On October 18 and 19, after settlers again began stealing olives in the valley above At-Tuwani, the people of At-Tuwani decided to begin picking their olives early so that more olives would not be lost to the settlers.

This time, with the presence of our team and support from Rabbis for Human Rights who coordinated with the Israeli military, the people of At-Tuwani were able to harvest their olives and regain use of that valley. The team participated in the olive picking, and there were no problems, even though the settlers could be seen in the forest above the olive grove. On October 20, soldiers declared the olive grove a closed military zone and ordered that the harvest must end by noon.

Olive picking continued into November with accompaniment by team members. Many days there were settlers nearby up in the forest chanting and making their presence known. Soldiers came by regularly. On November 14, when Israeli military authorities told the villagers they needed permission from the military to harvest their olives, a villager told them, "It is our land. We need no permission to go on our land." The families said they believed it was because of international presence that there was no trouble from the settlers.

On December 9, settlers again attacked the Tuba children as they walked near the settlement outpost. The soldiers quickly loaded the children into their jeep and drove through the stones being thrown by the settlers.

1. Quoted by Ali Abunimah. *One Country: A Bold Proposal to End the Israeli-Palestinian Impasse* (New York: Metropolitan Books, 2006, p. 27).

2. Antigona Ashkar. *Violence, Harassment and Lawlessness against Palestinians in the Southern Hebron Hills* (Jerusalem: B'Tselem—The Israeli Information Center for Human Rights in the Occupied Territories. July, 2005, p. 21).

The Journal
December 13, 2004-February 28, 2005

December 13, 2004, Monday

I arrived back in the West Bank and Hebron Saturday evening for my tenth trip here. After spending the night in Hebron, I headed for the Beqa'a Valley just east of Hebron, where I have spent so much time during the past ten years. It was wonderful to visit old friends, to visit the Sultan and Jaber families, but it was disturbing to see the expansion of the Kiryat Arba settlement, the confiscation of more Palestinian land in the valley, and the increasing oppression of the Palestinian people. I saw demolished grape vines and grapes rotting on the vines because the Israeli military had prevented the Palestinian farmers from selling their grapes.

This morning I walked into Hebron in time for team worship and then immediately left with the whole team to travel to At-Tuwani for a joint CPT team meeting. CPT now works out of both Hebron and At-Tuwani, with team members moving back and forth between Hebron and At-Tuwani. Some team members are considered part of the "Tuwani core" and spend more time in At-Tuwani. I have been asked to spend most of my time this winter working in At-Tuwani. I am excited about living in a Palestinian village.

At-Tuwani is only ten miles south of Hebron. We could get there in ten minutes from Hebron if we went on the new Israeli settler road that goes right by At-Tuwani. However, for Palestinians, this is not possible. For Palestinians, there now are only two roads into and out of Hebron, a city of 140,000 people: one to the north and one to the west. We went the long Palestinian way, one hour or more, first west to Dura, and then south through the Al Fawwar refugee camp, through the large (seventy thousand) town of Yatta, and then back east through Karmil, and on to At-Tuwani.

This is a difficult road because at many places along the way the road has been demolished or blocked by the Israeli military. We had to drive very slowly over the bumps, rocks, and holes in the road. The road was very narrow at places because of the huge piles of dirt and boulders along the way that just a week ago completely blocked the roads. Each time the Israeli military has blocked the roads, the Palestinians reopen the road, as they have done repeatedly over the past four years. Our taxi stopped about a mile from At-Tuwani because of the rough roads. Israeli bulldozers had torn up the good road, so we walked through the mud, crossed over the new Israeli road (Route 317), and walked through more mud and then on the fairly good dirt road up the hill to the village.

I was excited. I could hardly wait to get here. From previous trips to Yatta, I remembered the rugged mountains, distinctive buildings, farms, and villages along the way. Everything looked familiar as we approached At-Tuwani: the Ma'on settlement in the distance with its distinctive tan stucco houses and red tile roofs—a trademark of many of the settlements, actually small villages that dot the Palestinian landscape, the outpost in the pine trees on top of the hill near the village, the shape of the ancient stone houses. I remembered being here for a demonstration on January 21, 2000. I recognized many of the places as we walked into the village to our one room little house villagers built for us in the middle of the village.

After our team meeting I joined Joe Carr and a Dove (Since members of Operation Dove do not want their names used, I will refer to them as "the Doves"), for "school patrol," an activity that has become the focus of our work here. At about noon

School children being accompanied by soldiers.

we were on our way up the Humra Valley to watch for the children leaving school and walking home. We were on the other
side of the valley from where the soldiers accompany the children past the settler outpost. The area where the children walk
is a closed military zone, so we cannot be there. The settlers can
be there. Our role is to let the soldiers know we are watching
them. We hope to have "the grandmother effect," as people tend
to be on their best behavior when their grandmothers are present. There are things no one would do if their grandmother is
watching. The soldiers know we are watching them and that we
will report on what happens.

Soldiers accompany the children because of the intervention
of Ta'ayush and Machsom Watch members, Israeli activists who
set up a meeting in October between Knesset members and military officials to discuss the problem of school children being
attacked. Machsom Watch played a key role in this because of
their good contacts with the military through their daily interac-
tions with military officials at checkpoints. Hana Barag and
Chagit Bak were especially influential. Machsom Watch is an
organization of 500 Israeli women. Every day some of them go

to military checkpoints to observe the behavior of the Israeli military. In 2003 they visited checkpoints three thousand times.

That meeting included ten Knesset members, members of the Committee on Rights of the Child, a Knesset committee responsible for the protection of children in Israel. The committee included both right and left wing members, including members of Shas and Likud. The right wing members were especially incensed when they learned that the military was passively standing by while Israeli adults attacked children as they tried to go to school.

The Knesset members berated the top military officials present. It was quite an embarrassment for the Israeli government to have the truth exposed that settlers can give orders to the Israeli military, attack soldiers and police, and prevent the military and police from doing their job of protecting people. The Israeli media gave the story wide coverage. Out of those meetings came an agreement that the military would accompany the children every day and that the military would meet regularly with this committee. Israeli activists say that one reason this plan worked was because the military became accountable to this committee. The beatings and attacks had the opposite result of what the settlers intended.

Since then, our team has continued to go out each morning and afternoon on adjacent hills to watch as soldiers accompany the children, and, by our presence, let the Israeli authorities know that we are watching them. The team also sends regular reports to the Knesset committee, OCHA, Machsom Watch, and Ta'ayush to keep them informed of what happens each day.

After a short wait, an Israeli military Hummer drove down the road across the valley toward At-Tuwani, stopped at the edge of the village, and waited for the children to come from school. Soon the children were on their way home with the Hummer ahead and two soldiers walking with five children, their M-16 assault rifles at the ready. I had a lot of mixed emotions as I watched the absurd scene before me. I was glad the children were being protected but not that soldiers were doing it, or even that the children needed protection.

We came back to the village and helped carry cinderblock for the workers who were building the walls for the new medical clinic. It was originally thought that being present at the building of the clinic would be the primary focus of our work in the village. We now spend less time at the clinic since the military has stopped harassment at the building site, making our presence there less necessary. Working there helped me connect with some of the men of the village.

The people of At-Tuwani felt the need for a clinic because the nearest hospital is thirty minutes away in Yatta, if the Israeli military allows the people to drive to Yatta. Often the roads have been closed and the only way to Yatta is walking or taking a tractor through fields, which means a much longer trip. Since the building does not have a permit (no buildings in At-Tuwani have a permit), the military had ordered work on the clinic to stop and had confiscated materials and equipment. There was fear of arrest and fear that the structure would be demolished. The villagers wanted support for their decision to continue work on building the clinic.

The clinic is being built beside the deep well from which villagers get their drinking water. There also are cisterns in the village where water is collected in the rainy season. Drawing water from the well with a rope and a bucket is considered women's work, a cultural norm our team does not follow. Often the village well is a gathering place for the women of the village. I am amazed at how the women carry those five-gallon plastic buckets so gracefully on their heads up the steep hills to their homes.

This evening a group of village children came to our little room for help with their English homework. I learned that many evenings we are blessed by the presence of children wanting help learning English. As we sat together on mats on the floor, the children took turns filling out the answers in their workbooks. Palestinian children study English, starting in the second grade.

After the children left, a group of village men, a sort of unofficial village council, came to talk with us about our work here. They expressed appreciation for our presence and explained that our presence is important and that they want it to continue. In fact, they said they will not let us leave. They stressed the importance of our work monitoring school escorts, supporting the clinic, and accompanying farmers. They also want us to work with other villages and to do more media work. They made it clear that an important part of our work is drawing the attention of the world to what is happening here. They are eager for media attention.

December 14, 2004, Tuesday

At seven o'clock this morning we team members headed up the valley for school patrol, greeting villagers on the way. It wasn't long before we saw the soldiers and five children coming over the hill from Tuba. I got to meet the students, whose ages ranged from six to twelve. They do not need to come here to school. They could go to another school in the opposite direction, but they are willing to daily face the threats of settlers as an act of resistance to the settlers wanting to drive them out, and because the school in At-Tuwani is a better school. I was reminded of watching Palestinian school children in Hebron walking through tear gas in order to get to school. I am honored to work with these children.

At eleven o'clock we headed out by foot to the village of Tuba to do our afternoon school patrol there, and for me to get acquainted with the people there. It was a brisk walk of at least an hour and a half over and down mountains and steep terrain on the long path. What a thrill to walk through these rugged mountains, to look south to the Negev Desert and east to the Dead Sea. We saw gazelles running ahead of us.

We walked the long way around and over the mountains so that settlers would not see us. It could be quite dangerous for us if they saw us. Joe talked about huddling together to soften their blows if the settlers did attack us. What a horrible way to live. But this is what the villagers have been facing for the past twenty years. The walk was also sobering as we passed the abandoned villages of Humra, Sarura, and Khoruba, villages that were abandoned in 1997 because of constant harassment from settlers. I thought, "This was ethnic cleansing, a serious war crime, but why had I never heard of these villages?"

It was eerie to walk past the homes and the fields that once were farmed by the people who used to live there. We saw freshly cultivated fields that have recently been confiscated by Ma'on settlers. We walked past the remains of the Ma'on outpost and Dov's house that was demolished in 2000 by the Israeli military.

We got to Tuba in time to watch the children coming over the hill, accompanied by both soldiers and police. It was a thrill to see those children again. Omar abu Jindeeya, father of some of the children, watched with us and then invited us to his home for tea. He and his wife, Zahreia, have ten children and live in a big, beautiful cave his grandfather carved into the rock. Their home felt warm and inviting. Tuba is a village of nine homes and sixty people. It is much more primitive than At-Tuwani, but the people are just as friendly.

Since the late 1990s the people of Tuba have been under constant pressure from the nearby Ma'on settlement. The village has lost half of its annual income because of land confiscation and settler harassment. They have lost 140 acres of their cropland. Because they refused to abandon their homes, the Israeli military came in 1997, took their belongings, dumped them two miles away, destroyed their tents, cisterns, livestock, grains, and livestock pens, and closed the entrances to their caves. The villagers dug out their caves and continued their simple life.

Omar and his brother, Ibrahim, grew up in Tuba. Their grandparents were refugees from Garateen, a town of maybe one thousand people across the Green Line in what is now Israel, one of the 418 Palestinian towns and villages flattened in

1948 in a huge campaign of ethnic cleansing by the Israeli military. Many people from Garateen now live in the area around Yatta and At-Tuwani. Their family was driven from their home in 1948 and, in the 1990s, driven from their caves in the wooded hill now occupied by the Havot Ma'on settlers. Now the Israeli government wants to drive the abu Jindeeya family from their homes yet again.

Both Omar's wife, Zahreia, and Ibrahim's wife, Imtere, have been badly beaten by settlers. In 2000, Zahreia was traveling with three children on the road near Ma'on when two settlers, one with a gun and one with a club, attacked her after she refused to give up her donkey. Zahreia was severely beaten, her baby fell from her arms, and the other two children ran home.

Back in At-Tuwani this evening, I visited Nasser and Kiefah Adara and their three boys (Salim, 12, Basil, 9, and Samieh, 5). I had lots of fun playing with the boys and getting to know the family. Nasser is our landlord, and Kiefah has started the women's cooperative in the village. Kiefah wrote a postscript to this book.

※

Kiefah was born in 1976 and grew up in Yatta. She dropped out of school after the eighth grade. Her marriage was arranged at sixteen. She was very scared and spent much of her time crying at the beginning of her marriage. Village life in At-Tuwani was difficult for her at first. The village at that time had no electricity and still has no running water.

In 2000, ERM (Environmental Resource Management), a British aid group, did some educational work in the village, including summer camps for children and workshops for women, including teaching women how to conduct meetings.

Kiefah, then twenty-four, came alive and caught a vision for women's liberation. She helped organize summer camps for the children. She started a women's co-op this past summer to develop both economic enterprises and educational programs for women. One goal was to create space for women to learn and grow. The first step for the women's cooperative has been producing and marketing the beautiful traditional cross-stitch needlework done by women in the area.

In spite of resistance from some village men, Kiefah has continued to organize and educate, creating space for women to grow. She understands that change comes slowly. With support and help from her husband, Nasser, she renovated an old family stone house in the village, which is now known as "the museum," a place for women to meet and sell their traditional needlework and other crafts. Kiefah arranges for the teaching of traditional crafts to the younger women of the village and surrounding villages. Most of these items, small purses, pillowcases, or fancy traditional dresses, are sold to groups that visit the village, which provides vital extra income and a degree of independence for the women. The women's group began with seven women and now includes twenty-seven women.

Kiefah is a traditional Muslim woman who understands the oppression of women. I have never seen her without her headscarf. She, also, is a patient visionary who has a vision for the liberation of women. It is true that Muslim women here are oppressed but no more than Western women who are objectified, set up to compete with each other, and treated horribly by men. In comparison with most Western women, Kiefah is a liberated woman. She and her children share the same life. She lives in a vibrant community. She goes out into the hills with the sheep. She understands oppression but has a different vision of liberation than do Western women. Instead of being individualistic and self-centered, her vision of liberation includes community and submission to God.

December 15, 2004, Wednesday

Two Israeli women from Machsom Watch came today to be briefed on recent events here before going to a follow-up meeting tomorrow of the committee of Knesset members and military officials who are responsible for monitoring the military accompaniment of the school children.

✳

I met Hafez Hereni who has worked closely with our team since our first day here. He has been present in many of our difficult and joyous times. Hafez is an outgoing, gentle, sensitive person, and the one permanent resident in the village who speaks fluent English. He started university education, but like many Palestinians, had to quit because of money problems.

The story of Hafez and his family is the story of life in At-Tuwani. Like the abu Jindeeya family, the Hereni family has roots in the village of Garateen in Israel. Hafez's mother, al Hajji Fatima, still talks about life in Garateen. In 1980, when the Hereni family went back to the village that was bulldozed in 1948, they found some hay from 1948 under some of the stones. Now they, like other Palestinians, are forbidden to even cross the Green Line and enter Israel.

Hafez has two brothers in the village, Saber and Ghanam. His mother, al Hajji Fatima, is a feisty 74-year-old woman. In 1986, when settlers stole a flock of sheep, Fatima, along with other villagers, went after the settlers and got to the gate of the settlement before the sheep got there. There was a fight with settlers shooting their guns in the air and beating one older village man. The shepherds recovered all except two of their sheep, which they later got back through the help of the Israeli Civil Administration.

In 1986, two years after the settlement began, Hafez, then eleven years old, and his brother, Ghanam (13), went up the hill toward the settlement with their sheep. Three settlers with guns came toward them. This was the first time they had seen settlers and naively assumed they were fellow human beings coming to talk. A settler began beating Ghanam, who was in bed for a week after the beating. Hafez ran away when another settler came toward him. Hafez became very fearful after this, always afraid that the settlers might attack.

In 1987, settlers took much of their land. There is now an apricot and peach orchard on their land, across the settler fence. Before the settlers actually stole the land, they had been stealing the wheat harvest from that land for a few years. A military bulldozer was used to prepare the ground for that settler orchard.

In 1990, things became worse. The Hereni family uprooted olive trees that settlers had planted on their land. The next day settlers destroyed the same number of Palestinian olive trees. That same week settlers came while Saber was plowing and told him it was their land he was plowing. Settlers attacked Saber and broke his arm. Saber filed a report with the police but nothing happened. This was the beginning of a yearly struggle over who would plant which fields.

In 1992, while settlers were plowing a Hereni field, Fatima went after the settlers with a big rock. Her family stopped her and calmed her. A settler came and talked to the family. He showed them a map that indicated huge areas belonged to the settlers. The Israeli Civil Administration later admitted the land did not belong to the settlers, but the settlers were determined to take the land. By this time, most of the Hereni family land was stolen.

For one month in the summer of 2002, the family experienced harassment from Israeli soldiers almost every night. Many nights soldiers raided their home and other homes in the village. The children were terrified to be woken in the night by soldiers screaming at the family. But it got so common that the children would get up and walk out the door as soon as the soldiers came in the house. The soldiers often destroyed things in the homes. They also brought in a tank to make lots of noise in the night. In response, Ta'ayush people started sleeping in the village. If the soldiers knew Israelis were present, they would not attack. But one night Israeli activists were able to film the soldiers' mayhem. This made the Israeli press, and the harassment stopped.

April 2004 was a difficult time for the family. One day, some

Ta'ayush people were in the village for a meeting. Fatima had gone up the hill behind her house with the sheep. Hafez was told that settlers had approached his mother. Hafez knew that when settlers come, there is trouble. Often someone gets hurt. Hafez ran up the hill and saw eight settlers. At least one had a gun. A settler had pulled off Fatima's headscarf and the settlers were trying to take the sheep. The Israeli peace activists came running up the hill. One Israeli filmed the action.

As Hafez approached, a settler started to shoot at Hafez's feet. Dirt hit Hafez in the face. The settler told Hafez, "There is nothing I can do now. I will have to kill you." Blood was running from the hand of an Israeli activist who then tried to talk with the settler, who stopped shooting. Israeli soldiers and police appeared on the scene. Blood was coming from Fatima's mouth. A settler had taken her shepherd's rod and beaten her with it. After she fell down, settlers hit her with rocks as she lie on the ground. One rock hit her on her right cheek and one on the back of her head. But she got up and ran after her sheep. When things calmed down, soldiers offered her water. She refused the water and told the soldiers, "I don't want your water. You are the same people who try to kill me, and now you want to make me better."

A Palestinian ambulance took her to the hospital. The next day, family members took Fatima to the Kiryat Arba police station to make a complaint against the settlers. Settlers told the police that the shepherds had attacked them, but Ta'ayush had the tape of what had happened. They showed the videotape to the police and made their complaint, but the police did nothing. Hafez told me that when he saw the tape, he was shocked at what he had been through and what danger he had faced.

Three weeks after this incident, Israeli soldiers came to At-Tuwani with a backhoe and demolished Saber's and Ghanam's homes. The family watched in disbelief. Then in July settlers destroyed fifty of their olive trees and put dead chickens into their cistern to poison the water.

December 17, 2004, Friday

It must have been twenty degrees this morning, something unusual for here. The ground was frozen. The rain ended last evening and the wind blew from the north, so I knew it would be cold. This morning, however, the wind came from the south, so it warmed up.

There have been special work projects in the village when the men of the village get together to make improvements to common areas in the village. This morning the men were building a stone wall along the street below our house. I helped gather rocks from the olive grove beside the street. Palestine is blessed with stones. There are stones and rocks everywhere. It was great fun working and drinking tea with the men and boys of the village. What a blessing common work can be.

Team members have been working in At-Tuwani on five-day rotations. Today was the end of my five-day rotation so I came back to Hebron.

December 20, 2004, Monday

Like in At-Tuwani, school patrol has also been an important part of the work of the CPT team in Hebron. Both settlers and soldiers have repeatedly harassed Palestinian school children in Hebron. Dianne Roe and I went on school patrol this morning at the Qurtuba girls' school in front of the Beit Hadassah settlement. Why were we there, I wondered? Here were beautiful Palestinian children going to school. Almost beside them, beautiful Jewish settler children were going to school. Genetically they are practically the same. Something horrible has been imposed on them.

Everything was quiet this morning. But it has not always been quiet. The Palestinian children have repeatedly been attacked, not only by settler children, but also by settler parents. Just a few days ago settler children tried to attack Palestinian children here.

In addition to a dozen Israeli soldiers and police, there also were international observers (TIPH) to monitor the situation and discourage overt violence. It was quiet, but the fear, the oppression, and the separation continue. Tomorrow morning the soldiers, police, and international observers will again be here to remind us all of our common humanity. When will this apartheid system be discarded and a commitment made to respect each other and share this beautiful land?

Israel has been building a wall, what Israelis call a security barrier, along the western side of the West Bank. The route of the Wall does not follow the Green Line, the 1967 border between Israel and the West Bank. Instead, it curves and snakes around in order to take most of the good Palestinian farm land and the aquifers, without taking Palestinian villages and population centers. Palestinians consider the real purpose of the Wall to be land confiscation and the expansion of Israel's borders, taking as much as half of the West Bank. Israel wants to take the land but does not want the people who live on the land. The Wall is being built entirely on Palestinian land.

Abdel Hadi Hantash from the Land Defense Committee came by this morning. Our team has worked closely with him over the years on issues of home demolitions and land confiscation. He reported on more land recently being confiscated for the Wall. He said that the latest projection is for the Wall to go south of At-Tuwani. That would be good news, for it would spare the people of At-Tuwani a lot of grief. The route of the Wall has been of great concern for the people of At-Tuwani.

The projections have been that the Wall would go just north of At-Tuwani, which would put the whole line of settlements south of Hebron and much of the South Hebron Hills on the Israeli side of the Wall. That would cut At-Tuwani off from the rest of the West Bank and would surely mean the confiscation of all the land south of At-Tuwani, and probably removal of everyone from the village. If it is true that the Wall will go south of At-Tuwani, I wonder, why this change? Do the Israelis know that we would make a lot of trouble for them there? Is our presence a factor? Is the growing nonviolent resistance in the South Hebron Hills a factor?

December 23, 2004, Thursday

I came back to At-Tuwani yesterday. Seven children came from Tuba today. The school closed early today at half past eleven, but the soldiers didn't come to accompany the children. John Lynes, an English Quaker, and I waited on the hill above the village until after two o'clock and then walked over to the edge of the village to talk with the children who were patiently waiting there. John called the military but still no one came. The agreement between the Knesset committee and the military included a provision for calling the military if soldiers were late. I called a little later and the man said the soldiers would be there soon. But before the soldiers arrived, the children gave up and left to walk the long way home. We talked with the soldiers who finally arrived at quarter after three. They were friendly.

December 24, 2004, Friday

I got a ride to Karmil and went to the mosque for Friday prayers. The prayers were a time of deep worship for me. I felt God was very close. I could not understand much of the sermon, but I did understand the comments about America and Israel, Afghanistan, and the recent massacre by American soldiers in Fallujah, Iraq. I felt much pain concerning what America is doing in the Muslim world. I also thought of Peggy who is in Iraq with CPT.

It was disturbing to see swastika graffiti on the wall outside the mosque. I was horrified, but I also understood. Occupation and oppression bear bitter fruits. Some Palestinian boys pointed a toy pistol at me today. I asked them if they were settlers, and they said no. I told them that they were acting like settlers. Unfortunately, we become what we hate.

I was then invited to Nasser and Kiefah's home for lunch. I had a wonderful time relaxing with the family. I ended up spending the rest of the day with the extended Adara family. What a beautiful Christmas Eve. The other team members wanted to be in Bethlehem for Christmas, so I will be the only one here for three days. I want to experience Christmas here with the shepherds. For me, this simple, ancient village is the real Bethlehem.

Bethlehem today is a modern, bustling city with noise, pollution, and traffic jams. At-Tuwani is a small village where people live in much the same way as in ancient Bethlehem. Whole families live in one small room and life is simple. At-Tuwani, however, has more in common with the past than ancient stone houses, women drawing water from the one well and carrying it home on their heads, or shepherds watching their flocks in the surrounding hills. Like Bethlehem of old, At-Tuwani is an occupied town. Instead of Roman soldiers, now Israeli soldiers are present, controlling and oppressing the inhabitants of Palestine.

December 25, 2004, Saturday

It was a joyous, wonderful Christmas. There was no school today to honor the birth of Jesus. Muslims honor Jesus and believe he was the Messiah. My plan was to go out into the mountains with the sheep because I wanted to be with shepherds on Christmas Day. It didn't work out as I planned. We didn't know that Israelis were coming today to plant olive trees.

At about nine o'clock we saw soldiers and police down by the settler road. Soon we saw a big truck loaded with olive trees, a gift from Israelis for the villages around here. The truck turned up the road to the village but was stopped by soldiers and police. Apparently the olive trees were seen as some kind of security threat. I remembered King Herod also had considered the baby Jesus a security threat. Why would anyone fear babies or olive trees?

Some villagers and I headed down to see what was happening. I made my presence known to the Israeli police in hopes of encouraging them to allow the olive trees into the village. The olive trees were finally allowed into the village after a long discussion between the driver and the police as Israeli military jets thundered overhead. I thought of the Roman soldiers who used to occupy this land. The police ordered that the truck could only be in the village for thirty minutes, so a dozen of us quickly unloaded about a hundred trees. That was fun.

It wasn't long before twenty-five people from Ta'ayush drove up. They were going to plant some of the trees in the Bedouin village of Kasm il Karam, east of here, on the other side of the Karmel settlement. I decided to join them. Police stopped us down by the road. They did let us go but warned us that we all needed to stay together so they would not have extra work. They followed us and kept watch on us the whole time. I wondered, were we engaging in threatening activity? Were they concerned about what we might do, or what settlers might do to us? Who makes the threats here?

The farther east we went the more rugged and desert-like the hills looked. We passed a number of Bedouin encampments and saw many camels. Soon we got to a school where we were to plant the olive trees. There was no soil in the schoolyard, only rock. But we dug little holes and planted the trees. I couldn't believe the trees would ever grow there and later learned that the trees would need to be replanted. But it was a symbolic action on the part of the Israelis.

We then went to another Bedouin village where we gathered in a big room with a fire pit in the middle, a meeting place for Bedouins from the surrounding area. About thirty Bedouins were there, plus the Israelis and some local Palestinians. We drank tea and listened to speeches. I wished there could have been more dialogue between the Israelis and the Bedouins instead of speeches by politicians.

Afterwards, we went to Susiya, a Palestinian village southwest of At-Tuwani. All the houses and caves in the village have been demolished by the Israeli military. The people now live in tents like Bedouins. We gave them some olive trees but did not plant any since it was raining. We gathered in a large tent where they served all of us a big meal of couscous and lamb.

What a wonderful way to celebrate Christmas. The season of Advent leading up to Christmas was about anticipating the coming of God's kingdom, a new age of peace and justice. Today I experienced a foretaste of that new age. Israeli peace activists (wise men?) from Ta'ayush came to the South Hebron Hills bearing gifts of olive trees to show their respect to people who are supposed to be their enemies. Here I was with shepherds and Bedouins, with Israelis coming with olive trees to symbolize their desire for peace, with Jews, Muslims, and Christians breaking bread together. Here were people who have accepted the message of Jesus. Today we dreamed of the time when all oppression will cease and those nasty guns and clubs will be turned into plowshares.

As I walked back toward home, two big trucks turned onto the road toward At-Tuwani. They were bringing flour, chickpeas, sugar, and oil from the United Nations (UN) and the European Union (EU) to be shared with the people of the area. Each family received one or two 100-pound bags of flour. People from Tuba and other villages were waiting for the trucks. Omar was here with his donkey to carry his portion home to Tuba.

I asked, "Why do these people need to be fed by the world?" Over half of the Palestinians in the Occupied Territories are being fed by other nations. According to the UN, real food consumption per capita among Palestinians has fallen by 25-30 percent in the past few years, and chronic malnutrition is on the rise. The Palestinians are resourceful people. They have been coping with this emergency by eating fewer meals, buying cheaper food, selling assets, getting assistance from relatives, and sometimes removing their children from school.

Because of the Occupation and the systematic attempt by Israel to subdue, crush, and defeat the Palestinians, the Palestinian economy is in ruins. Factories are closed, unemployment is high, and freedom of movement is restricted. At the same time as massive amounts of food are provided to the Palestinian people, massive amounts of their own food are lost each year due to land confiscation or loss of access to land, destruction of crops and livestock, crops rotting in fields because of loss of access to markets, restriction of movement, destruction of assets, and denial of access to water.

I thought back on my visit to the Beqa'a Valley last week where I learned that although this was a good year for grapes, the Israelis prevented the Palestinians from selling their grapes. Most of the grapes rotted on the vines. There was no point in picking the grapes if they could not be sold. This was especially disgusting since those Hebron grapes are the most delicious grapes I have ever eaten. Eighty percent of the grapes in the Beqa'a were never harvested this year. In the past, those grapes were sent to Jordan, Gaza, the northern part of the West Bank, and Israel.

This year the Israeli government made a political decision to close all those markets. The Israeli military closed roads, imposed curfews, and prohibited Israeli juice companies from buying Hebron grapes. This was a great loss for the Palestinians, probably twenty-five million dollars just in the Hebron District. In the Beqa'a Valley, between one and two hundred thousand dollars were lost, plus all the costs of producing those grapes in the first place. This is economic terrorism.

I learned that my friend, Mahmoud Jaber, shipped twenty tons of grapes to Nablus this fall. Because the Israeli military closed roads, the grapes sat on a truck for four days in the hot sun. Mahmoud ended up receiving a little over two hundred dollars for those twenty tons of grapes, not enough to pay for the transport. Mahmoud was deeply distressed by this loss and died of a heart attack soon after this. After hearing this story, I went over to Mahmoud's house and expressed my condolences to the family. We talked about the night I spent with them two years ago while settlers rampaged nearby after Palestinians killed Nati, a settler who started an "illegal" outpost across the road.

I was filled with anger. Grapes rotting on the vines are part of a concerted effort by the Israeli government to impoverish the Palestinian people. Because of loss of income, because of farmers not being able to produce food, malnutrition rates are rising among Palestinians. Palestinians can no longer grow grapes on huge areas where vineyards have been confiscated, demolished, or killed by settlers spraying herbicides on the grape vines.

Under international law, it is the responsibility of an occupying power to provide for the basic needs of the occupied people. Israel is in violation of international law not only by not providing for the food needs of the Palestinian people, but also by preventing the Palestinian people from feeding themselves. The Israeli government deliberately created the Palestinian hunger problem. By feeding the Palestinian people, the international community is subsidizing the Occupation. I do not suggest that the world let the Palestinians starve. The international community, however, must not allow this injustice to continue. Maybe it is time for Israel to be held accountable for their illegal activities and for the mess they are creating.

My day ended with supper with a family in At-Tuwani. I spent much of the time playing with the children, including getting quite silly. Christmas came to At-Tuwani this year. Even the Muslim schools were closed to honor the nativity. For me, At-Tuwani is the real Bethlehem.

December 26, 2004, Sunday

I went alone partway up the hill for school patrol but couldn't see anything because of the fog. I walked down the hill and met the children. There were nine children today.

I was invited to Nasser and Kiefah's family again for breakfast this morning. Nasser told me that when the idea of an international team living here was first suggested there was a lot of fear and suspicion. Maybe we were Israeli spies. Maybe we would steal from the people. Now, he said, everyone here has learned to love us and appreciates how we relate to the people here. It seems clear that we are accepted here. I told Nasser that I want an open, honest relationship with him. I want him to tell me if anything we do is a problem. He said he would be honest with me. Actually, he has been honest with me. He keeps correcting me on both my Arabic and things I do.

Nasser and I spent part of the morning grazing his sheep near the Ma'on settlement. We saw a settler on a four-wheeler, but there was no problem. I saw an ancient tomb, probably from the Roman period, hewn out of a rock on the hill above the village. There were maybe one hundred small circles carved in the rock, one circle apparently for each person buried in the tomb. I stood there in awe.

We came back into the village and were told that there were settlers above the village, near the settler outpost. We rushed up there and found a dozen Palestinians between the village and the settlement in a field where villagers had recently planted 150 olive trees. I worried that the settlers will want to destroy those olive trees. I learned that there were three settlers there in the field just a half hour earlier and had left when the Palestinians came toward them. We could see the settlers standing among the trees below the settler outpost.

We sat there on the rocks for maybe an hour, sending a clear message to the settlers that the villagers will not be intimidated. I am deeply impressed with the strength of these Palestinians. It is the settlers with their guns and clubs who are acting cowardly. One of the Palestinians offered me a baseball bat. This was in jest, but obviously they are prepared to defend themselves as they have in the past. I told them that my ugly face should be enough to scare the settlers away.

We called Ezra to tell him what had happened. Soon Israeli police came to investigate. A bit later, soldiers came in a Hummer. Two got out and approached us, politely greeting us with "Salaam alykum." I was impressed with the way these soldiers greeted the Palestinians with respect. They listened to what had happened. I doubt anything will come of this, but it is one more report about the ugliness of the settlers. Maybe one day the stack of reports will be so huge that the Israeli government will say "enough." Actually, the Israelis could stop this harassment any time they wanted to. They could put the settlers under curfew every time they caused trouble. That is what they do to the Palestinians, but the Israeli government does not use the same standards or laws for Israelis and Palestinians.

It would be a mistake to think of the settlers as lawless. Although often they appear to be a law unto themselves, the settlers have merely been following plans drafted by the Israeli military for gradual confiscation of the whole area. The Israeli government planned the line of settlements that runs past At-Tuwani. These settlers are the shock troops for the military. As one Israeli soldier told me, "We hate the settlers. They are bad people, but they are doing our work for us." The real reason the settlers are not prosecuted for theft, violence, and intimidation is that they are carrying out Israeli government policy.

My role in each of these encounters with police and soldiers has been to stand nearby, say nothing, but make my presence known. I let the Palestinians handle everything. I am only a support to them. It is their struggle.

December 27, 2004, Monday

I had breakfast again with Nasser and Kiefah. They are supposed to be supplying our team with bread each day, but every day when I ask them for bread, they refuse to give me any. They simply insist that I must eat with them. I have not eaten one meal by myself the past three days since the other team members are gone. Maybe they are not sure I could take care of myself. But I love their hospitality.

December 29, 2004, Wednesday

I spent yesterday afternoon and last night in the Beqa'a visiting friends and was surprised to experience culture shock. I couldn't believe how rich the people in the Beqa'a seemed. They have very little, but they have more than the people in At-Tuwani. The houses in the Beqa'a seem so big now. Most of the people in At-Tuwani have one small room for each family. This morning Jerry Levin and nine Americans connected with Holy Land Trust in Bethlehem came to the Beqa'a for a tour. After hearing the Jaber family members tell their story, we came to At-Tuwani where I helped give the Americans a tour.

NBC journalists came yesterday morning and went to Ma'on to film the Tuba school children being escorted to school. Ma'on settlers stopped them at gunpoint. Israeli police supported the settlers by forcing the journalists to retreat, even though they had a permit from the Israeli military to film there. The journalists then filmed the children from above the village.

I also learned that a settler from the Avi Gail outpost attacked shepherds near Mufakara yesterday and threatened to kill one shepherd. Police came, but the shepherd decided not to press charges against the settler after he came to an agreement with the police that he could graze his land and that the settlers must stay away from his land. The shepherd then invited the police to his home and said he would kill a sheep for them.

December 30, 2004, Thursday

I didn't sleep well last night after receiving a phone call that my wife, Peggy, would be arriving here today. I was too excited to sleep. She arrived in Amman, Jordan, yesterday on her way back to Iraq. It was decided that before returning to Iraq she would come here first. She has been working with CPT in Iraq since 2002. Peggy tells about her work with CPT in Iraq in her book *Iraq: A Journey of Hope and Peace* (Herald Press, 2004).

I headed for Hebron this morning, met Peggy there, and together we returned to At-Tuwani for another honeymoon. As we walked up the road to At-Tuwani, Peggy realized that when she rode on a tractor from Karmil to Jinba three years ago, she had passed through At-Tuwani. The village looked familiar to her.

We received a royal welcome in At-Tuwani. The women were especially eager to get a glimpse of this woman they had heard so much about from me. After greeting everyone, we were invited to Nasser and Kiefah's house for tea. We were then taken to Na'im and Sabha's house for the evening. A lot of people were there, both women and men, including Saber, the mayor. They prepared a feast, machlube, to welcome Peggy. When we were ready to eat, all the women went to another room. Peggy said she had a marvelous time with the women, all snuggled together under blankets in the cold house.

I could hear a lot of laughing, including Peggy's, coming from the next room. I feel quite honored that they would receive Peggy in this way. The motivation for that honor probably is complex, including appreciation for the presence of our team, and probably appreciation for Peggy's work in Iraq.

A big jackhammer and bulldozer started work on the road to Jinba today, thanks to a grant from ERM, a British aid group. The road is so rocky that even tractors have to go very slowly. A car would not make it. When we arrived here this afternoon a military jeep drove into the village. Saber talked to the soldiers, who gave an order that work on the road stop. Team members observed the conversation but did not get involved. There is to be a meeting of Palestinian leaders in Yatta in the morning to discuss their response.

December 31, 2004, Friday

Peggy and I were given a day off, so we left at ten o'clock this morning to walk to Jinba, a village about five miles south of At-Tuwani. Three years ago, Peggy and other CPTers spent three days helping protect the people of Jinba from settler attacks during the barley harvest. She was eager to get back to Jinba to see the people there. We knew it would be a long walk up and down mountains, and it was. The walk through the mountains was breathtaking in more ways than one. The barren, rocky hills with small patches of fields are a testament to the determination of the people here to eke out an existence from these mountains. We saw shepherds grazing their flocks on the mountains around us. There wasn't much grass there between the rocks, but the sheep do find a bit to eat.

We saw where the jackhammer and bulldozer had done some leveling of the extremely rough road. They must have done a mile and a half yesterday. That the Israelis do not want the only road to surrounding small poor villages to be improved says a lot about the attitude of the Israeli government toward the people.

We also saw the various settler outposts on the hilltops along the way. From these outposts come the settlers who almost daily harass the Palestinian farmers and shepherds. We walked past fields of barley, wheat, and lentils that the settlers have burned each year just before they are ready for harvest. We saw wheat fields that just recently had been torn up with the tires of settler tractors and a huge area torn up just two days ago by a military tank. We walked past abandoned villages where the Palestinians have given up because of the continual harassment from settlers.

A group of people in three white SUVs drove toward us on the road. I immediately took them for Israelis. Were they settlers? I took off my CPT hat and Peggy took off her scarf so that we would not be identified with CPT or the Palestinians. It felt too scary to meet settlers alone far away from any other people. When one vehicle stopped, I walked up to them and greeted them in Hebrew. When they asked what we were doing here, I said we were enjoying this beautiful land. We told them we were from America. No more questions asked. We had apparently passed as American Jews and raised no suspicions.

We were not quite sure of our directions when we got close to Jinba and mistakenly took a left turn which led to Mirkez, a small village of tents and caves. A Palestinian man greeted us and told us Jinba was the village in the other direction. He insisted we drink tea with him. Soon a woman with her face covered came and sat with us. Then another woman brought tea. Her husband came and sat with us. He had a sore throat and headache and took some of the oranges and lemons we had brought to give to our hosts in Jinba. I was impressed and honored that he felt free to take some of our fruit.

We were ready to leave, but they insisted we wait a bit. Soon another woman came with a meal of bread, jam, scrambled eggs, olives, and olive oil. She spread the food on a mat on the ground and we had a delicious meal. When we left, they sent bread with us. We invited them to visit us in At-Tuwani.

Soon we were walking up the hill toward Jinba, another small village of caves and tents. Jinba was an important Roman fortress and has been a major center of commerce ever since. As late as 1980, there were two thousand people living in Jinba. Now there are around one hundred residents. In 1985 the Israeli military came and destroyed two thousand olive, fig, almond, and grape trees. Many of these trees were large and dated back to the Ottoman period. That explains why I did not see one tree here today. In 1987, the Israeli military demolished forty homes, many of which were ancient stone houses. Three stores, the mosque, and a swimming pool were also demolished. Today there is not one house in Jinba. The people all live in caves and tents. The Israeli military has strictly forbidden anyone to build a house in Jinba.

There was a good road from Jinba to Yatta, but the Israelis demolished that road in 2002. The only other way to get from Jinba to doctors, hospitals, schools, and other services is the rough three-hour tractor ride through At-Tuwani. In 2003, a Jinba woman died in labor during the tractor ride to Yatta.

Miriam, maybe sixty years old, saw us coming and came down the hill to greet us. She remembered Peggy as the American farmer who knew how to harvest barley. Peggy apparently made quite an impression on the Jinba farmers with her ability to do hard physical work harvesting the barley. They were surprised that an American woman could do hard physical work. They harvest the barley by hand, stooping down to grab the barley and using sickles to cut the grain stalks.

Peggy told me that at one point a group of Israeli soldiers drove up to the field where they were working. Everyone became tense. No one knew what to expect. Would the soldiers force everyone to leave the land, as they have often done? What trouble might the soldiers cause? Peggy and Zleekha, their translator, looked at each other and together knew what to do. They took the initiative in trying to break the tension and get the encounter with the soldiers off to a good start. They walked up to the soldiers, put out their hands, and welcomed the soldiers, saying, "We're glad you came. We could use your help. We have a lot of work to do." The soldiers declined the offer. However, this led to a friendly conversation and joking around. As the soldiers got ready to leave, they said, "We have a lot of work to do too. Maybe you could help us?" Peggy responded, "But we only work nonviolently."

We soon met another woman, Huwaida, in whose cave Peggy had stayed three years ago. Miriam and Huwaida are married to brothers, Musa and Issa. Huwaida brought out mats from her cave for us to sit on. They served us tea and said the men had gone to Yatta for Friday prayers and would come back tomorrow. We felt a bit awkward, but welcome. We enjoyed viewing the gorgeous valley below us.

Ibrahim, a neighbor, came home on a donkey with his four-year-old son, Ahmed. When Peggy came here from Karmil on a tractor three years ago, Ibrahim's wife, Nadia, was in the trailer with her week old son, Yunis, and one-year-old Ahmed who is now four. Soon we also met Nadia and little Yunis.

Ibrahim told us that a week ago on Thursday, three Jinba teenagers were tending their sheep when three settlers from the nearby Itimar settlement, armed with one rifle and two pistols, approached them between ten and eleven o'clock in the morning. One of the settlers aimed his rifle at the three youths as the settlers stole three sheep. Ibrahim said the police did nothing. Each year the people of Jinba lose much of their crops and flocks to settler violence and thievery.

Some of their loss is also from the military. Each year the Israeli government sprays some of their fields with herbicide to kill their crops. This also results in sheep dying and people getting sick.

Miriam then led us to her cave, an incredibly welcoming room carved out of the rock on the hillside hundreds of years ago. We were treated to sheep cheese. We watched as Miriam sat on the floor preparing supper. She began by putting chunks of dried sheep cheese in a bowl with water and mixing it up with her right hand. She added tomato, onion, and oil and poured it into a pot on a fire. Peggy helped her break up bread in a bowl. The soup was poured over the bread and mixed, and soon we were treated to a delicious meal. Huwaida came and ate with us.

Before long, Miriam put out the mats and we went to bed.

January 1, 2005, Saturday

Happy New Year. When I went outside in the middle of the night, I was impressed with all the lights in Israel on the other side of the Green Line, just a mile or two away. Everything was dark on the Palestinian side.

Huwaida spent the night with us. She and Miriam acted like young girls at a slumber party as they giggled and talked much of the night. Miriam woke Huwaida at five o'clock to tend the sheep. I went out with them and talked with some neighbor men who told me the first home demolition was in 1985. There have been many house and cave demolitions since then. I could see the rubble of many of the houses.

We had a breakfast of cooked fresh sheep milk made into curds, bread, and olive oil. We then left and started our walk home, greeting people on the way. We met five brothers from

Mirkez, who were gathering brush for their fires and insisted we go back home with them, but we declined.

When we got to the top of the last hill before At-Tuwani, we saw the bulldozer smoothing the road. We chatted a bit with the driver. We walked a little farther and saw a settler security truck approach and drive past to the left of the road. We knew that meant trouble. Soon we saw team members coming toward us to check on the bulldozer. We decided to keep walking toward home and were impressed with the new smooth road to At-Tuwani.

As we approached the village, we saw the jackhammer at work behind the school, making some play space for the school children. Soon police and soldiers arrived for another confrontation at the school. There were at least twelve Israelis and maybe thirty villagers. The Israelis had guns. We learned that police came again yesterday and threatened that if the bulldozer and jackhammer were moved even one foot, they would be confiscated. The men decided to defy the order and resume work this morning. We stood and watched the scene by the school, standing where the villagers wanted us to stand, so that we were not involved but visible to the police and soldiers.

The standoff ended with the police arresting the owner of the equipment. He was later released. We also learned that after consulting with the settler security man that we saw on the road, the soldiers ordered the bulldozer back to At-Tuwani. The soldiers do what the settler security man tells them to do.

The people here do have a letter from the military stating that they have permission to repair the road. That is not the same as a permit, however. They did not try to get a permit because they knew they couldn't get a permit. They simply decided to go ahead and do what needs to be done. The next step will be for them to discuss this with their lawyer.

I suggested that lots of us, Israelis, internationals, and Palestinians, go out with picks and shovels and continue repairing the road. Have lots of media here. What a story that would make. The Israeli government will not allow even minor repairs on a horribly rough road while Israeli settlers drive on the new road nearby. This would create a dilemma for the Israelis. If they allow us to repair the road, we win. If they do not allow us to repair the road, that visually exposes the racist policy of not allowing Palestinians to have even decent dirt roads.

A lot of people came to At-Tuwani for a goodbye meal for Saliim and Sarriya Adara, the parents of Na'im, Nasser, Yassir, and Aisha Hereni, who are leaving tomorrow to go to Mecca for the pilgrimage. This evening we were part of another send-off for them.

January 2, 2005, Sunday

A Dove and I went up the hill for school patrol. Two others left early and walked to Tuba to meet the children there. They called and said that an armed settler came between the waiting soldier jeep and the children. The settler threatened the children who shouted to the soldiers for help and ran back toward Tuba. Omar and his son came out and they all started walking toward the jeep. They could still see the settler. When the soldiers finally got out of the jeep and started walking toward them, the children ran toward the soldiers. The children, along with three soldiers walking with them, then continued their walk toward At-Tuwani with settlers on the hill above them in the trees yelling threats and making weird threatening noises. Three settlers and a dog also followed two of our team members part of the way back, shouting threats at them.

This story, like everything else here, makes no rational sense. The soldiers and police do nothing about fellow Israelis threatening school children, yet the children run to the soldiers for protection, the very same soldiers who are protecting the settlers and threatening the future of all Palestinians here. We watch from adjacent hills because we are not allowed in the area, but the settlers who threaten children and soldiers are allowed in that area near the children. The Israelis prevent Palestinians from improving their roads and even demolish many roads, but Israelis have new modern roads.

Peggy and I spent the evening with Nasser and Kiefah. Kiefah wanted to talk with us about the oppression women experience in At-Tuwani. Some women are controlled by their husbands, have no freedom, and can't leave their homes. She said that other village men are different. They allow their wives freedom and are not threatened by strong women. That led to a discussion of Islam and women. She said that the oppression of women is tradition and culture, not true Islam. The coming of Islam originally brought liberation for women.

I have done some study of Muslim feminists, so I, in my arrogance, thought I could teach her something about Islamic feminism. I quickly realized that she already knew what I was only learning. She was aware of the idea that the conservative commentaries (Tafsir) have taken on more authority for some Muslims than the Qur'an itself. I thought about how the same thing happened in Christianity, with the freedom for women in the Early Church being subverted by later male leadership. I thought, "Yes, women are oppressed here, but women are also oppressed in Western culture. Oppression takes many forms."

Tom Fox and John Lynes came today. We were blessed by Tom's visit with us. He has been working with CPT in Iraq and wanted to experience a bit of our team life in Palestine. He had been a member of the U.S. Marine Band but then left the Marines, became a Quaker, and devoted the rest of his life to working for peace. Tom is a tall, quiet, unassuming person. He came to us with an eagerness to learn both about the suffering of the Palestinian and Israeli people and about how our team is responding to the oppression all around us. He asked lots of questions about our work here, comparing the situation here with what he has been experiencing in Iraq, in order to take those insights back to his work in Iraq.

Note: Little did we know that in less than a year's time, Tom would be kidnapped in Iraq. Later he was killed and his body found in Baghdad on March 9, 2006.

January 3, 2005, Monday

Tom, Peggy, and I went on school patrol this morning. It was raining and extremely muddy on the freshly bulldozed road. The children were late, arriving at 7:45 in a military jeep. The jeep stopped before getting to the normal stopping place. The children got out, and two soldiers got out. The soldiers waved goodbye, but apparently the children insisted that the soldiers walk with them because the two soldiers then did walk with the children the rest of the way. We met the children who told us there were no problems. I am so impressed with these children. Every morning they face the threats of the settlers, the rain and cold, and the long walk because they are determined both to go to school and to resist the occupation.

John, Peggy, and I went out on school patrol at 10:30 because school was dismissing early today. School let out just as we passed the school. We waited a long time in the cold and rain. We called the military and police. The soldiers finally came at 12:30. One soldier walked with the children in the rain. We came back wet and frozen.

Peggy spoke to a group of village women this evening about her work in Iraq. There was an enthusiastic response. The women could easily identify with the oppression of the Iraqi people. These women are serious about changing the world, and are not afraid to take risks. Settlers recently beat one of them as she tended sheep out in the mountains.

January 10, 2005, Monday

Peggy and I left for Hebron last Tuesday morning where we spent some time being part of the Hebron team and visiting Palestinian friends in the Hebron area. Our Palestinian friends had many questions about Iraq for Peggy, and some expressed a lot of fear and concern for her. Much of the conversation with one family centered on having fear, trusting in God, and acting in faith. Peggy told them that it is love that overcomes fear and that the only way she can continue her work is to daily pray for love. This family also struggles with fear as they daily face threats from settlers and soldiers.

How beautiful it is when Christians and Muslims can share their faith together, when they can talk about how their faith affects their lives. That is so much better than arguing about differences in belief.

I said goodbye to Peggy this morning in Jerusalem as she got a taxi to the Allenby Bridge on her way to Amman and then tomorrow to Baghdad. I realize how dangerous it is to be in Iraq but have no doubt that she is called to go there. I am grateful I can have a small part in supporting her in her calling and view our times of separation as times of fasting. I don't like our periods of separation, but being convinced that she is following God's call for her makes it much easier. What is better, more fulfilling, more joy-producing, than doing what God calls us to do?

Bill Baldwin and I got a bus to the Bethlehem checkpoint and waited to meet a bus with Lutheran seminary students. We led them on a tour of Hebron and then At-Tuwani. We first went into Hebron to the Ibrahimi Mosque and then to the synagogue side at the Cave of Machpelah. While waiting to go into the synagogue, Israeli soldiers harassed a Palestinian Christian woman from Bethlehem who was with us. She felt humiliated by being singled out and having her identity card challenged. The only reason she was singled out was because she was Palestinian. We all gathered around her and the soldiers. I sensed that the soldiers were quite embarrassed by what they felt they had to do. They seemed to know that what they were doing was racist and wrong. That is encouraging. They actually apologized to her. We ended up being denied entry into the synagogue.

The noon call to prayer rang out from the minaret above us as we waited. A Jewish woman, maybe fifty years old, who was praying outside at the corner of the building, immediately began screaming and wailing at the top of her voice and continued her wailing until the end of the call to prayer. Although

I could not understand her Hebrew, it seemed that she was crying out to God in defiance of the Muslim faith, calling on God to rescue and preserve the Jews from the Muslims. Or, maybe she was cursing Islam. My heart was filled with compassion for that woman. I have no doubt about the sincerity of her prayer. She loves God, wants to serve God, and probably truly believes that God loves only Jews.

I experienced a deep longing that this woman would be able to rejoice that Muslims also call out to the God of Abraham, Sarah, and Hagar. I wished that she could see the Muslim faith as a confirmation of the faith of Abraham, that before God the Muslims are not only her cousins, but sisters and brothers, loved alike by God. I was reminded that faith can free us, or it can imprison our minds and hearts.

Soon we were on our way to At-Tuwani in a splendid new bus on the new Israeli bypass roads, for a ten- to fifteen-minute ride south of Hebron. I wished we would have taken the Palestinian roads. I felt very uncomfortable using my privilege to do things the Palestinians are not allowed to do. When we got to At-Tuwani, suddenly the seminary students became Palestinians because our bus was unable to drive into At-Tuwani since the road was too torn up by the Israeli military for the bus to get through. The seminary students had to walk through the mud just like Palestinians have to do. We had only one hour, much too short a time, but we gave them a tour and they saw the real Bethlehem.

We saw a military jeep by the bus as we walked down the hill. I had seen a settler security vehicle in the area when we walked into At-Tuwani, so I assumed that the settler informed the military about our presence. There was no problem, but the soldiers wanted to know who we were and why we were in At-Tuwani. Our presence reminded the soldiers that the world is watching what they are doing here.

January 11, 2005, Tuesday

This is the beginning of a three-week school vacation. We plan to spend this time visiting other villages in the area. Bill and I walked about a half hour southwest to Mufakara and met a shepherd who invited us for tea, bread, and sheep butter. His wife was washing the children's hair. We sat outside his cave overlooking a spectacular valley between two large, rocky mountains to the south. We also had a view of much of the rest of the village. All eleven village families live in caves. The shepherd took us into his cave, which felt warm and inviting. He said his cave is new, only about one hundred years old.

Soldiers came to the clinic this afternoon at one o'clock and ordered work to stop. When I got here yesterday I noticed that they had started building the pillars for the second floor. They now have permission for one floor but have decided to go ahead with a second story. They want the second floor for a meeting room. These people are great. They keep pushing the boundaries. Someone said they will wait a week and then probably start again. The soldiers apparently are watching everything the people here do.

I have been having fun telling people that I am very unhappy when they ask me how I am doing. They immediately recognize that I am joking about Peggy not being here. It gets a laugh every time.

January 12, 2005, Wednesday

Bill and I walked the long path to Tuba. It was a long, two-hour walk on the donkey path, crossing over gorgeous mountains. We met various people on the donkey path, people who now have no other way in and out of their villages because of closed roads or being prohibited from using the good roads. When we approached anyone on the path, I always called out *Salaam Alykum* to them to ease their fears. It must be scary for them to meet North Americans way out in the mountains. How could they know we are not settlers?

After two hours we were in Tuba. We visited with Omar's brother, Ibrahim, and his family. Omar and Zahreia came over to see us. We had a lunch of bread, olives, olive oil, and dibs. They wanted us to stay the night. I sure wanted to because I was really tired, but we needed to get back. The path was long and we were weary, but the mountains were inspiring.

January 15, 2005, Saturday

I took Nina Mayorek and Vivi Sury, two Israeli women from Machsom Watch, on a tour of Hebron. They wanted to experience how Palestinians live. I seem to have become desensitized to the settler Hebrew graffiti everywhere around the old city. I became more aware of it today as I accompanied the two Israeli women through the city. They told me it is so disgusting they did not want to translate it for me. They pointed out that there is no difference between this and the anti-Jewish graffiti of the Nazi era. "What is the difference," they asked, "between a Star of David and 'Death to the Jews' or a Star of David with 'Death to the Arabs'?"

There seemed to be an extra large number of soldiers on the streets today. There were soldiers everywhere. Every time I walk through the market and encounter six soldiers on patrol with their guns held high, ready to shoot, and see them point their guns around every corner, I am appalled by the horror the soldiers must be experiencing and causing. I am also troubled by the incredible arrogance of sending these eighteen-year-old Israeli youth into Palestinian neighborhoods with such a show of force.

I recoil in horror every time, and it is difficult for me to greet them in an open, friendly manner and see them as people instead of as enemies. I know too much about the atrocities they regularly commit. Today I was in even more turmoil as I walked with these two Israeli women and sensed their fear of and disgust with what the soldiers were doing. I also remembered that Israeli soldiers have trained American soldiers to do the same things in Iraq.

I had a long talk with two soldiers as I waited for the women this morning. They wanted to know what I am doing here so I told them. They seemed very supportive. They agreed that guns will never solve anything, and they hope to work for peace after their military duty, but they feel they have a duty to their country. One of them, whose father came from Iran, said his sister has been picking olives with the Palestinians since doing her military duty.

Soldiers also have consciences. We have seen soldiers in Hebron being nasty and not allowing children to go to school until their commander leaves the area. The soldiers then allow and even encourage the children to go to school. Often Israeli soldiers have confided in me that they do not approve of what they are doing and think their actions are counterproductive, but for various reasons, they have chosen not to resist. One soldier told me he has a wife and two children and does not want to go to prison. Some soldiers think they can counteract some of the harshness of the military.

Note: To learn more about the reactions of Israeli soldiers who spent time in Hebron, see the website of Breaking the Silence, a group started in 2004 by a group of Israeli soldiers who had done military duty in Hebron and are now documenting the atrocities in which they participated.

January 16, 2005, Sunday

I got into a big conversation today about the recent Palestinian election with a group of Palestinians, including a member of the Palestinian Legislative Council. They said that abu Mazen, the successor to Yassir Arafat, has no power. Israel and the United States have the power and will do what ever they want to do, and are not inclined to give much to the Palestinians. Abu Mazen's assigned role is to keep the Palestinian people under control.

I suggested that abu Mazen's role need not to be Israel's servant or to keep the Palestinian people under control. Rather, his role could be to lead the Palestinian people in a nonviolent campaign to end the Occupation, which would include a serious struggle of civil disobedience, like everyone destroying their identity cards or defying curfews. Will abu Mazen have the vision to lead the Palestinian people, or will he play the game defined for him by U.S. and Israeli interests?

I went to the Beqa'a Valley and visited the Sultans. Beheh, their youngest son, and I decided to walk up the hill across the road where just three years ago an illegal settlement outpost had been started. On Friday evening, January 17, 2003, two Palestinians came to the outpost and killed Natanel Ozeri (Nati), the founder of the outpost. In response, settlers rioted and caused much destruction of Palestinian property in the area, while I watched from a Palestinian home across the road. I remember surveying the massive damage to Palestinian property following the rioting.

We could not have walked up this hill two years ago, even though it is Sultan land, because settlers probably would have attacked us. Even the Sultans could not go on their own land near the outpost. We walked past the place where some settlers had wanted to bury Nati before his body was snatched away by other settlers, taken to Jerusalem for burial, and then brought back and buried in Hebron. Settlers still come here every Friday to remember Nati.

We then came to a pile of rubble, the remains of the small outpost the Israeli military demolished after Nati's death. I felt a deep sense of awe as I stood silently in front of the rubble of Nati's house. I thought of the shattered dreams both of Nati's family and of Palestinians whose homes have been demolished. I thought also of how distorted and misplaced Nati's dreams were, how they caused so much suffering and grief for both Palestinians and Israelis.

There had been trouble from the beginning. Nati harassed, threatened, and destroyed the property of his Palestinian neighbors. He prevented neighboring farmers from going to their land near the new outpost and stole a tractor, tools, and animals. He and his friends destroyed many trees and four hundred grape vines and assaulted more than twenty of their neighbors.

Nati was a leader in Kach, a right-wing Israeli organization named a terrorist organization by both the Israeli government and the U.S. State Department. He wrote the biography of Baruch Goldstein, the settler who massacred twenty-nine Muslims as they prayed in the Ibrahimi Mosque in Hebron in 1994. His wife's father got a life sentence for killing Hebron University students.

I thought of his friend, Dov, who was killed near At-Tuwani, and the suffering and grief he caused. I thought about how much I care about the settlers. I thought about how both the Beqa'a and At-Tuwani are intertwined and now are part of my life. I remembered how Nati and Dov were among the settlers who had camped out in front of the Sultan home in December 1999, demanding that the Israeli military demolish the house and give them permission to start a new settlement on the Sultan land. I remembered living with the Sultan family to help protect them during that time of terror. (I recorded this in *Hebron Journal*, pp. 194-221.)

January 18, 2005, Tuesday

When I left the apartment in Hebron at noon, I noticed a soldier out on Shuhada Street pointing his gun at me. I said, "Don't point your gun at me." At first he seemed to not understand, so I said it again. He raised his gun and aimed it more directly at me. I said, "I am a human being, a person. Don't point your gun at me. Didn't your mother teach you to respect people?" He then disappeared around the corner. I wonder what he was thinking.

People keep asking me about Peggy. I am always touched by that. What a gift it is to be allowed to do this work. Even if Peggy does nothing in Iraq, just her being there in the middle of the violence as a protest against violence is in itself a powerful witness.

January 20, 2005, Thursday

Today is the first day of Eid al Adha, the most important feast in the Muslim calendar, a remembrance of Abraham's readiness to sacrifice his oldest son, whom Muslims say was Ishmael. I went with villagers to visit extended family in the village of Ar Rifa'iyya along the settler road between here and Hebron. First we went to Eid prayers in the small mosque there. I appreciated the chanting and the prayers. Around us were very common and simple people who warmly welcomed me.

After prayers I was led down into the village and invited into a room with some men. After five minutes we went out and sat on chairs around a fire. I didn't understand what was happening until they led a large Holstein cow toward us. Then I understood. It is customary to sacrifice an animal on the Eid. They were going to kill the cow. I learned that the cow had belonged to Grandmother Adara who died recently at age 103, and the cow was literally to be divided among the family.

It was quite an event. They brought out butcher knives, and soon the cow was tied up and its throat was slit. I felt sorry for the cow. Although I had misgivings, I felt I should help. At least thirty of us were involved, including the women, who had their roles. They cleaned the stomach and prepared for cooking while the men cut the meat into pieces, divided it into three piles, and then gave each family their share. One-third goes to poor people. I thought all these people were poor. I was impressed with how everyone was included, how power was shared, and how everyone worked together. There was no boss. Decisions were made by a lot of talking back and forth.

One of the men took me for a walk across the road from where I could see the Karmel and Ma'on settlements, At-Tuwani, and the whole surrounding area. I saw many demolished homes, the settler roads, and the nearby military tower and outpost. Practically every home in this area is subject to Israeli demolition. That felt so horrible to me. The village is right along the settler road and gets a lot of harassment from both settlers and soldiers.

At about eleven o'clock I was told we were leaving to go just across the hill to the edge of Khallet al Maiyya, the village where Waheed Sultan's wife, Dalal, is from. I thought about her and the Sultan family. This is another connection between the Beqa'a Valley and the South Hebron Hills. We went to Ni'man's house, the brother of Nasser, Yassir, and Na'im.

About twenty people were there, and as soon as I saw the camel I knew what we were going to do. In spite of feeling really bad for the camel, I once again felt a need to participate. Again we cut up all the meat and put it in three piles and divided it between quite a few families. I was given two bags of meat, but gave them to someone in need.

It was clear to me today that an important part of our work right now is building relationships. I did a lot of that today. It is a bit frustrating, as I am unable to keep up with all these relationships, but now I can go to Ar Rifa'iyya and people will know me. I do not know what this means for the future, but I believe it will be relevant somehow. Maybe I will never know. I also sense the importance of the door to the Islamic world that has been opened to me.

Because other roads were closed, we drove more than five miles over terrible roads to get to Ni'man's house just across the valley, not more than a half-mile from Ar Rifa'iyya. The road home was even worse. We could have been home in five minutes on the settler road but had to go more than a half-hour on horrible, bumpy, rocky, potholed roads at no more than five miles an hour. I felt a lot of anger and told everyone in the car how disgusted I felt at this indignity.

I also made a lot of jokes. I kept telling them to turn left toward the good road. They kept telling me, "No, that is *Mamnuah* (forbidden)." When we finally got to a better road, I told them to stop, that Palestinians are not allowed on such good roads. They all got a good laugh out of that.

I also made a theological point. I said two roads, one for Israelis, one for Palestinians, is *haram* (a horrible sin) because it is a racist policy in denial of the oneness of God. If God is one, then it is unthinkable to have a good road for Israelis and a rough road for Palestinians. Those separate and unequal roads are a mockery of the heart of the Judeo/Christian/Islamic faith.

It occurred to me that when we are discussing various topics and situations, I often make simple theological observations, like referring to the goodness of creation, the importance of grace, and the oneness of God. The Muslims here also often make theological observations, as for example, people continually referring to the goodness of God. In fact, the Arabic language is laced with theological terms. Maybe an important part of what it means to witness is to keep raising basic spiritual questions.

January 21, 2005, Friday

After worship, we spent time in our team meeting talking about how to respond if we meet settlers out in the mountains when we are with the shepherds. One option is to leave the area. When the shepherds see settlers, they run. But there are problems with running. We get scattered, and we give the message we are weak and afraid of the settlers, and that we are on the Palestinian side. If we meet the settlers, we will walk toward them in an open, friendly way, greet them, and show them we are not threatening them and not intimidated by them. If we are at a distance, we may decide to leave the area, but not run.

We talked a while about cameras that the Palestinians want us to have because they are important for documenting what happens. On the other hand, I feel especially unsafe meeting settlers if they see I have a camera. I do not want to do anything to upset them if I am alone with them out in the mountains. Cameras can be a form of protection by letting settlers know that what they do will be filmed, but cameras can also inflame the anger of the settlers and increase our risk. Confronting settlers here feels different from confronting settlers in Hebron. There I was on public streets with some sense of protection from all the people around me. But I also have a desire to meet settlers here. I really want to talk with them.

When I was in Hebron this week, I read the book *Storm of Terror: A Hebron Mother's Diary* (Ivan R. Dee, Chicago, 2002), by June Leavitt, a woman who lives in Kiryat Arba. The book describes many of the events I describe in *Hebron Journal*, but from a very different perspective. I was especially interested in learning about the author's son living in the settler outpost here and about Dov's death here. I want to meet her and her son.

Since I promised the people in Tuba I would visit them during the Eid, I got permission from others on the team to go today. I got stopped before I left and had to first eat at Mfathil and Jamla Rabai's house. I had a delightful time sitting in the sun eating with the family. I feel so accepted here.

It was a long walk to Tuba on the narrow donkey path, so narrow that at places I had to be careful not to slip and go tumbling down the mountain. I felt a lot of anger that I could have walked to Tuba in fifteen minutes past the settlement, and anger for the many Palestinians for whom this is their only way to get to stores, schools, doctors, etc. This narrow path across and around the mountains is new, created only three years ago, because it was never needed before, since there used to be roads Palestinians could use. I met and talked to various shepherds along the way as they were grazing their sheep.

Suddenly, I came upon a donkey grazing alone in a field. I wondered why the donkey was there, from where it had come. As I approached the donkey, it started walking away. As it started moving, I heard a baby crying. There was a child in the saddlebag! "I must do something," I thought, "but what?" I then saw another shepherd who thought the donkey was from Tuba. So I walked behind the donkey, encouraging it to keep moving on the path toward Tuba. The baby kept crying. When we got closer to Tuba I saw another shepherd returning to Tuba with a large flock of maybe 150 sheep. I yelled to him. He came, jumped on the donkey, and rode back toward his flock of sheep. Apparently the donkey had wondered off from the flock. I guess the shepherd knew the donkey would return home. He didn't seem worried. And I didn't do anything heroic.

I got to Ibrahim's home totally exhausted. Ibrahim and Omar had not gotten back from Yatta. I tried to relate to the children but didn't do well because I was so tired. I fell asleep there on the mat in the sun and woke up when Ibrahim got home.

I watched the family do their chores, bring the sheep back from grazing, and feed the sheep. As I watched the flocks go to the safety of the sheepfolds for the night, I was reminded of many biblical images of shepherds and sheep. I thought of people being like sheep, blindly following their leader. As a flock of sheep moves about, the sheep are all close together, with each sheep not looking where it is going but simply following the sheep in front of it.

As it was getting dark, I was invited into their tent for prayers and then a supper of lamb and noodles. It was delicious. People are eating more meat during the feast. Maybe that helps explain the Catholic and Orthodox Christian practice of fast and feast days and not eating meat on fast days. Poor people eat meat mainly on special occasions.

Omar and some of his family came over and we had a wonderful time talking in the tent.

It was wonderful not having electricity and, therefore, no TV. We could just talk with each other. I visit so many homes here where the whole family is glued to the TV. So often, the television set is at the center of the home. It colors every interaction in the family. I often wish we could just talk with each other. How can we win this struggle for a new social order if the TV brainwashes everyone with its theology of redemptive violence, crass materialism, and sexism?

I have started turning my back to the TV and refusing to watch it. One of the many things that disturb me about TV is how everyone is portrayed as super rich. All the homes are elegant. What does it mean for these poor people to watch that? It must be destructive. What does it mean for women to see all the women on TV portrayed as glamorous? What will be the long-term effects of TV on this culture?

We had a lot of fun joking, but they seemed to appreciate when the conversation turned in a more serious direction. We talked about what it means to serve God, about not worshipping money, about giving everything we have for peace and justice. I was quite aware that the children were listening and soaking in every word. It was wonderful sitting together in that small circle, huddled under blankets in such an intimate way, with just a kerosene lamp for light. We have sacrificed so much intimacy in having electricity, bright lights, and big warm homes.

January 22, 2005, Saturday

Ibrahim turned on his battery radio at about five o'clock this morning to listen to British Broadcasting Corporation (BBC) news in Arabic. There was lots of news about Palestine and Iraq. We then had breakfast in bed. Actually, we ate sitting on the mats we slept on.

Ibrahim showed me an order from the Israeli police from last July ordering him to stop farming another five acres of his land. It surprised me that this order came from the police and not the military authorities. So the Israeli police are also directly involved in stealing land.

January 23, 2005, Sunday

The owners came this morning and took away the bull-dozer that had been sitting here since January 1 when Israeli authorities demanded that the Palestinians stop work on the road to Jinba. This means that for now they have given up on repairing the road. That brought up a lot of anger in me that I have to deal with. Why can't Palestinians fix their road?

We talked about spending more time in other villages in our team meeting today. Out of that discussion, the team decided that a Dove and I should go to Jinba to spend the night and check on what is happening there. So we had a brisk walk in the cold wind. It looked like it would rain, but the rain held off until we got to Jinba.

When we got there Musa and his family were finishing chores with the sheep and tightening down a tent in preparation for wind and rain. Soon we were drinking tea in Musa and Huwaida's cave and then eating a delicious supper. When we finished eating we went over to his brother Issa and sister-in-law Miriam's cave where we all had a long conversation and spent the night. I told them how when Peggy and I were here, Miriam and Huwaida chattered all night. That got a big laugh.

As Musa and Issa shared some of the history of Jinba, I was thinking that this is just one of more than a thousand villages where one can hear the same stories, stories that can be repeated in every Palestinian village and town. Why does the U.S. government continue to support these crimes against humanity? Ethnic cleansing is wrong no matter who does it. We learned that their fields had not yet been sprayed with herbicide this year.

I asked about what the Wall will mean for people here. Issa replied, "I don't care about the Wall. It makes no difference to me. Either way, the Israelis want us to leave and take our land, but we are not leaving."

I laid on my mat in that beautiful ancient cave and felt the weight of oppression these families are enduring, but my heart was also filled with joy as I thought of these beautiful, gentle, strong people who are simply trusting God for their future. As I lay in that cave, I felt I was in the womb of the earth, surrounded by God's love and care.

January 24, 2005, Monday

I woke up feeling incredibly happy. As we ate a simple breakfast of bread and sheep yogurt, Issa said that Jesus was present with us. I also sensed that as we broke bread and drank tea together. Issa said, "There is not a Jewish religion, a Christian religion, or a Muslim religion. There is one God and one religion.

We are not separate." Those words encouraged me. Can we call all people to that one faith, that one Lord? I sensed this oneness of Spirit with these Muslims in Jinba. The Spirit of Jesus is alive and incarnated in the people here. I am humbled by these gentle people.

It had rained all night, so the long walk back to At-Tuwani was through mud. It was hard going but also fun.

When we got back, two Doves left to visit the village of Jawiyya, across the road from the Ma'on settlement. The village has a long history of harassment from both settlers and soldiers. They have demolition orders for their tents and buildings. A shepherd told the Doves that he was out near the Israeli road with his sheep this morning when a settler security man with a gun drove up, stopped his car, and shouted at him to leave the area. As is common for shepherds here, they leave the area immediately when settlers approach them. Their vast experience tells them that if they don't leave, either they or their sheep get beaten, or they get arrested. Sometimes sheep are killed and sometimes stolen. What an exercise of raw power over the Palestinian shepherds! How can we affect this imbalance of power?

A shepherd from Mufakara came and said settlers came toward him today, but he and his sheep escaped. He seemed quite troubled. He asked us to accompany him tomorrow. That led to a short discussion with him. We said we want to do more than just watch for settlers. It seems that the main role shepherds see for us is to be on the lookout for settlers, so that the shepherds can run away with their flocks when settlers approach. What more could we do? We suggested that if we see settlers, we immediately tell the shepherds who will leave, but we will stay to face the settlers. He agreed and asked us to come to Mufakara at noon tomorrow.

That led to a big discussion among us after he left. How ready are we to face the settlers? At what point would we leave the area? Under what conditions do we walk toward the settlers? How would we respond to the settlers? Now I need to deal with my fears. I am not quite ready to meet those settlers. I hope I will be ready tomorrow. My greatest fear is that Hebron settlers may be there and recognize me and vent their anger from the past on me. Over the past ten years, I have experienced a lot of hate from the Hebron settlers. I would rather start from a neutral beginning when meeting settlers way out in the mountains.

January 25, 2005, Tuesday

A shepherd from Mufakara came by and told us to come and accompany them tomorrow instead of today. We sent the two Doves over to Jawiyya again to accompany shepherds. After maybe an hour they called and asked us to come over to join them. They were across the road from the Ma'on settlement where soldiers had arrested a shepherd.

When we got there, we saw six soldiers. This was my first encounter with Itimar, a short, blond soldier who seemed to be in charge. Everyone seemed relaxed as we waited for the police to come. We were on the telephone calling Israeli support people, police, media, and U.N. officials. There was some good

Shepherds heading out to the hills.

conversation between shepherds and soldiers, including some joking. The shepherds are quite adept at relating to soldiers. When I asked one of the soldiers what was happening, he told me that these Palestinians know that this land does not belong to them, that they are trespassing. "You don't know these Arabs," he said. "They are bad people. They do terrible things all the time. We see what they are doing every day." When I questioned him, he said that all this land belongs to the Jews. It has belonged to the Jews for thousands of years. The Arabs are thieves, living on Jewish land.

Another soldier said that the whole problem here is caused by the presence of us internationals. "Before you came in September there were no problems here," he said. When I questioned that, he said that we don't know what is happening here. The soldiers see everything, even what is happening inside Arab homes. He denied that any land is being confiscated or Palestinians being attacked. When I pointed out examples of problems happening here every day, he denied that they were true. He said I was completely wrong in what I was seeing. I wondered, does he really believe that? Is he so taken in by military propaganda?

This soldier was articulating the myth of Israeli innocence, the idea that Israel has done everything in its power to establish peace. They withdrew from Lebanon and turned over parts of the West Bank to Palestinian control, but every step Israel has taken for peace has been rewarded by more violence from the Arabs. The Arabs do not want peace. They have refused every generous offer from the Israelis and offer only violence in return for gestures of peace. The myth of Israeli innocence rejects any legitimacy to Palestinian grievances, making respectful negations near to impossible.

The Doves told us that they had come up the hill with a number of shepherds and their flocks. After about ten minutes, a settler security car stopped, watched a short time, and drove back into the settlement. Soldiers arrived not long after that and shouted in Arabic for the shepherds to leave. The shepherds started to slowly leave. Settlers watched from the road, but stayed in their car. The Doves walked toward the soldiers and greeted them. Itimar politely explained that it is forbidden for the shepherds to be here. When a Dove asked him why, Itimar responded that the settlers are afraid because there are so many people here. He said it might be possible for just one flock to come tomorrow.

It seemed like it was all over, but then a shepherd brought his flock back and some of his sheep ate a bit of the young barley that the settlers had planted in the shepherd's fields. The settlers have been planting these fields since 2000. Two settlers, one with a gun, became very upset and demanded that the shepherd be arrested. So the soldiers obediently arrested the shepherd.

That resulted in a big discussion of who owns the land. "Do the settlers have a deed for this land?" we asked. "Unless the settlers have a deed to the land, there is no problem with the shepherds being on their own land." We had just talked to an Israeli human rights lawyer, Limor Yehuda, with the Association for Civil Rights in Israel (ACRI), who said that if Palestinians own the land, or even if no one owns the land, as long as Israelis do not own the land, the shepherds may go on the land because the land is open to everyone. Only a military order (closed military zone) can keep shepherds out, and the military needs some reason for that.

One of the settlers then walked toward an elderly woman and her flock. The woman picked up a rock. Immediately a soldier ran toward her. The woman then left with her flock.

One of the owners of the land, an older man, came and began shouting at Itimar, who kept telling him to shut up. I was impressed that he was not one bit intimidated by the soldiers. I wondered what difference our presence was making. How would this situation have been different if we had not been there? Would the soldiers and settlers have been more aggressive? Would the shepherds even have been here?

Two Israeli police came at about eleven o'clock and began

to assess the situation. After about fifteen minutes the police announced there would be no arrests, so we started to leave. The shepherds insisted that we go to Jawiyya with them for tea, which turned out to be a delicious meal, with us sitting on mats in the sun, surrounded by the villagers.

The villagers told us that most of the Ma'on settlement was formerly their land. One shepherd said his family lost more than 200 acres to the settlers. They said there are about forty houses in Ma'on, most of which are empty. The shepherds are worried that the settlers may soon start building on Jawiyya land across the road from the settlement to get a foothold on that land in order to expand from there.

We got back home at four o'clock and spent some time evaluating the day. We all were excited about what happened. We had a big discussion about our role in these situations. How much leadership should we give? Should we mainly observe and let the shepherds take the leadership? I wondered if maybe some of us had been too assertive today. In the end, I think we were in agreement that we should give little leadership. We concluded that part of our work is to make the Israelis follow their own rules.

We could be onto something big here. With the help of lawyers, the media, and the international community, maybe we can establish the right of the shepherds to be on their own land. Maybe then we can extend that right to other areas. Today we helped expose the injustice of shepherds not being allowed on their own land.

January 26, 2005, Wednesday

I heard loud booms all day yesterday from the south where the military is doing training exercises. Many of the booms were tank shells exploding. The firing continued during the night, along with the sound of jets and helicopters overhead. This continued most of the day today. How disgusting! They are preparing to kill people. They are preparing for war. Why are they not preparing for peace? All that activity must be costing huge amounts of money, paid for by U.S. taxpayers. I can think of other uses for that money. I also thought about the destruction and desecration of God's creation all that bombing is causing.

Ezra brought a group of six members of the Irish Parliament to At-Tuwani for a tour. We all met down by the clinic where everyone was served tea. After some speeches, we walked up to the school. That was the chance for us team members to share a bit from our perspectives. The parliamentarians seemed very interested and supportive. I think they got the picture of what is happening here.

We were planning to go to Mufakara at noon but were told that we are to go tomorrow. Before we could do anything, we saw shepherds and soldiers up the hill from the school. Villagers asked us to go up there immediately. We walked out to beyond where we do school patrol. There were three flocks of sheep grazing there, all from At-Tuwani. We learned that the reason for the presence of the soldiers was that two settlers on a four-wheeler had seen the shepherds and had probably called the soldiers. By the time we got there, the soldiers had left. We sat with Juma and chatted as we watched the flocks grazing.

✳

Juma Rabai is thiry-one, born in 1974, a quiet man with a strong spirit. Juma's house is on the edge of the village, the house closest to the settler outpost, so his family is especially vulnerable. His father worked in Israel to support the family. Juma left school after ninth grade to help support the family after his father became sick with leukemia. Juma then worked in agriculture in Israel for twelve years.

When the Ma'on settlement began, his father tried to build relationships with the settlers. At times the family was able to graze their sheep inside the settler fence. But beginning in 1986, his family began experiencing repeated settler attacks and attempts to steal their sheep. A settler tried to attack his father in 1986, but his brothers protected their father. In 1988, this same settler shot at his brother. His brother ran toward a neighbor's house. The settler kept shooting, with the last shot hitting the door of the neighbor's house.

In November 1999, Juma's family went to plow their fields. They met thirty settlers and three soldiers at their field. Juma and his cousin went to the soldiers and asked why the settlers were on their land. The settlers then attacked. They threw rocks at them and the tractor, and came and beat them. Juma was hit on the head and was unconscious for ten minutes. He and his cousin were injured and bleeding. The soldiers watched and did nothing. The soldiers even shot at the family as they walked over the hill. They had to wait for one and a half hours for the soldiers to get an ambulance to take them to the hospital.

In 2001, four settlers on horses approached Juma's father, who was old and sick and could not walk well. One of the settlers attacked his father with a horsewhip. They tried to catch Juma's brother, who ran away, but lost one of his shoes in the flight. Settlers took the shoe and cut it into pieces.

In 2002, Juma went to plow his land. Settlers, soldiers, and police came. The police confiscated his tractor, took it to the military base at Susya, and held it for more than a month. The police offered Juma a deal. They would give back his tractor if he signed a release, giving his land to the settlers. He obviously refused, but ended up paying a $250 fine to get the tractor back. Here, it seems the police are also thieves.

Later in 2002, his brother, home from the university, was sitting reading under a tree. A settler came and attacked him. His brother was arrested and fined over $100.

Juma's father was very sick in 2002. They took him to a hospital in Hebron, but the doctors said they could not help him. They released him to die at home. On the way home, four settlers stopped their car on the settler road, took his father out of the car, pulled the tubes out of his body, and assaulted the others with their gunstocks. Soldiers came and did nothing. Juma's father died twenty days later.

The settler attack on CPTers on January 18, 2003, was on Juma's land. It was his tractor that was overturned by settlers.

On April 17, 2003, five settlers approached the family as they were shearing sheep. The settlers all had guns. There was a standoff. The settlers tried to burn their wheat. The family called the police, but the police did not come. Other villagers came. As it was becoming dark, the settlers attacked and started shooting. Hathra, Salman Rabai's wife, was injured when she tried to stop the settlers.

In July 2003, ten masked settlers came out of the forest and attacked shepherds with slingshots. Hathra was again injured. Police came and did nothing.

In August 2003, the family had gone to a wedding in Yatta. When they came back, they heard shooting and saw Juma's son was bleeding. Bullets were hitting the ground around them. The settlers then left in a settler security car. The boy's wounds were superficial, but one person had a head fracture from falling. At two o'clock that same night, soldiers came on Juma's roof where he was sleeping, knocked him down, and asked for his identity card. They beat his brother. The soldiers took the ID cards with them and said they would be back at seven o'clock in the morning. Juma called Ta'ayush. They came with an Israeli journalist before the soldiers arrived. Juma told the Israeli activists to hide because if they were seen, the soldiers would act politely.

When the soldiers came, they spoke very rudely to the family and tried to beat his brother. The Israeli activists came out of hiding, after which the soldiers quickly gave back the IDs and left.

In March 2004, twenty settlers approached Juma when he was out with his sheep. Juma knew one of the settlers. They were shooting their guns and had dogs and slingshots. They damaged one Palestinian car with rocks and cut the tires. When the soldiers came, the settlers left. After talking with the soldiers, the commander told the Palestinians they had to leave the area. Juma told them they would not go anywhere until the police came.

The commander said, "If you do not leave in five minutes you will see something bad."

"What will you do?" Juma replied. "Go ahead and kill us." Soldiers then started beating the sheep. At this point Ezra and a journalist came. The police came and took a few settlers to the police station. The police told Juma, "You plan these problems with Ezra to stir up trouble."

"No," Juma replied, "you do nothing, so I call journalists."

I asked Juma how this has affected him. He said it has not been easy. He feels a lot of pressure inside. He could explode, he said, but he understands that is what the settlers want. "If we act like the settlers, we will suffer even more." He said his hope is in God. "Light comes after the dark."

Juma pointed toward his fields just below the settlement outpost across the small valley. Two years ago the settlers started plowing his fields there. Now he is not allowed on that land. He said this whole side of the wooded mountain occupied by the outpost belongs to his family. He pointed to his cistern that settlers poisoned with gasoline in August, just five months ago. Amazingly, I heard no bitterness from him.

✳

We noticed that the shepherds were taking their flocks closer to the settlement outpost. Juma explained that the grass is much more abundant there since it is seldom grazed. He said they would not be grazing there today if we were not present. We followed the flocks as they slowly made their way down the mountain toward At-Tuwani. Juma invited us to his house for lunch. I was really hungry and tired.

As soon as we finished eating, Juma told us that Mufakara shepherds wanted us immediately at Khoruba, up beyond where we had just been. That sounded terrible to me. I was really tired, but we again trudged back up the mountain. We saw no one. We went on the long path past the abandoned village of Sarura and saw shepherds in the distance. They called to us, and as we went around the mountain we saw that it was Mufakara shepherds and their flocks. They said they had seen settlers several times, and one time the settlers had flung rocks at them with slingshots, a common method of rock throwing. No one was hit.

With our presence, they wanted to take their flocks further up toward the settlement outpost on the other side of the next mountain. Settlers had confiscated all the fields in that valley six years ago and were now farming those fields. We slowly made our way up the valley toward the outpost as the sheep found a bit of grass between the rocks. We tried not to be seen by settlers. When we got within half a mile of the outpost, we saw three settlers. They looked like young teenagers. Immediately the shepherds and their sheep took off running. I was impressed with how fast those sheep could run. Apparently the sheep understood the danger and were ready to run. I thought of Abraham and David grazing their sheep in these hills and being on the lookout for lions and other predators that could attack their sheep. Maybe they also were ready to run.

It didn't feel right to us to walk toward the settlers and try to talk with them this time. But we didn't run. We slowly followed the shepherds down a valley and up the next mountain. We sat down with the shepherds and watched the three settlers with two valleys between us. They in turn were watching us. With that distance between us, I felt quite safe.

I felt terrible. Why this animosity between Jews and Arabs? They are cousins. Why should they fear each other? I thought of the bitter fruits being produced by the Zionist vision. The founders of the Israeli state understood and agreed that negotiating with the Arabs to take most of their land was impossible, and that there would be constant trouble as long as the Palestinians had any hope of resisting Israeli control. The only answer was to completely crush the Palestinian people. Only after the Palestinians begged for mercy and were willing to accept any conditions the Israelis wanted to impose could there be any negotiations.

The Israeli problem here now is that the Palestinians have not been crushed. In fact, they are stronger now than they have ever been: numerically, politically, intellectually, and in international support. The Israeli plan is not working.

This reminds me of a conversation with an Israeli soldier on December 31, 2003. He told me how God gave all this land, including Jordan, to the Jews. "Israel has been very gracious but made a big mistake in 1948 in agreeing to share the land. Israel is now in a war with the Arabs and will take it all." He opposed all negotiations.

"The Arabs will be beaten into submission until they beg for peace. The Arabs are evil and violent. They all are liars. They can never be trusted. They even kill Jewish children, something Jews would never do. All Arabs are terrorists." The truth, however, is that Israelis kill at least ten times as many Palestinian children as Israeli children are killed by Palestinians. The Palestinians are not innocent, and neither are the Israelis.

It did not need to be this way. The Jews could have come here in peace. I know how gentle and welcoming these people are. Instead, the Israelis came with their guns and stole the land. Now there is no end in sight to the animosity their thievery continues to create.

It was fun walking with the sheep and the shepherds back up to Mufakara. They invited us for tea, but we declined. We came back home and I had a nap.

We were invited to spend the evening with other villagers waiting for Saliim and Sarriya to come back from the hajj in Mecca. They had put up a big tent for the welcoming home activities.

They were waiting all last night and all day today. The couple did not have a cell phone, so we did not know where they were. We ate with the men and talked around the fire. They had fun as I practiced saying, "*Hajj Mabrurr wa siun maskull*," a statement of blessing for people returning from the pilgrimage. I kept getting it wrong.

At about ten o'clock we saw three cars coming up the road. Excitement filled the air. Soon there were fireworks coming from the cars and fireworks exploding on the roof above us. Wow! Everyone greeted the pilgrims as we were served dates, coffee, and food. Saliim talked and talked about his experiences. This was the big experience of his lifetime.

January 27, 2005, Thursday

Villagers killed four sheep this morning for the welcome home party. My job was to keep the fire stoked.

The other team members went over to Jawiyya again this morning. We could see them as they went up the hill across the road from Ma'on. We saw settlers approaching and the shepherds running away. The three team members stayed there as settlers approached them. Soon soldiers were there. I was concerned about what was happening but felt the need to go to Mufakara as I had promised.

The shepherds had already gone up the mountain with their sheep when I got to Mufakara. They wanted to graze their sheep near Avi Gail, the next settler outpost southwest of At-Tuwani, composed of about five mobile homes and a big water tower. We stayed well below the outpost where we could not be seen. It seemed we were playing cat and mouse. I was to help watch for settlers. We moved down the mountain to a road that took us to the far west side of the settlement. Two shepherds had gone up on the next mountain from which they could safely see the Avi Gail outpost and warn us if any settlers came toward us.

It felt to me like I would want to stay there and greet the settlers if they came. That felt right to me. It felt different than yesterday. We really do need to be guided by God's spirit in each situation.

We snuck up the mountain and got within three hundred feet of the fence around the outpost. The grass was tall and lush. It looked like it had not been grazed for years. The sheep had a great time getting actual mouths full of succulent grass instead of getting a short blade of grass here and there. Since other shepherds were watching from the other side, my job was to keep low where I could not be seen, relax, and enjoy the beautiful scenery and the several hundred sheep grazing all around me. Occasionally, I reached out and touched them as they grazed right beside me.

After about half an hour the shepherds on the next mountain called that someone was coming. Immediately the shepherds and sheep started running down the mountain, up the road in the valley, and up the next mountain. I started walking up the hill toward the outpost. Soon I saw three soldiers. I looked at them through my binoculars as they looked at me through their binoculars. I waved to them as I walked toward them. They didn't wave back. I was concerned that they not see me as any kind of threat. After all, they did have M-16s.

I shouted "Shalom, shalom," as I got closer. They shouted, "What do you want?" I called back, "I want shalom." They asked again. Again, I said I wanted peace. They would not allow me to come closer than maybe a hundred feet from them. Again they asked what I wanted. Again I said, "Shalom."

They said they also wanted peace, but the Arabs do not want peace. "The only thing the Arabs want is to kill Jews," they told me. I saw no point in arguing with them. They were speaking out of fear and ignorance.

I asked them, "How can we work for peace?" They said they didn't know. They had not yet found the answer. They asked where the shepherds were from. I didn't answer that. I said I lived in At-Tuwani. I wanted them to know that. They seemed surprised. One of them seemed to know about us.

They kept reminding me that I could not approach them. I asked why. "Orders," they said. I said I wanted to shake their hands. They said, "It is forbidden."

They suggested I leave, which felt right to me, so I wished them shalom and started walking around the mountain. I was

Lillies of the valley.

feeling depressed as I walked away. Both sides are so afraid of the other side. Is there any hope? Then I saw the first big red flowers of the season growing between the rocks. Some people say they are the biblical lilies of the field. Those flowers don't pay any attention to our fears. They do not have guns. They only know that the land belongs to God. So, maybe I can have hope too. I met the shepherds on the other side of the mountain who laughed as I told them what the soldiers had said, that the shepherds wanted nothing except to kill Jews. It was rather ridiculous.

When I got back to At-Tuwani people insisted that I rejoin the party and eat. I met lots of extended family members who had come to congratulate and welcome back the pilgrims. They had lots of questions about our team. I came back to the house and immediately had to play some soccer and marbles with the children who were here. No other sixty-five-year-old man is treated like they treat me. The children always expect me to play with them. What a gift that is.

Problems started across the road today when settlers came, some on foot and some in a car. One settler ran toward our team members, yelling at them and throwing stones. The team members didn't know that there were two other settlers on the other side of the hill who attacked sheep and shepherds. Several shepherds were slightly injured. The shepherds said they do not want to go back to the area unless they have more support. They are concerned about getting killed and about their pregnant ewes running and having miscarriages. How much protection can we offer them?

After a Dove videotaped a settler, he approached her with a rock in his hand and held it a few inches from her head and told her, "When I come back in five minutes, I will kill you." At this point, soldiers arrived. The first thing the soldiers did was to talk to the settlers and get their story. The settler who threatened the Dove went back into the Ma'on settlement. Police and a Druze man from the DCO came.

After talking with the police, it was decided that the Doves would go with the police to the Kiryat Arba police station to file a complaint about the death threat. That took into the evening and they went to the CPT apartment in Hebron for the night. They had waited six hours and were not taken seriously. The police said that since the settler had not used a gun and had not actually hurt her, there was no problem. Would they make the same response if a Palestinian had threatened to kill an Israeli?

After discussing the day, I went back up to the party. There were lots of people I didn't know. I prayed with the men who then sat around and talked. Some young men from Yatta began questioning me about why our team was here and what we are doing. I assumed I was talking with Hamas members. Soon we were discussing nonviolence. I mentioned the importance of getting their stories out to the rest of the world. They kept challenging me. They said we should be going to the settlements and working with the settlers since that is where their problems are coming from. I felt supported when I told them I want to go spend time in the settlements. They wanted to know my analysis of the struggle here. The conversation was intense and deep.

Later the conversation turned to telling jokes. It was interesting how they took turns and with how much gusto they laughed. They insisted I tell a few jokes I know in Arabic.

January 28, 2005, Friday

I helped unload a big truckload of clothing from "Friends of Israel," an American Christian Zionist group. Israeli activists regularly get these things, even though they are intended for Jewish immigrants to Israel. I imagine the American Christian Zionists would be horrified if they knew that their clothes were being given to Palestinian Muslims. I thought, maybe there is a bit of justice in the world.

I went with some of the men to Karmil for Friday prayers and rode back on a tractor and wagon. A Mufakara shepherd also came back with us. He and I immediately left and walked to Mufakara. His wife served us a lunch of bread, scrambled eggs, sheep yogurt, and olives. We then headed up the mountain and met other shepherds with their flocks. We headed back to where we were yesterday on the other side of Avi Gail. Again we sneaked around the side of the mountain trying to keep our heads down so we would not be seen. I asked myself if I was ready to meet the settlers. Was I ready to get beat up today? We were not there long before we saw a soldier up on the hill, so we left the area. It seems significant that the shepherds didn't run like yesterday.

After we got up to the top of the mountain closer to Mufakara, we saw two settlers coming toward us on a four-wheeler. I was worried. I asked if I should go to talk with them. The shepherds seemed unconcerned. They said, "No, just stay here." The settlers looked us over as they drove by within maybe two hundred feet of us. When they had gone, I told the shepherds I was confused.

Why didn't they run? They explained that they are not so concerned when they are on undisputed land. It is when they are on what settlers have or are in the process of taking that the settlers really get upset.

This got me to thinking. Why are we going out with the shepherds? Is it only to help the sheep get better grass? Or is it for something more than that? Our task is not to get the sheep better grass, but to be a catalyst in helping make it possible for the shepherds to graze their sheep without fear even if we are not present. Each year the Israelis take more and the shepherds have less. Can we do something to reverse that? Can we help roll back those boundaries? We have a more important task than helping shepherds to sneak onto their land.

It was good to spend a lot of time with Faadal today. He took me under his wing and tried to be my teacher about Islam. He said he likes me and wants me to go to heaven. That touched me. This 30-year-old shepherd is illiterate and lacking in social graces, but I quickly learned that he has a gentle heart. He walked back to At-Tuwani with me through the abandoned village of Ir Rakeez where we met one of the two families who have just recently moved back to that abandoned village. That is encouraging.

I went over to visit Hafez this evening. He expressed a lot of gratitude for the conversation I had last evening with guests around the fire. He said there has been a lot of suspicion about our presence here, especially from people who do not live in At-Tuwani, and indicated that I helped answer a lot of their questions. Hafez told me people here call me Jaber (my name from the Beqa'a) Adara. I am considered part of the Adara family. I feel honored.

January 29, 2005, Saturday

Today was the first day of school after a three-week vacation. There were nine children from Tuba with three soldiers walking and one jeep. I got to greet the children. They seemed happy.

A shepherd came to our house at ten o'clock and insisted that all three of us go with him to accompany Mufakara shepherds. Kathy Kapenga and Barbara Martens felt they were on call for the shepherds from Jawiyya and could not go. I really did not want to go. I was tired and I wanted to get ready to go to Hebron. Finally we agreed that I would go with him.

We went with three flocks of sheep up to the near side of Avi Gail and watched the sheep graze on some fairly good grass there. We tried to keep low, but we could see right into the outpost. The outpost is three years old, and is named for Abigail, the local woman King David married over three thousand years ago. Mufakara people originally built the road into Avi Gail.

I had an excellent view from the mountaintop of the line of settlements and outposts extending from the Karmel settlement to the Susya settlement. It became starkly clear how the Israeli military is using this line of settlements and outposts to cut off the South Hebron Hills from Yatta and the rest of the West Bank.

For a long time we didn't see anyone in the outpost, maybe because it was Sabbath. After about an hour we saw one soldier in the outpost. He was watching us. But this time the shepherds didn't run. I was prepared to meet the soldier or settlers if the shepherds left. Shortly before we quit for the day, one of the shepherds suggested that I go to the outpost and talk with the soldier. I hesitated. I wasn't sure I wanted to do that, but then decided I should go. After all, he suggested it, and I am really not interested in playing cat and mouse. I said yes. He conferred with the others, but they decided to not have me go. That whole scene felt good to me. I wasn't calling any shots. The shepherds were making the decisions.

On the way back to At-Tuwani I met about fifteen Mufakara children on their way home from school. They greeted me enthusiastically. Some of the girls who had been quite bashful in their homes were especially friendly today. They seem more outgoing when they are not at home.

Barbara and I got a ride to Hebron with Ezra and two other Ta'ayush people who had been visiting today in the South Hebron Hills. I felt uncomfortable driving on the Israeli road, with accepting a privilege that Palestinians do not have, but also appreciated the opportunity to spend that time with these Israeli activists. We dropped off the two Ta'ayush women at the Kiryat Arba police station to check on another Ta'ayush activist who was arrested in Susiya this morning for photographing a soldier. "But they don't arrest settlers who engage in violent behavior," I thought.

It was interesting driving through the Kiryat Arba settlement and down into the Old City in Hebron with Israelis. I also felt weird walking into the old city. I felt like I was on another planet, coming from the South Hebron Hills. I really did not want to come here. I don't want to be in the city. I feel out of place. I am a country boy. I identify with the shepherds.

January 30, 2005, Sunday

I went to Bethlehem this morning to worship with the Emanuel congregation, got a taxi to the Beqa'a Valley where I spent the afternoon visiting a lot of friends, and then walked back to Hebron after dark. Actually, I had an armed, military escort home from Kiryat Arba, which didn't make me feel any safer. As I approached Kiryat Arba I decided to check with security there for a phone number for my friend in Kiryat Arba. I took off my CPT hat. The man in the booth said he didn't have a phone book but that I could get the number at the coffee shop in Kiryat Arba. That sounded good. So, without my CPT hat, and without having my backpack checked, I walked right into Kiryat Arba, greeting everyone in Hebrew. The woman in the shop gave me the phone number and I was on my way. I'm sure everyone thought I was Jewish.

I walked out of the settlement and ignored the soldiers sitting in a jeep, guarding the entrance. I turned left to go to Hebron, something a Jew would not have done after dark. I knew that would concern the soldiers. I didn't get far before the soldiers yelled at me. I ignored them and kept walking. It wasn't long until they pulled up beside me in their jeep. I greeted them in Hebrew. They only asked me where I was going and followed me as I walked. I greeted all the Palestinians along the way.

When I got to Worshipers' Way, the street Kiryat Arba settlers use to walk into Hebron, I knew the soldiers would expect me to go that way instead of through the Palestinian neighborhood. I wanted to walk through the Palestinian neighborhood. The soldiers stopped me and let me know I could walk down Worshipers' Way. I said I knew that, but liked this road.

What could they say? Who are mere soldiers to tell a settler what to do? I was sure they thought I was Jewish. They left and soon soldiers in another jeep stopped beside me to ask where I was going. Then soldiers in still another jeep followed me down to the area around the Ibrahimi Mosque/Cave of Machpelah. There I put my CPT hat back on as I walked into the Old City.

February 1, 2005, Tuesday

I came back to At-Tuwani this afternoon and learned that about a dozen people from Ta'ayush were here today to plant olive trees. Arik Ascherman from Rabbis for Human Rights was with them. They went to the village of Ma'in, west of At-Tuwani, and planted two hundred olive trees because settlers had recently destroyed two hundred olive trees there.

One young Israeli with the Ta'ayush group said the last time he was here he was in uniform and had a gun. He was very afraid Palestinians would kill him. He believed what the military had told him. Now he was here among the Palestinians without a uniform, without a gun, and he was not afraid.

The number of children coming to school the past few days from Tuba and now also the neighboring village of Maghair al-Abeed increased to fifteen. That is exciting. But I also learned that on both Sunday morning and afternoon, the soldiers drove the children in their jeeps past threatening settlers. Yesterday, settlers appeared with a dog when the children were going home from school.

February 2, 2005, Wednesday

We left at half past six this morning to go out on school patrol and went out to the top of the next hill east from where we have been watching each day, near the abandoned village of Khoruba. From that hill we were closer to and had a better view of the settler outpost. We could see the children walking on the distant ridge top from Tuba toward Ma'on. It was really exciting to see them in the distance. We could not see them as they approached the place where they meet the soldiers, but soon we saw them again as they came over the hill just below the outpost. They were accompanied by one police jeep followed by a settler security vehicle. There were fifteen children this morning.

We learned a number of things from an international aid worker who came and joined us as we waited for the children. The military is upset that there are now fifteen children. They are upset that work is continuing on the second floor of the clinic, in spite of repeated warnings to stop work. They are upset that the Palestinians started improving the road to Jinba. The Israelis want less people using the road, not more.

The aid worker expects the Israeli government to soon announce that the Wall will be built south of here near the Green Line instead of north of here as had been expected. That will be very threatening to the settlers, who will feel betrayed and very angry. That could make for a dangerous time here. The settlers may want to take their anger out on the Palestinians, or on those who support the Palestinians.

The goal of the Israeli government is to remove people from the area. Making services available to people in the area makes it easier for the Palestinians to stay and more difficult for the Israelis to remove them. The goal of the Israelis is to roll back services in the area. That is why there is a demolition order on the school. That is why none of the villages in the area are allowed to hook into the Israeli electrical grid or water system. That is why the Israelis have demolished so many cisterns and wells in the area. With water, land, roads, access to schools and medical care, the people will stay. In fact, the population here has been slowly increasing in the past few years due to the increases in services. The school and clinic in At-Tuwani are factors in At-Tuwani becoming a hub for the area.

The Israelis have a big problem here. There are some services here, and those services are expanding. International donors have been building schools, clinics and toilets. The work of the British aid group, Environmental Resource Management (ERM) has been extremely important. Building cisterns and wells makes it more possible for people to live here. It is not easy for the Israelis to demolish these structures because to do so makes the Israelis look really bad to those donor countries. Israeli attempts to remove the people from here by denying access to water and other services have failed.

International investment here has made a huge difference. Add the presence of international activists here, and one can easily see that removing the Palestinians from the area is becoming more difficult. This insight helps explain why our presence here is such an aggravation to the Israeli authorities.

What more can Israel do to the Palestinians? They are not crushing the Palestinian spirit. Expelling the Palestinians would now be very difficult. If they did expel all the Palestinians, the Israelis would be even less secure than they are now by having created even more enemies and opposition.

We again spent a major amount of time in our team meeting this morning discussing what to do if settlers approach us when we are out with the shepherds. Since each situation is different, we need to evaluate each situation. Are the settlers coming toward us? Does it look like they are organizing something, like making phone calls? Are they wearing masks, and do they have weapons? How many of them are there? Are the settlers angry at the shepherds or at us? Are soldiers present? Are we visible to other people? I find these discussions very helpful in my thinking through how I will respond.

We went back to Khoruba for school patrol this afternoon.

I was quite aware that we were in more danger in that place. We were closer to the outpost and the settlers could be hiding and waiting for us there. But it felt right to be there. The children passed by us with no problems. There was one police jeep and a settler security vehicle. We were somewhat concerned when we saw two settlers below the outpost, but the children passed by with no trouble.

A man in a settler security vehicle parked above us on the road and watched us and the shepherds who were below us. Soon soldiers in a jeep and a white pickup truck joined the settler security man. After conferring with the settler for about ten minutes, the soldiers in the white vehicle drove toward the shepherds and the jeep came toward us. The four of us separated, with two Doves going down toward the shepherds.

The other Dove and I approached the soldiers who were walking toward us. The soldiers were friendly. We shook hands and started talking. One asked to see what we had on our video camera. I did not want to show it to him, so I joked and asked him if he thought he would look very handsome on the video. He didn't push the issue any further. This is a new group of soldiers, and they wanted to know what we were doing so we told them a lot about our work. We talked about guns and nonviolence. I told them the story of the former soldier who was here yesterday. I told them about Israeli activists who come here regularly. They seemed impressed and supportive.

February 3, 2005, Thursday

All four of us went on school patrol this morning. On the way we heard chanting from the outpost. We went to the far hill again at Khoruba and soon saw the children coming in the distance. We stood there expectantly waiting, wondering if they would be safe or if they would be attacked by settlers. We never know.

About the time we saw the children and two soldiers walking in front of them up by the outpost, a settler came down out of the trees and started walking on the road toward the children. I was worried when the children were in a dip in the road where we could not see them. Then we saw the settler playing his guitar and singing very loudly. He seemed to be directing his singing toward the children. It felt hostile, mocking, and degrading. He stopped singing as soon as the children passed.

Rich Meyer, who is the CPT staff person for the Hebron project, came to spend a few days with us. Rich and I went out on school patrol. We walked up the hill and noticed that four flocks of At-Tuwani sheep were up near the settler trees where yesterday afternoon soldiers told them they were forbidden to graze. I was glad to see that they are not intimidated. Actually, there were more shepherds there today.

After seeing the children disappear over the distant mountain, a settler walked down out of the trees toward us and stopped. He seemed uninterested in us and walked away. We spent some time with two shepherds and their flocks.

February 5, 2005, Saturday

It was really cold and windy when the four of us went up to Khoruba again this morning, but no more for us than for the children who were walking. There was a chance for snow last night, but we didn't get any.

We had a discussion of nonviolence and loving our enemies when we got back to our cold house, and how that relates to loving, or at least not hating, the settlers. I said I hoped that if Palestinians were attacking someone like Dov, I would stand in front of Dov to protect him. What would happen if we had an opportunity to protect settlers? How would that change our relationship with the settlers or with the Palestinians? What dialogue would that open up with the people here?

Three people from Ta'ayush came here this morning for a meeting requested by the villagers, who want more coordination and dialogue with Ta'ayush about their plans before they undertake actions here. Villagers have been concerned that some Israeli activists come and do their thing here, but neglect to consult with the local people beforehand. The people here want to share decision making. We team members wanted to talk about our need to be accountable to the people we are working with. Sometimes it seems that Palestinians are being used in the ongoing battle between the Israeli right and the Israeli left. Are we here out of love for the people, or for some other concern?

Many of the At-Tuwani men were present for our meeting. We discussed the need for accountability and coordination of our activities. Just talking about these issues seemed to give everyone new hope.

We were all invited to a village home for lunch. It was deeply moving for me to eat again with Israelis, Palestinians and internationals, with Jews, Muslims, and Christians. That is a foretaste of the coming kingdom of God, of how things could be. It was a bit of reality breaking into our twisted world. We had our differences, but we were not afraid of each other.

I went to visit Hafez this evening. I wanted to share a concern about our meeting this morning. The villagers agreed with the Ta'ayush suggestion of increasing the size of our team to six. I was uncomfortable with that decision because there was no way a Palestinian in that meeting would have felt free to disagree. Hafez agreed with my concern and said he would raise the issue with the people here. I also shared an article with him that I had just written about At-Tuwani. I felt complimented and trusted when he offered some helpful criticisms.

February 6, 2005, Sunday

The four of us went up to Khoruba again this morning. A cold wind was so strong that it took some effort to stand there. My discomfort was rewarded by the joy I felt when we saw the silhouettes of the children coming over the far mountain, when we saw them in the next open area, and then again when they came around the bend by the trees and the outpost. What a thrill to see those fifteen children brave the wind, cold, and settlers to get to school. We hurried back and met the children just below the school. They looked so happy. They said they saw us watching them. I felt a great joy in seeing them and also a deep sense of responsibility toward them. They know the horrible dangers they face, yet they trust that we adults will somehow protect them. Although standing out there on the next hill seems so small and insignificant, they seem to feel protected by our presence.

Our presence is hardly a solution, however. Something needs to be done to remove the threats to the children. Some time ago Israeli military authorities suggested that the Palestinians transport their children with a tractor and wagon. The Palestinians pointed out that the tractor would make a lot of noise, attract even more settlers, and require still more military protection for the children. The Israelis quickly dropped that idea. One team member joked that maybe the soldiers could airlift the children with the Apache helicopters that we continually see flying over the area.

We noticed this afternoon that the children all moved to the side of the military jeep away from the settler trees. After the children had passed by we saw two settlers above us in the trees and three settlers over below the outpost. It felt very uncomfortable. We watched helplessly as the children went past the outpost without incident.

Soon we saw two settlers on horses and with a dog coming out of the trees. While the one on a white horse rode away from us on the road, the other settler on a brown horse headed toward us. We quickly agreed that we would walk toward the settler and greet him. I feel more comfortable in being proactive, not passive.

When he came near I greeted him with "Shalom, shalom." He was about sixteen. He gave no response. Then he asked where we were from. I said we live in At-Tuwani. As he turned to leave, I again said, "Shalom, shalom." I am glad I overcame my fear and greeted him. Who knows when we may meet again.

After we were sure the settlers had left we went around the mountain to join the Mufakara shepherds. They seemed really glad to see us. We spent about two hours in the wind and rain going around the mountain and up toward Ma'on. We saw no settlers. I think the weather kept them away. We came home wet and cold.

Two Doves spent the day at the Kiryat Arba police station being interviewed again about the death threat on January 27. They went with six shepherds from the area who were also making complaints. This time they felt that they were taken seriously. The Palestinians, however, had to stand outside for an hour and a half in the cold wind and rain. Finally the police gave each shepherd five minutes to state their complaint.

During this time a notorious young settler from the Susya settlement came out of an office in the police station and saw the shepherds. He did not say anything, but he looked very angry. Two shepherds from Susiya were there to make a complaint about this very settler. After the settler left, a police officer told the shepherds that the young settler, along with others from Ma'on, will be arrested tomorrow. We are not holding our breath.

The police in Kiryat Arba today said that shepherds may graze their sheep to within one hundred feet of settler outposts. We spent some time strategizing about how we can test this by bringing flocks of sheep near the settlements. A villager will talk to shepherds from Mufakara and Jawiyya about coordinating grazing near settlements. This sounded really exciting. Maybe the purpose of our playing cat and mouse out in the wind and rain has been to build trust with the shepherds, an important first step.

February 7, 2005, Monday

I left early this morning to get to Hebron in time for worship and team meeting. I met Diana Zimmerman who was in At-Tuwani during the October 9 attack and Sally Hunsberger. Matt Chandler came this afternoon for a short visit before returning to Iraq.

February 10, 2005, Thursday

I went to meetings in Jerusalem and Bethlehem today. When I crossed the checkpoint from Jerusalem to Bethlehem, I walked up to the Wall that was being constructed near the checkpoint. I was filled with anger and disgust. Words cannot describe the horror, the depravity, the arrogance of building that Wall of hate, that Apartheid Wall, that confiscation, expansion Wall. I looked at the twenty-eight-foot-high Wall, higher than the Berlin Wall, that snakes around the hillsides, confiscating huge tracts of Palestinian land, dividing families, isolating people, and cutting people off from their land. It is hideous.

There was a policeman standing there with his M-16, guarding workers. I spewed out some anger in front of him. I said, "This is disgusting. This is racist. This is apartheid. Aren't you ashamed of what Israel is becoming?" I doubt it did any good, but I could not be silent in the face of such evil. The policeman pretended to ignore me, but he had to have heard everything I said.

February 11, 2005, Friday

Matt and I came back to At-Tuwani today. We accompanied a shepherd with his sheep, right up to the trees by the outpost. People here are getting bolder every day. He said if settlers come, we should just watch. We then went to his house for tea.

Yesterday at eleven o'clock, Barbara and Sally accompanied four flocks of sheep and their shepherds over the hill to near the Ma'on settlement. There were maybe twenty-five Palestinians involved. It wasn't long before a settler security man came. He was shocked to see so many people present. "What are you doing here?" he asked. "This is our land," the shepherds replied. "No, it is not your land. You must leave," retorted the settler. The children began singing, and the settler left very angry.

Soon soldiers arrived. They were not in a good mood. They questioned the shepherds on their claim to the land. They asked to see deeds. The shepherds called Saber who came one and a half hours later with the deeds. The soldiers told the shepherds, "You think you are important because you have internationals here with you." The shepherds offered tea to the soldiers, but they refused the tea.

People from the DCO came and agreed that the land belongs to the shepherds. They said there would be a meeting on Sunday to decide where the shepherds may and may not graze their sheep, a meeting to which the shepherds are not invited. The shepherds told the authorities, "You can make whatever decision you want, but this is our land and we are going on our land. We do not need your permission to go on our own land."

February 12, 2005, Saturday

After worship we got into a discussion about using the police in our work. After I expressed some uneasiness about using the police, a Dove pointed out that in the case of the settler who threatened to kill a Dove on January 27, we do not want to punish the settler, but he does need to be held accountable. The shepherds here do not have any means for obtaining justice.

We want to give a message that the violent, oppressive behavior of the settlers is not acceptable. For far too long the Israeli authorities have looked the other way and allowed settlers to do anything they wanted. I do see a clear difference between standing up for others and using the police to protect oneself, but I am still not convinced that real social justice will come through violent authorities.

We have been given an opportunity to raise issues of basic human rights, both to the authorities and through the media. The police are starting to listen to us, and we have the impression that they are starting to listen to the shepherds. Shepherds tell us that this is the first time they feel the police have listened to them. Our presence here seems to be changing the power equation. But it is important that we not look to the police as the answer. We must build the answer.

Yesterday we promised Mufakara shepherds that we would

go there today. This morning there were predictions of snow. It was raining hard, but when there was a break in the rain Matt and I decided to walk to Mufakara. It sounded crazy, but we went. We ended up spending three hours there in a cave sitting around the fire talking with the shepherds and eating lunch with them. We were having a great time.

We started walking home but then saw other Mufakara shepherds over toward the Ma'on outpost. They called for us to join them. They asked us to stand between them and the outpost and watch for settlers. After about half an hour we saw a settler with orange pants and a gray-checkered jacket who watched us for a few minutes and then started coming toward us. We warned the shepherds and they started moving away. We decided to stay and watch. The settler came closer, maybe within four or five hundred feet. There was a valley of confiscated wheat fields between us. He seemed to be checking out how many flocks were with us. He then ran back into the outpost.

Right after that it started raining again. Soon there was a high wind with rain, sleet, and snow. It was miserable. We decided the settlers would not come back in this weather, and the shepherds were heading toward home so we decided to call it quits. We walked into the blistering wind with the sleet stinging our faces. It was horrible. I could hardly see where I was walking. Then it started snowing harder. I thought this was the beginning of something big. We took a shortcut through a field and our feet sunk deep into the mud. By the time we got to the path, the wind had died down and soon it stopped snowing. It was actually a pleasant walk down the road, except we were soaked and cold.

No sooner had we arrived at home when a neighbor came and told us that someone saw two settlers heading toward the shepherds up at Khoruba where we had been and that we should get back up there. "Oh, no," I thought. "We should have stayed longer. We abandoned the shepherds in their time of need." No other team members were ready to go. Although cold and tired, I felt I had no choice, so I headed back up the mountain toward Mufakara where I met the shepherds as they arrived home. They had seen the settlers, but there was no problem. So maybe it was best that we were not up there to meet the settlers. It is hard to know what decisions are right. We can only hope that we are open to God's leading.

February 13, 2005, Sunday

A neighbor came after worship and told us that most of the At-Tuwani shepherds were going up to the north side of the Ma'on settlement where they had their encounter with Israeli authorities last Thursday. We all walked over toward Ma'on, up over the hill and down the next valley where settlers are now farming more than three-fourths of the way down the small valley. The shepherds were already going up the next hill below the Ma'on settlement. There were about eight flocks of sheep, tended by both female and male shepherds. Some women were also gathering herbs from the rocky terrain. All four of us walked halfway up the hill to be above the shepherds in case settlers came toward us. The grass was much taller there.

At 10:18, three soldiers stopped down by the road and began to walk toward us. They both yelled and motioned for us to go down to them. We didn't see any reason to walk down, so they had to walk up to us with their M-16s at the ready. Itimar was quite angry with us. We didn't go to them when they called to us. They said we were not allowed to be where we were. They also said we looked suspicious up on the hill where we could not easily be seen.

I thought, "Yes, you are right to be suspicious of us. We are simply accompanying shepherds on their own land, but we realize that may threaten Israeli confiscation of that land." They also said there were too many sheep together, which they thought to be unusual and suspicious. "Yes," I thought, "if the shepherds are not isolated they have more power and that also is a threat to the Israeli goal of removing the people from here."

It quickly became clear that the shepherds were not going to do any pushing today. They are taking this very slowly, one small step at a time. They immediately agreed to stay on the lower part of the hill. I thought that at least we established our right to be on this much of their land. I reminded the soldiers that this is Palestinian land but didn't push the issue.

Matt and I moved to the upper part of the valley to watch for settlers, with two Doves below the shepherds. At 11:05 a settler on a four-wheeler came down from Ma'on, stopped, probably to make a phone call, and then drove to a place two hundred feet up the mountain from us. I wasn't worried about that one settler. The shepherds continued grazing their sheep.

At 11:10 a settler security man named Gdalia drove up the road, stopped, and waited. I assumed he was waiting for soldiers to arrive. At 11:20 the three soldiers we met earlier drove up and got out of their pickup truck. The bearded Gdalia, a large man, about fifty years old, originally from South Africa,

Israeli soldiers, Palestinian-owned sheep, and the wooded settler outpost in the background.

got out of his truck and talked to the soldiers. I realized that this was the settler security person we have been seeing most every time there has been trouble. By this time most of the shepherds were near the soldiers across the valley. A shepherd called for us to come over to them.

When we crossed the valley, Gdalia, with his M-16, ordered me to "Take your people back to At-Tuwani." I thought it rather odd for him to expect a foreigner to give orders to Palestinians on whose land he was a guest.

I said, "They are not my people. I am their guest, and this is their land." He didn't like that.

He said, "This has been Jewish land for over three thousand years. The Arabs have no right to be here. They have to leave." He was very angry. I am sure he ordered the soldiers to remove all of us. But none of us were leaving. And this time the soldiers were not following his orders. He was actually quite powerless even though he had an M-16 assault rifle. He was not even free to attack us. He jumped into his truck, roared away toward Ma'on, nearly running over several sheep. He didn't go far before he turned around and came back. He was a frustrated man.

Itimar again confronted us. He said that he had told us that the valley was the borderline. We were not allowed to be on the other side of the valley where we had just been. All of us had heard him say earlier that we could be halfway up the other hill.

We stood waiting for the police. Except for Gdalia, there was a positive attitude on the part of everyone. The soldiers were relaxed, the shepherds confident that justice was on their side. There was lots of interaction between all parties, except for Gdalia, who remained stiff and angry. I felt sorry for him.

Three police came at 11:40. They first talked to Gdalia and the soldiers. Then they talked with the shepherds. Most of the conversation was in Arabic. I stood around playing journalist, taking notes with my pen and paper. After joking with one soldier, I continued writing. The soldier then asked me if I was writing about our jokes.

It was an amazing picture. The shepherds were peaceful, disturbing no one. They were just grazing their sheep on their land. Foreigners (Israelis) armed with M-16s, trained and prepared to kill, had just invaded the shepherds' land. The shepherds met them on a different level, rendering all those guns useless. This was nonviolent action at its best: disarming the opponent, making their weapons useless, changing the power equation, and transforming the whole scene. The shepherds were fighting on terms on which they had some chance of winning.

At 12:04, three higher-up police arrived in two vehicles and began conferring with all parties. One of them said to me, "Why don't you first take care of your problems in America?" I explained that we stand in the middle of violent situations in many places, including North America. I then pointed out to him that there were sixteen heavily armed Israelis present to keep simple shepherds from having access to their land. I reminded him that America was paying for this huge Israeli commitment of personnel here today.

The result was the police again telling the shepherds that they could not go over on the next hill, that there will be a meeting soon with the DCO, and that the military will decide where the border will be.

I felt some anger at the idea that the occupying military will tell the local people what portions of their own land they will be allowed to use. But I also chuckled to myself. "Do you occupiers really believe that these shepherds will passively accept your edicts?" One shepherd told me, "We don't care where they draw their lines. We will continue to go on our land."

We are in the middle of an exciting nonviolent campaign, led by people who, though not trained in nonviolence, have a deep understanding of nonviolence. They are simply doing what they know is right. Maybe that is what nonviolence is all about: simply doing what we know is right. We are witnessing a very productive use of civil disobedience. Each day the shepherds take another small step. Because of the confrontations with sol-

diers and police out on Palestinian land, the issue of whether or
not the shepherds can graze that land is now being discussed at
different levels within the Israeli power structure.

Matt reminded me of Gandhi's salt march. Why can't
Palestinian shepherds graze their sheep on their own land? Our
program of accompanying school children from Tuba has been
so successful, I believe, due to the fact that we are confronting
such an outrageous situation in which adults try to violently prevent children from going to school. It seems so simple. Children
should be able to go to school without being beaten by adults.
Shepherds should be able to go on their land.

Shepherds told us that tomorrow we will all focus on the
south side of the settler outpost and the next day at Avi Gail.
Wow! I am excited by all this, but also realize how dangerous
our situation is. I know enough of the violent history of settlers
and soldiers here to know that overt Israeli violence could begin
again at any time, even though we internationals are present. At
any time the military could come and start demolishing At-
Tuwani homes to punish the villagers and "teach them a les-
son." There are many kinds of collective punishment available
to the Israelis, something illegal according to Article 33 of the
Fourth Geneva Convention.

This afternoon I was leading a tour for some Mennonite
Central Committee workers on the hill above At-Tuwani. I got a
call to go to Mufakara to tell the shepherds there that we will be
meeting tomorrow morning near the Ma'on outpost, combining
flocks from both Mufakara and At-Tuwani. When we got to
Mufakara, a shepherd told us that a settler attacked him this
afternoon and threatened him with death. The settler, around
twenty-five, with a red beard and brown eyes, told him, "I know
where you live. If I see you here again I will come to your home
and kill you." Other team members had seen three settlers arrive
in the Khoruba area after school patrol. The settlers were very
angry and took off after the shepherds. Our team filmed the settlers but did not witness the death threat.

We stayed a while in Mufakara, chatting with the shepherds while being surrounded by maybe thirty children. Our presence was exciting for these villagers who have little contact with the outside world.

February 14, 2005, Monday

Matt and a shepherd went to the Kiryat Arba police station to show the tape of the settler who attacked and threatened the shepherd with death yesterday.

We left at half past nine to go up to Khoruba with the shepherds. There were about ten shepherds and at least three hundred sheep. We were grazing on land that they had not dared to go on for four years. I was expecting soldiers and police to come, but we never saw them. We saw settlers watching us from several places in their car, but the settlers never got out of the car.

We created a dilemma for the settlers. Should they call police and soldiers? Either way they faced difficulties. If they didn't call the authorities, they were conceding the land to the Palestinians, at least temporarily. If they called the soldiers, they risked authorities allowing the shepherds to be on their own land, which would mean a big defeat for the settlers. Either way, they lose. Today we reestablished in some small way the right of the shepherds to be on another piece of their land. I congratulated every one on our small victory.

There was continual bombing during much of the day with some really loud booms. It was practice military bombing south of here, near Jinba. I thought of Peggy in Baghdad during the bombing there. It sure sounded like a war. There were lots of military jets and helicopters in the air. How ironic. Here I was with simple, peaceful shepherds who have no desire to hurt anyone, on some of the most beautiful land on this earth, listening to the bombs of the people who want to steal this land. These Israelis are blowing up these beautiful mountains in their preparation for war and conquest, yet the Western media tell us these shepherds are terrorists.

February 15, 2005, Tuesday

At 7:25, soldiers in a Hummer came around the corner by the settler outpost at a fairly high rate of speed and turned toward the ruins of Dov's house, turned around, and went back. I was worried that there may have been settlers on the other side of the hill where we could not see. But there was no trouble. There was one police jeep with fifteen children following. I ran down the hill and met them. They seemed happy.

Two Doves accompanied the shepherd to the Kiryat Arba police station to make a complaint about the death threat on Sunday.

The shepherds from Mufakara and At-Tuwani again combined flocks and went to where we were yesterday. We got much closer to the outpost than yesterday, all the way over to the road that leads up to the ruins of Dov's house. I stood below those ruins, at the ruins of what had been the first settler outpost here, now a pile of rubble. I thought of Nati and Dov, of rubble, destruction, and wasted lives. I thought of the bitter fruit of hatred and racism.

I was nervous. Would settlers attack us? What was going to happen? It was a thrill to see all those flocks of sheep all over those hills. By the time the shepherds left it was time for school patrol. After we saw the children walk across the last hilltop, we watched Gdalia in his white pickup truck drive around the hills where the shepherds had just been, seemingly looking for the shepherds. But the shepherds were gone. I was glad.

On the way to Hebron I noticed a large gathering of people in Dura, people mourning for a boy shot and killed by Israeli soldiers near the Ibrahimi Mosque yesterday.

A soldier pointed his M-16 at me as I walked past the Beit Romano checkpoint in Hebron. That was too much for me. I shouted at him, "Don't you dare point your gun at me." He immediately lowered his gun. I then walked up to the two soldiers and started a conversation. I told them that after Israeli soldiers had killed a boy yesterday, they needed to be more careful with their guns. That led into an intense discussion of nonviolence. The one soldier was pretty hardnosed, but the other soldier said he saw the futility of guns and is looking for a better way, even considering Christianity. He told me Jesus showed a better way. We talked about Jesus, Gandhi, and King. We parted, wishing each other shalom.

February 16, 2005, Wednesday

At about quarter after eleven Sally called and said settlers had attacked them near Khoruba, where we were yesterday. She then called back again saying that Johannes was seriously injured, and taken to a hospital. Johannes, whose mother tongue is German, is a twenty-three-year-old Dove from northern Italy.

I later learned that Sally, Johannes, and a Dove had gone to Tuba this morning on school patrol and stayed to accompany Tuba shepherds who were joining the At-Tuwani and Mufakara shepherds. Two team members were with the At-Tuwani shepherds. They could see each other across several hills. At eleven o'clock Diana called Sally to say settlers were attacking. After a settler shot his gun, a Dove called the military and police. The settlers retreated when soldiers arrived. Diana realized they were near the place where she and others were attacked on October 9 last year.

A masked settler approached the three team members returning from Tuba. They tried to engage the settler in conversation, but he would not talk. He wanted the video camera. The settler went toward Johannes who tossed the camera to another team member. It was like a game of football as the team tossed the camera back and forth to keep it away from the settler. The Dove hid the camera behind a shrub when the settler was not looking. The settler punched the Dove in the face, chest, and groin. The settler then approached Johannes, punched him in the face and knocked his glasses off. Johannes just stood there, so the settler hit him in the chest. The settler appeared to be leaving but turned around and kicked Johannes in the face with a karate-like kick. Johannes crumpled to the ground.

Soldiers came and described the event as a fight. Sally told the soldiers, "This was not a fight. Johannes was just standing there and the settler came and beat him up." Soldiers took Johannes and two other Doves in a Hummer to the Soroko Hospital in Be'er Sheva. Police took Sally and Diana to the Kiryat Arba police station to make a report.

Only Barbara and I were at the apartment in Hebron. We decided that I would return to At-Tuwani immediately, so here I am. I thought I was going to be in Hebron for three days. Now I am back in At-Tuwani.

It was a sobering ride here. I was heading into the unknown. I thought of the two Doves, two decent people who had no reason to be beaten. I wished it could have been me instead. I thought of the settlers, so zealous and so misguided. How could we touch something in their souls? Maybe only by letting them beat us? I asked if I was ready to be beaten. Was I ready to die? I felt a deep peace as I thought about it. If they kill me, *ilhamdililah* (Praise God). What is my little suffering compared to all that these Palestinians have suffered? I felt I was ready to face the settlers.

Since the shepherds were still up at Khoruba with their sheep, I headed up there. I walked toward the shepherds and greeted each one as they were starting to head home. I decided to walk up the hill and greet the soldiers. I called "Shalom, shalom" to them and they allowed me to approach their truck and jeep. I got a mixed response. Itimar offered me orange drink, which I accepted. Others were more reserved.

My approach was to ask them what they thought was the answer, how peace could come here. One immediately said, "Separation." I thought, "Apartheid." When I suggested that I would like to go into the settlement and talk with the settlers, they said, "That would be impossible, they would kill you." I thought to myself, these soldiers do not have a very high opinion of these settlers. But they also expressed a lot of fear of the Palestinians.

They demonstrated that fear a few minutes later when those soldiers drove their jeep down to the edge of the mountain and scrambled down into the valley. The shepherds asked me to go down to intercept the soldiers because some villagers were there gathering herbs. I soon saw three villagers standing with their hands behind their necks. I asked the soldiers what was happening. They explained that they saw these three young men and were afraid they might have guns and be preparing an attack on the soldiers. They said they were searching the area in case the villagers had quickly dropped their guns somewhere when they saw the soldiers coming.

The soldiers were afraid. I would be afraid too if I was walking on someone else's land with an assault rifle. I wanted to remind them that it is the settlers and soldiers who have guns and attack people, but I kept quiet.

It became even more ironic when an hour later we saw three teenage settler girls walking close to At-Tuwani and then toward the settler outpost. They seemed to be giving a message that all that land belongs to them. Even those settler girls recognize that it is safer for settlers to walk close to At-Tuwani than for Palestinians or internationals to walk close to Ma'on.

I joined the maybe dozen villagers out in the field where the settler girls had just passed, a place easily visible from the settlement, to send a message that we were not intimidated by the settlers. I had some fear that the villagers might be in some danger tonight, but no one seemed concerned about that.

I got a call from Sally saying she and Diana finally got to the CPT apartment in Hebron from Kiryat Arba where they gave statements to the police about the attack today. We learned that Johannes had a broken jaw, a serious eye injury, and hopefully, no brain damage. He will stay in the hospital for more observation and tests.

At-Tuwani buzzed with excitement. Five people from the International Solidarity Movement (ISM) and three women from the International Women's Peace Service (IWPS) came. Ezra and Ta'ayush people came. Two more people from Operation Dove came to join us. We felt a lot of support.

We all met in the clinic meeting room (the second meeting there) this evening and started with speeches from Saber and Ezra. Saber began by saying that he was sorry for what happened today, but that it is part of the reality here. We decided to go back tomorrow to the same place we were today. Saber warned it could be dangerous but standing together is our best insurance policy. Saber also talked about how things have changed here since our team came. Villagers used to hide when soldiers and police came into the village. Now they are standing up, cooperating, and working together. They are no longer in a defensive posture. Now they are taking the initiative. Our task now is to take the story of At-Tuwani to the world. To do this, we are taking actions that will expose the ugly face of the Occupation. Will the world notice? Will the world care?

February 17, 2005, Thursday

Five of our guests went with me on school patrol this morning. The visitors were horrified that the children had to endure such hardship and cruelty. They said it was unbelievable. That jolted me. Have I accepted the totally unacceptable situation here? We could see one soldier jeep ahead, and three soldiers walking with the children.

On the way back, I took the guests to Mufakara where we sat on the rocks and drank tea with villagers. By the time we got back to At-Tuwani it was time to go out with the shepherds. I saw Israeli police down by the clinic. They were questioning Ghanam about his van. I later learned that when the police came, they went to the clinic and asked who owned the van. The workers were from Yatta and did not know. When they were unable to say who owned the van, a policeman slapped one of the workers in the face. The police claimed the van was stolen. It turned out that the police had gotten one digit of the serial number wrong. Ghanam had the correct papers and proved that the van was not stolen. Ta'ayush will follow up on this and make a complaint to the police about this abuse.

We saw a group of journalists up toward the settler outpost so we walked up there and were met by Israeli soldiers. Itimar was in charge. He said the whole area was a closed military zone, that we could not go anywhere. He said there were soldiers at the top of the mountain, and they would take care of the shepherds, who already were at the top of the hill.

That was the beginning of a whole day of people not accepting his orders. We quickly decided that three of our group would sneak away and head up on the other side of the valley. I argued with Itimar, saying we were international observers and had a right and a responsibility to be with the shepherds. I asked him why he was restricting the shepherds when it was the settlers who attacked us yesterday. I went on to explain that in the past the military has not done a good job of protecting Palestinians. He didn't like that. I asked to see the papers making it a closed military zone.

Finally he said we could go up to the top of the mountain where we could see, but no farther, and we had to stay far to the west, away from the outpost and away from the soldiers and shepherds. I told him I could agree to that if he would also keep all the settlers out of the area. He agreed.

When we got to the top we could see the others with the soldiers and shepherds. The shepherds were arguing with the soldiers who were not allowing them to go any farther. I called a team member who said we should join them. I felt free to do that because I saw settlers there. Itimar did not keep his agreement.

The soldiers were trying to keep the shepherds from going any farther than the top of the hill. The shepherds would not accept that. The village women especially were pushing for more radical action. One shepherd and his mother got into an argument because he was trying to stop his mother from defying the soldiers' orders. It wasn't long before the shepherds and their sheep were walking past the soldiers and over the top of the hill, going right down into the Khoruba valley where for four years they had not been allowed to graze. The poor soldiers stood helpless and powerless with their M-16 assault rifles. I felt sorry for them. But there was nothing they could do. They were not going to shoot nonviolent shepherds with media and internationals present.

This reminds me of the time on February 14, 2002, when soldiers would not allow Palestinian children in Hebron to go to school. After much discussion with the soldiers, two of us CPTers consulted with the children and agreed to simply ignore the soldiers, walk right past them, and go to school. The children followed us as we marched past the powerless soldiers. Because of the international presence, they were not going to shoot a group of non-threatening schoolgirls. Their M-16s were rendered useless.

We walked down the valley with the sheep. Soon the shepherds were moving east across the valley to the next hill where they had been the past two days. The shepherds had not been allowed in some of that area for the past six years. The soldiers moved over there, above the shepherds. Some of us stood between the soldiers and the shepherds. By this time, five Israeli activists arrived and started arguing with the soldiers. The police arrested two of the Israeli activists (one was released) and one shepherd, ironically the one who had been trying to keep his mother in line. We were told that the police punched one of the Israelis in the face.

I guess I was in a bit of danger of arrest, but I was never really ordered to leave. I did keep asking all the police and soldiers why the shepherds could not be on their own land. A Palestinian came and showed the police his deeds to the land.

A Hummer drove over the rocks and the rough terrain toward the sheep to drive them to the other side of the valley. The sheep ran away. Eventually all the shepherds went to the other side of that valley. That was interesting. The soldiers were still permitting shepherds to be on some of the land. I call that a victory.

I was quite direct with the soldiers and police. "Why is it the settlers beat people, and because of that you put further restrictions on the Palestinians but no restrictions on the settlers? The settlers stir up trouble, and the Palestinians are punished. This is incredible. Why are the settlers allowed to go on Palestinian land, but the shepherds are not allowed on their own land?" I asked them why they were not up by the settlement keeping the settlers from coming on Palestinian property. They did not respond.

I told them this is a strategy I have been witnessing every time I have come here in the past ten years. The settlers stir up trouble, and the Palestinians are punished. Ilan Pappe has documented how this Israeli strategy dates back to the 1940s when Israelis began their program of ethnic cleansing. See *The Ethnic Cleansing of Palestine* (Oxford, Oneworld Publishing, Limited, 2006, pp. 39-85).

Two settler women stood on the hill just above us. I wanted to go talk with them, but an Israeli woman went up instead even though the soldiers told us we could not go. She came back crying, deeply shaken by the hardness, the racism, and the close-mindedness of the settler women. It was hard for her to believe that her fellow Israelis could be so bigoted and cruel.

Villagers brought food to us, so we sat on the hillside eating with the shepherds while the soldiers sat eating on the hillside on the other side of the small valley. I wished we could have been eating together. In some ways, it was a peaceful scene. The shepherds were happy about the gains they had made today. The soldiers were relaxed as they sat and ate. I later told the soldiers that I wished we could have been sharing our food. "No," they replied, "you would not want to eat the horrible crap we have to eat."

We were told that Johannes lost his glasses yesterday, so I asked the soldiers if I could go to where Johannes was beaten to look for them. I had to wait, but later, police gave permission for me to look for them. I didn't know where to look and later learned that a teenage shepherd knew where the beating took place, so at half past one we walked over to where the soldiers were sitting and again asked permission to go look for the glasses. Itimar said no, that only police could give permission. I didn't accept that. I kept asking why we could not look for the glasses. Before long, Itimar gave in and three soldiers accompanied us over to the next hill. We found the place, saw the blood, but didn't find the glasses. We found out later that Johannes actually has his glasses.

I am glad we looked for the glasses. It helped humanize the situation for the soldiers, and it was another opportunity to push the soldiers back another step. We also got another opportunity to go on that land and had a good time talking with the soldiers. I talked mostly with a guy who was born of Iraqi and Moroccan Jewish parents. I told him he was an Arab. That seemed like a new idea to him. There has been a systematic attempt in Israel to negate Jewish-Arabic culture.

We saw a young settler walk down the hill above where the soldiers were sitting. A Dove and I decided to walk toward him and try to talk to him. I expected the soldiers to stop us, but they didn't. We got within maybe two hundred feet of him, called "Shalom, shalom," but he just cursed us. The only word we could understand was "Nazi." He looked about sixteen and had long, light-colored hair. We kept telling him we wanted to listen to his concerns, but he kept cursing us. As he walked away, we turned back.

Gradually the shepherds started heading home, but some lingered on the top of the hill above At-Tuwani. We noticed Gdalia, the settler security man, go to the soldiers, and it wasn't long before soldiers came to us and demanded that the shepherds move farther from the outpost. It was rather obvious that the soldiers were following the orders of the settler. The shepherds made a token compliance, and the soldiers didn't push it. Gdalia drove down to us. I greeted him, but he didn't respond. He seemed angry. The shepherds and soldiers engaged in conversation. The soldiers even accepted orange slices that a shepherd offered to them.

Soldiers sometimes bring up the subject of Dov and that a Palestinian killed him. This afternoon when we asked them if they thought Dov was a good man, one of them replied, "No, not necessarily, but we like people like Dov because they do our work for us."

We followed the shepherds down the hill, walking on the road by the trees that surround the settler outpost. Just a week ago, they would not have gone on this road.

Salman's wife, Hathra, insisted we stop at their house for tea, which turned out to be a meal. I was really tired and took a nap there in the sun on the mat they had brought out to us. When I woke up, a number of men had gathered there and were discussing the day's events. After a bit of chatting, I left. They said they would let us know about plans for tomorrow.

February 18, 2005, Friday

Since it was Friday there was no school, and we were told that there would be no action with the sheep today. A little later a villager said we should go up to the top of the hill and check on what was happening. Three of us went up the road toward the trees and the settler outpost. This was the easy way, but more likely to get us into trouble. Sure enough, up near the top we saw police who called to us. We walked toward them and met them half way. They asked where we were going. We said we were going up to the top of the hill to check if there were problems. They assured us that there were no problems, that the police and soldiers always do the right thing and have everything under control. "Oh, really?" I thought. We said we just wanted to check, that we didn't plan to be there long. The police said we could go.

We went up and saw Mufakara shepherds where we were yesterday, with soldiers on the opposite hill, just like yesterday. We saw the settler security vehicle above the soldiers. Gdalia drove toward us as we started to leave and then drove toward the police above us. He stopped to talk with the police as we walked below them. I imagined he was complaining to the police about our presence. We waved to the police as we walked by. The police waved back to us. Gdalia did not wave. He must have been furious that we were walking where we had not been allowed to be just a week ago, and with the permission of the police.

I think it was important that we went up there this morning. We reminded the Israelis that we are watching them, we reestablished our right to be there, we connected with the police in a positive way, and we reconfirmed to the shepherds that we are available.

We got back to At-Tuwani just in time to catch a ride to Karmil. I spent about two hours in Hebron typing out an article and checking email.

Soon I was on my way to Jerusalem. Nina Mayorek, a Machsom Watch person for whom I gave a tour of Hebron recently, picked me up at Tantur and took me to her home where I spent the night. I felt right at home. I even knew many of the books on their bookshelf. Nina has been deeply moved by Peggy's book. We did a lot of talking about her upcoming speaking tour in America along with a Palestinian Christian and a Muslim woman. She is a biochemist who does research on diabetes. Nina poured out her heart to me about how the Occupation is destroying the soul of Israel. "The moral depravity of the Occupation has penetrated the hearts of the Israeli people," she said.

February 19, 2005, Saturday

We left at half past six to meet other Machsom Watch women at Liberty Bell Park in Jerusalem. On the way, we drove by the Palestinian village of Waleja on the Green Line west of Jerusalem. The Palestinians there have not received Israeli IDs, so they are illegal in their own homes. There has been continual military harassment of the village, including home demolitions, arrests, etc. They had been forced from their homes in 1948, not far from where they now live. Israelis confiscated most of their land. They are in constant danger of being expelled from their present homes in Israel's ongoing campaign of ethnic cleansing.

Soon we were in a bus with about fifteen women headed to At-Tuwani. I had a microphone and talked the whole way about the history of our work in At-Tuwani and important places along the way, like the Beqa'a. We got here at about eight o'clock and were met by villagers who served us tea.

We went to the school and talked with the principal. We learned that seven or more settler women had tried to attack the children this morning. They threw stones at the children, but no one was hurt. The soldiers quickly got the children into a jeep, and sped away. Some police came to the school to ask about the women trying to attack the children this morning, but they did not talk with the children, even though the children were waiting to give their accounts to the police.

The Israeli women asked lots of questions and got a lot of information. Hanna Barag in particular asked lots of questions and took careful notes. She helped set up the meeting with Knesset members and the military last October, and will be meeting with those Knesset members and military personnel again tomorrow. She plans to present what she learned today.

At half past nine, while we were at the school, we saw soldiers near the outpost. It wasn't long before we saw a group of ten or more settlers in the trees. Soon there were soldiers, police, and Border Police all around. I could see at least twenty of them. I wondered what was going on. The Palestinian understanding is that the settlers had gathered a large group in the woods to attack shepherds and internationals when we went up there today. That sounds scary. Attacks on Sabbath can be nasty.

If the settlers had attacked us, it could have been serious, but the soldiers and police had gathered to restrain the settlers. What the settlers did not know was that for some reason, maybe God's protection, the shepherds had decided to go to the Avi Gail outpost today. The settlers' plans were futile, and the soldiers had contained the settlers. Some of our team went to Avi Gail with the shepherds. There were about six soldiers there and a few settlers inside the outpost, but there were no problems. The shepherds grazed on land where they had not been for five years.

One of the Machsom Watch women expressed how angry she was at the settlers. I confessed to her that my biggest struggle here is with anger. She then asked me how I deal with my anger. I said, "First I need to recognize and confess that I am angry. Suppressing our anger is not helpful. Second, it helps to know that I am doing something about the injustice, that I am not helpless and powerless. Anger combined with feelings of powerlessness is destructive."

"Third," I said, "I have to turn to God and ask for love." The third answer was very difficult for her to hear, both because of my mention of God and prayer, and because of my mention of love. She said she could not possibly love the settlers. She could never do that. I said, "I also am unable to love them. I have to continually ask for that love to be given."

I referred to Martin Luther King Jr.'s writings on the importance of loving our enemies and to the example of one night King coming home after midnight after a difficult day and getting a phone call from a white racist who said he was going to kill King and his family. King broke that night. That night he turned to God for help, realizing that he could go no farther on his own strength. I also cannot do this on my own strength. The work of CPT is a spiritual struggle rooted in faith and prayer. We do not have the strength to engage in the struggle on our own power. We are weak cowards. We have to turn to God for strength, to tap spiritual resources beyond our own strength. Our personal prayer times and daily times of team worship are essential to our work.

It is commonly known that people become what they hate. When we encounter really nasty actions on the part of participants in the Israeli/Palestinian conflict, we can get sucked into the conflict and switch from being peacemakers to being belligerents in the conflict.

A spiritual danger we face in our work is to become Manichean, to see people in terms of good and evil. Because they think they are good and their enemies are evil, many people believe they must do everything they can to crush their opponents. How easy it is to see either Israelis or Palestinians as evil and join the struggle to defeat the side we consider evil. Instead of thinking of victory versus defeat, we can seek ways of transforming the conflict.

The CPT vision, which has deep Christian roots, recognizes the reality of evil and oppression, but also understands that the struggle begins in our own lives. CPT is involved in resisting the powers of evil, but it is not only evil and oppression "out there" that we struggle against. We also must deal with the oppression that exists in our own lives.

Thus, we are all in need of great humility as we confront oppressive structures.

After the women left at eleven o'clock, villagers told me I should not go up to Avi Gail but rather keep an eye on things here in the village. I watched for a while from the school and then went up to Juma's house and joined the people there, including three Ta'ayush women who were keeping watch on the soldiers and settlers. About six soldiers and police stayed right above Juma's house.

The Ta'ayush women went with me on school patrol. The soldiers were half an hour late and accompanied by a police van. Three soldiers walked with the children. I worried about the children when they went out of sight by the settler outpost but trusted that there were more police and soldiers up around the corner. There was nothing more I could do.

I went back to Juma's house, ate lunch, took a nap there on the roof, and left when the Ta'ayush people left. We worried about what might happen tonight, so I told Juma we were willing to sleep in his house tonight if they wanted us for protection. Am I willing to do that? Am I ready to face those settlers in the middle of the night?

Juma told me that on Wednesday, shortly before the beatings, a settler, about 35-40 years old, came up to him and told him, "I will shoot you in the head." Juma replied, "Go ahead, and do it quickly." The settler left.

Two of us went over to Juma's house this evening to check on the situation there since their house is closest to the outpost. We were invited in to visit. Two elderly men who used to live in the abandoned village of Khoruba were there. I appreciated being able to connect that abandoned village with real people who had invested their lives there. They served us supper, after which many of the village men came to discuss where we should go tomorrow with the sheep. I keep being impressed with how democratic these people are. They each share their ideas and come to a consensus. They do not need Americans to teach them about democracy. It is the Americans who need to be taught democracy and nonviolence.

We decided to go to Khoruba tomorrow unless we see settlers in the outpost tomorrow morning. Juma didn't think it necessary for us to sleep in his house tonight. He will call us if there is any trouble in the night.

February 20, 2005, Sunday

We saw no settler activity in the outpost during school patrol, so the shepherds returned to Khoruba this morning. We went out at half past nine and stood between the shepherds and the outpost. It wasn't long before a young woman came down out of the trees with a baby carriage, a common form of protest for settlers. One of our team went up to talk with her. We noticed that when she got there both of them sat down. She was there about four minutes and came back. She reported that the woman told her this is the Holy Land, and it is only for Jews. The settler asked her if she loved Israel. She said she loved both peoples. When the settler learned that she was a Christian, the settler immediately ended the conversation.

The shepherds slowly moved closer to the outpost. Since there were no soldiers or police to be seen anywhere, I was feeling quite uneasy. What if settlers attacked us now? They must know we are here since the woman saw us. For a short time we saw another woman settler on the hill above us. At 10:52 we saw four settler men in the trees. Then four women with children and baby carriages came down from the outpost. I was feeling quite nervous. Would they attack us now? At 10:59 six settler men came down with dogs but then went back into the outpost. At 11:03 a police jeep came down out of the outpost. The shepherds didn't move.

Shortly after this, both Gdalia and soldiers appeared on the opposite hill. We walked toward the soldiers and talked with them. Itimar and the others seemed to be in a bad mood. From his remarks, I guessed that Itimar was in some trouble for not being tougher with us recently. The shepherds really did push him around. To be a good Israeli soldier one needs to be brutal. To his credit, Itimar is not brutal enough. We certainly have discouraged him from being tough. He said he was tired of his job.

Recently he had told us he wanted to make the military a career. I offered him my CPT hat if he would throw away his gun. I also offered the hat to the other soldiers, but they didn't take me up on my offer. "If you want a CPT hat," I told them, "all you have to do is get rid of your guns and take a month of nonviolence training."

We went back to the Palestinian side and sat with the shepherds. The soldiers, police, and settler women were on the other side. We sat and watched each other.

At 11:56, some sheep got into the wheat that settlers had planted on Palestinian land. A policeman came running down, yelling at the shepherd. He sounded horribly disrespectful and angry. I thought he was going to arrest the shepherd, but he only warned him. The policeman threatened to shoot the sheep if they got into the wheat again.

At 1:35 three older higher-ranking military officers and a

policeman came. They announced that this was a military fire zone and we had to leave immediately or be arrested. Only landowners will be allowed here, and only on Fridays and Saturdays with a special permit. The shepherds argued with them, especially an older woman and the two old men who used to live in Khoruba. I felt a lot of anger. Why don't they stop settlers from threatening school children, beating up internationals, attacking soldiers, and stealing from their neighbors? Do these soldiers really think we are that stupid? They are going to have a military firing area right beside the settlement? Maybe I am wrong.

Maybe they are planning to drive out the settlers by firing into the settlement and then give the whole area back to the Palestinians. Fat chance. This is another attempt at ethnic cleansing. I couldn't help but notice the tire tracks of the police and military vehicles in the fields of the At-Tuwani farmers. Not even the land is respected here, not to mention the disrespect for the people who live here.

I was overwhelmed with conflicting emotions as all the shepherds and sheep slowly headed back to At-Tuwani. I was angry and feeling defeated. The shepherds, however, did not look like defeated people to me. Their heads were held high. The faces of the shepherds spoke to me of hope and confidence. I stood there humbled. I have so little faith. These people understand patience. They actually trust that the future is in God's hands and not in the hands of those who seek to dominate, suppress, steal, and kill. Tomorrow they will push in a different direction. The Israeli goal of crushing them until they give up is not working. I thought of our time of worship this morning. We read Isaiah 65:18-19, 21-24, a powerful message of hope for a new social order of peace and justice for all.

February 21, 2005, Monday

We all went up the hill this morning to where we were yesterday for a big meeting announced by the Israeli authorities. All of the At-Tuwani shepherds and some of the Mufakara shep-

Israeli soldiers order Palestinian shepherds to leave.

herds were there, plus various Palestinian land owners. At 10:17, five military vehicles arrived. Some of them were from the DCO with some soldiers to protect them. The Israelis had M-16s and handguns. There were at least sixteen heavily armed Israelis who came to talk with the shepherds. This was a conversation? How can heavily armed people have a free, open conversation with unarmed people? The inequality of power was glaring. Of course, the Israeli authorities had no intention of having an honest conversation. Israeli authorities give orders to Palestinians. They do not have conversations with Palestinians.

By half past ten settlers started coming down the hill. At first there were three settlers, then about fifteen settlers watched by six soldiers. John and I decided to walk toward them to try to talk with them. The soldiers said the settlers would not talk with us. I asked them to tell the settlers we just wanted to listen and understand. The soldiers gave the message, but the settlers would not talk. We were standing maybe fifty feet from them, and they were neither cursing nor attacking us. I considered even that to be a breakthrough. We kept asking to talk but were ignored. I admired their discipline. I wondered what we could do to break down the wall between us.

At eleven o'clock we noticed shepherds moving out on the hill where they were yesterday when they were removed. The settlers noticed it too and told the soldiers to remove the shepherds. The soldiers obeyed the settlers and told the shepherds to move.

In the process of settlers going to talk with the soldiers, there were now settlers both in front of and behind us. I felt safe because they were not going to attack us with all these soldiers present. We kept trying to talk, but they ignored us.

We got a call saying that the Israeli government announced that they intend to build the Wall south of here near the Green Line. That sounds like good news for the shepherds here. I wondered how the settlers will respond to that decision.

The military people and the shepherds came back from a walk to talk about borders. Tarik, a Druze with the DCO, announced that almost all the land would be closed, except for Fridays and Saturdays when the shepherds might be able to get a permit to go on their land.

One soldier explained to me that since this is a firing range they are concerned that no Palestinians get hurt. Really? Are the settlers who live here not also in danger? I didn't say much, but I did ask Tarik in English why the shepherds can't go on their land. I told him that this is stealing, that every day Israelis steal more land. "Do you not have consciences?" I asked. I was ignored. This was not to be a conversation about the real issues.

At noon, all the soldiers left, but about fifteen settlers remained and prayed. John, who was raised Jewish but converted to Christianity, asked to pray with them but was refused. I again felt worried about being attacked. At 1:00 we sat and ate with the shepherds while watching settlers in the woods above us. I was quite nervous. At 1:25, two young settlers walked down toward the shepherds. There were no soldiers or police present. Would more settlers come? Would there be an attack? The two settlers walked past the shepherds who didn't move and continued walking toward the edge of the village.

About a dozen village women came out and screamed at the settlers. The settlers made a circle in the field and walked the whole way back below the trees and up into the outpost. Again, the shepherds didn't move. The settlers were making a statement. "Look at us. We are here. This is our land, and we will take it all." No Palestinian would dare to walk past a settlement like that.

We came back, and then at four o'clock a boy came and said we were to go up to Juma's house with our video camera. We headed up the hill and saw about twenty people in the field. I immediately knew what had happened. When we got there my fears were confirmed. Last night settlers destroyed the 150 olive trees that Saber planted about three months ago, trees that were donated by the YMCA and YWCA in Jerusalem. The trees were pulled out of the ground and broken. Young olive trees were scattered everywhere. Feelings of disgust welled up in me.

Suddenly I understood. Those two settlers walked in a circle in this field this afternoon to survey what they or their friends had accomplished last night. I had learned earlier today that the hundred olive trees that Ta'ayush people had planted over by Avi Gail on Saturday were also uprooted last night. The settlers were busy last night. I have been expecting trouble from the settlers. Villagers said they expect many more attacks from the settlers.

Soon soldiers arrived. We showed them the scattered olive trees. I asked Itimar again what the villagers are doing wrong. Why can't they be on their own land? Why can't they have olive trees? Why is it that settlers can steal, threaten school children, and beat up internationals and go free? Isn't there something wrong with this picture? He didn't answer my questions. What could he say?

This was a hard day for the people of At-Tuwani. They are not allowed to graze their sheep, and they can't plant olive trees.

The shepherds had a major setback, but they are still better off than they were a month ago. They can still go on land that until just recently was forbidden to them. The authorities today reconfirmed that much of the shepherds' land does in effect belong to the shepherds, even though they may enter it only on Fridays and Saturdays.

The shepherds are not sure what they will do next. Ezra will contact the lawyer. They believe the edict of today is illegal and will challenge it in some way, either by legal action or by nonviolent direct action. When asked what this means for the village, one shepherd responded, "What the soldiers and settlers did today is what we expect. They destroyed our olive trees, but we will plant more olive trees." Another shepherd said, "We will keep going back on our land even if they arrest us." I am humbled by these Muslim shepherds. Their faith is so much deeper than mine.

February 22, 2005, Tuesday

We went with the shepherds to Avi Gail today. Since it was a quiet morning, I did some writing and even got a nap, using a stone for a pillow. We had a nice lunch with the shepherds. I learned that they eat lunch together every day out in the mountains during the grazing season. These are great picnics.

Soldiers and police arrived just after two o'clock. The soldiers ran down the mountain to where quite a few shepherds were grazing their sheep. I was worried about what the soldiers might do, so I ran down the mountain as fast as I could. When I approached the soldiers, guys I have been seeing every day, they yelled in anger, "These people are too close to the settlement. They know that they are not allowed to go up to the settlement." I thought to myself, "Don't you have anything better to do than chase simple shepherds who are a threat to no one?" The soldiers ordered about ten of the shepherds to walk up the mountain to the road. I wasn't sure if they were under arrest. These shepherds were from Mufakara and Karmil. The At-Tuwani shepherds were a little further to the north.

Gdalia was there, acting like he was in charge. I was sure the soldiers and police came because he called them. When we got to the road the police took all identity cards and our passports. The policeman in charge was from Texas and was quite sarcastic. He asked why we don't go to Texas and protest the U.S. occupation of Texas. I said the Mexicans are taking it back. He said, "The shepherds do not need to be here. They can graze their sheep farther to the south, away from the settlements. This is not Arab land. These people are not even from here."

The police decided not to arrest anyone. We were all free to go. The soldiers then again pointed out where the shepherds may and may not graze. I must admit, the shepherds can get fairly close to the outpost. This is a victory. Gdalia stood there really angry. He had lost again. Not only were the shepherds not removed, their right to be there was reconfirmed. He would not talk with me. Even when I asked to talk about Dov and Nati, he refused.

The soldiers told the shepherds that they came this afternoon because a settler security guard had called them and told them that the shepherds had actually entered Avi Gail. That explains why the soldiers were so angry when they arrived. The soldiers and police soon realized that they were lied to and ended up being angry with Gdalia.

This also explains why a Mufakara shepherd was treated so roughly when he was arrested on the other side of Avi Gail today. The soldiers first went to the other side of Avi Gail this afternoon and arrested him when he was with his sheep over there. He said the soldiers handcuffed his wrists behind his back, shackled his feet, blindfolded him, and roughed him up. The soldiers were angry because they thought the shepherds were being really uppity by going into Avi Gail. They took him to the military camp at Susya and kept him there for three hours.

February 23, 2005, Wednesday
Matt and I went to Avi Gail and had a quiet morning with

the shepherds. We saw two demolished cisterns. The Israeli military demolished many cisterns here some years ago. This afternoon Matt and I walked down the road to meet Rich and the CPT delegation that will be here for two days. When we crossed the settler road, we learned that Israeli soldiers had closed the road to Karmil at two places at eleven o'clock this morning. They also closed quite a few other roads in the area today.

As I looked at those huge boulders blocking the road, I wondered why the Israeli authorities daily put these harassments on the Palestinian people. Why do they make it more difficult for the Palestinians to go to the hospital, more difficult to go to work, and more difficult to visit relatives? What have the Palestinians done to deserve all this suffering? Is this to punish the Palestinians for the gains they have made in grazing their sheep? I thought of the biblical story in Exodus 5 of the oppression the Hebrew people endured in Egypt, how Pharoah kept making their burdens harder. That is what is happening here. The Jewish people, who have known horrible oppression over the centuries, now keep increasing the burdens on the Palestinians.

I thought about my recent conversations with Israeli soldiers. They seemed incapable of seeing that maybe there was something unfair about the Occupation. They could not accept that maybe the Israeli military might be part of the problem. The Palestinians are the problem. The mechanisms the Israeli soldiers use to keep themselves in deep denial seem to be working well. They see only what they want to see.

Those big boulders blocking the road to Karmil tell a different story. Although they prevent Palestinian access to the settler road, the Israelis whizzing by on the new settler road do not even see those boulders. The Palestinians know they are there. They are the ones who feel the pain those boulders both represent and cause.

I took the CPT delegation on a tour of the village and then led nonviolence training for them. We spent a short time reviewing the philosophy of nonviolence. We then did a role-play to practice active listening in response to an irate settler ready to attack us. I had them each share in pairs about their fears. We then did some quick decision making, with one minute to decide how they would respond to a variety of settler threats and confrontations with soldiers. I tried to raise many of the issues we regularly face as we work here and give them some preparation for what they may encounter while they are with us.

Ezra came and wanted to open the road yet this evening. We thought we were going out on the road to accompany the bulldozer, but they were unable to find anyone who would bring a bulldozer this evening. They are planning to do it tomorrow.

I learned that Johannes is recovering in Italy. He will have his jaw wired shut for six weeks. His eye may heal without surgery.

February 24, 2005, Thursday

Rich and one delegate went on school patrol while the rest of us waited to accompany a bulldozer that was coming to reopen the road to Karmil. It ended up the Palestinians did not want us there. We watched from the hill above the village. Soon a bulldozer came down from Karmil, quickly opened a way around the huge boulders the soldiers had placed on the road, and headed back to Karmil.

We then went out with the shepherds. Rich took two delegates with him across the road with some shepherds from Karmil. When a settler arrived, they all ran away. The other delegates went with me up the hill toward the outpost. There was no major action planned for today.

The soldiers were late when the children were out of school. I needed to leave to go to Hebron to finish all my work before I would leave to go back to America. My time here was about finished. I walked down toward Juma's house where the children were playing and singing. I greeted each one of them, told them I was leaving, and sent greetings to their families. Each child greeted me and said goodbye. It was the most wonderful send-off I could ever imagine. I stood each day watching those children, sometimes in rain and snow, hoping and praying they would be safe. Now they were wishing me God's blessing. I started sobbing as I walked down the road. I was overwhelmed with feelings of joy and gratitude for the privilege of having been in At-Tuwani.

February 27, 2005 Sunday

I had a conversation with an Israeli woman as I went through Israeli immigration on my way home. She said, "Why can't we all just be nice to each other and get along?" "Yes," I said, "we need to treat each other with respect." It would have been fine if I had left it at that, but I, with my big mouth, felt the need to say that the conflict is more than a matter of just being polite with each other. I said a few words about the great imbalance of power in the Occupation and the horrible consequences of dominating other people, both for the Palestinians and the Israelis. I emphasized the emotional toll of the Occupation on the Israeli people.

Her polite, liberal veneer soon disappeared as she defended Israeli domination of Palestinians. She repeated the myth of Israeli innocence, the belief that Israelis have nothing to apologize for to the Palestinians. She went on to say, "We can't share power with the Palestinians because they are not ready for freedom and democracy." I was amazed at her words. I watched illiterate shepherds making important decisions about their lives in a very democratic manner. These shepherds understood not only democratic values but the power of nonviolence as well.

The message I heard was that since the Palestinians are not ready for freedom, Israelis must continue to dominate, suppress, humiliate, and control them. I thought of George Bush who also has the arrogance to believe that the United States must teach Arabs about democracy. I wish people like George Bush and this young Israeli woman could have spent the past three months living with me in the caves of Palestinian shepherds. I wish they could listen to the hopes and fears of these simple people. I wish they could have experienced the friendships between these Palestinians and Israeli peace activists who visit them regularly, demonstrating that peace is possible.

I wish I could have seen the same values expressed by Israeli soldiers and settlers, who live by the power of their guns. I watched these shepherds being bullied and pushed around by Israelis with guns. Although at times some soldiers were courteous, never once did I see Israeli soldiers relate to Palestinians in democratic, power-sharing ways. Most Israelis are living in deep denial. They refuse to see anything about their own actions that might be an obstacle to peace. The myth of Israeli innocence is quite strong. Everything is the fault of the Palestinians. Yes, the Palestinians have their faults, and some of their actions prolong the conflict, but the faults of one side do not justify the actions of the other side.

A well-educated Palestinian man was listening in disbelief to our conversation. It was difficult for him to hear that he is not ready for freedom, that he and his people are the cause of their own suffering. Both the Israelis and Palestinians I know want to live in peace and freedom, as do people everywhere. The problem is not the Israeli people. The problem is not the Palestinian people. The problem is that some people are dominating and controlling other people, and no one wants to be dominated and controlled.

Dominators resort to horrible means to maintain their control. Sorry to say, dominated people sometimes resort to horrible means to break free from their oppression. I spent the past three months working with both Israelis and Palestinians who want to end the system of domination and control. Maybe we could listen to them instead of those who think brute force is the answer.

What We Accomplished and How We Did It

As I look back on my time in At-Tuwani this winter, I am amazed at all that was accomplished. This is arguably the most exciting, successful, nonviolent campaign I have ever been part of. A group of untrained, partly illiterate shepherds led a sustained nonviolent campaign. I was constantly amazed at the depth of understanding of both nonviolence and democratic decision making these shepherds displayed.

Many people have argued that for nonviolence to work there needs to be a culture of nonviolence. Clearly, a culture of nonviolence exists in At-Tuwani and the South Hebron Hills. These shepherds understand resistance; they understand patience. They know how to cooperate, work together, and have a long history of resolving conflicts nonviolently.

Nonviolent action helps open new possibilities for all sides in a conflict. The status quo is upset, the power equation is changed, and the oppressed see new hope. Nonviolent action often results in discussions between the various sides and some kind of resolution to the conflict.

What were the results of nonviolent action in At-Tuwani during the past three months?

1. There is now a medical clinic in At-Tuwani.

2. Israeli soldiers and police are accompanying Palestinian school children instead of standing by as children are attacked.

3. Shepherds are now grazing their sheep in places they had not dared to go for the past two to six years.

4. The right of Palestinians to at least some of their land has been reestablished.

5. The power of the settlers, both in relation to the Israeli authorities and to the Palestinians, has been reduced.

6. The balance of power between the Israeli authorities and the villagers has been altered, resulting in a change of relationships between the Israeli authorities and the villagers. There have been fewer attacks and less harassment from soldiers and settlers. The villagers feel more confident, less afraid. Police are taking complaints more seriously.

7. A living school of nonviolence was created.

8. It is not clear how much the Israeli decision to build the Wall south along the Green Line is the result of nonviolent action in the South Hebron Hills.

9. The presence of internationals is having many effects on the village. The interest of the outside world is taken as an affirmation of the culture of the village and the importance of their struggles, which, in turn, gives new self-confidence to the people there.

We were not able to do everything. We had hoped to work on the issues of road closings. The Israelis prevent Palestinians from improving their roads and even demolish many roads, but these concerns got pushed to the side. However, those issues have not gone away.

How was it done?

1. The growing cooperation between shepherds was crucial. The shepherds met often to evaluate actions and plan next steps, which helped give direction and focus to each action. Due to the shepherds combining their flocks and going out together, it became much more difficult for Israeli authorities to isolate and stop them. Individual shepherds and flocks would have more easily been picked off one by one. The shepherds' solidarity meant they could not easily be stopped by settler threats and official force.

2. The villagers' deep religious faith and long-term view of history gave them the patience and hope needed to wage a sustained, long-term struggle, which, in turn, helped the shepherds overcome feelings of powerlessness and hopelessness. The religious faith of the internationals also was important, both in giving vision and strength to the internationals and also in fostering a deeper connection between villagers and internationals. Even though the internationals were Christian, the Muslim villagers respected the internationals for their faith.

3. The presence of internationals was crucial. The importance of this international presence is illustrated by the repeated complaints of Israeli authorities and settlers about there having been no problems in the area before the coming of internationals to the village. Obviously internationals did not create the problems. The presence of internationals exposed and revealed the oppression that had been there the whole time.

4. The ability of the internationals to earn the trust of the shepherds was extremely important. The trust that developed between villagers and internationals helped make it possible to take risky actions together.

5. After problems were identified, direct action was taken, including civil disobedience. Shepherds took their flocks on land they were not allowed to enter. Construction continued on building the clinic even though the Israelis ordered the work to stop.

6. It is significant that internationals took their cues from the Palestinians to whom they were accountable. They did not manage the campaign. Because of this, the Palestinians felt empowered by their presence.

7. Nonviolent action drew world media attention to the problems in At-Tuwani, which forced Israeli authorities both to ease the pressures they had been imposing on the people, and then to actually begin to place some restrictions on the actions of settlers against the Palestinians.

8. Violence directed at the internationals became a significant factor in gaining media attention and prompting Israeli

authorities to make changes. It seems that some kind of suffering is often required to accomplish goals. It is regrettable that the suffering of the Palestinians did not get the attention that internationals received.

9. The shepherds and internationals framed the issues. Should school children be able to go to school without being beat up by adults? Should shepherds be able to graze their sheep on their own land? By shepherds becoming more proactive, no longer were only settlers and the military framing the issues.

10. Significant dilemmas were created for the Israeli authorities. Would they allow settlers to beat up school children, or would they protect Palestinian school children? Would they force shepherds off their land, or would they concede that the land belongs to the shepherds? Would they crack down on the settlers, or would they continue to give the impression that the Israeli military takes its orders from settlers?

11. A significant factor in the success of nonviolent movements is the degree of support they receive from outside their movements. The support of Israeli activists was crucial for the shepherds. We worked closely with Israeli activists who helped with media attention and used their contacts in the military and government to great advantage. The presence of Israeli activists was a deep encouragement for the villagers.

Nonviolent action was able to transform repressive, potentially violent situations. Although the Israelis had lots of guns in confrontations with shepherds, those guns were rendered useless. Even though soldiers stood with their M-16's, shepherds walked right past the soldiers even when ordered not to pass. The soldiers sometimes stood helpless because they did not dare shoot with internationals and media present. Both villagers and internationals also were able to help soldiers relax in tense situations. In many cases, they ended up either joking with each other or having serious conversations.

One may ask how permanent are these accomplishments, and how dependent are they on continued international accompaniment. Nothing is permanent, but I believe it would be difficult for Israeli authorities to take away most of these accomplishments without a big struggle. If the team left tomorrow, much of these gains would remain. But continued international attention will be crucial until there is peace.

December 1, 2005-February 18, 2006

December 1, 2005, Thursday

I am now back in Palestine and can hardly contain my joy and gratitude. I came here with some wonderful preparation. Fasting the month of Ramadan this fall has again been an important time of spiritual preparation. On Friday, two weeks ago, I went to the mosque in Athens, Ohio, for Friday prayers and addressed the congregation, asking them for their prayers for Peggy and me. Then in the evening I went to Shabbat services at the synagogue and asked the Jewish congregation for their prayers. After this, we went to the gathering in Athens of our activist friends to send us off. In addition, Peggy and I spent Thanksgiving with our son Dale, his wife Debbie, daughter Rebecca, and their Church of the Sojourners community in San Francisco where we got our Christian sendoff. We feel very loved and supported.

We arrived in Amman, Jordan, last evening, and I left this morning to come to Hebron. Peggy plans to go back to Iraq for another four months, and, after two months, I plan to join her there for a month, insh'allah. A complicating factor is that four of our CPTers were kidnapped in Iraq on Saturday. Peggy had hoped to also leave for Iraq this morning but will wait in Amman and do media work there in hopes of helping get our teammates released. This kidnapping is something we knew could happen. We are committed to this work and accept that there are risks. I continue to be fully supportive of Peggy going back to Iraq in spite of the dangers.

December 2, 2005, Friday

I walked back into Hebron this morning after spending yesterday afternoon and evening visiting friends in the Beqa'a Valley. Jenny Elliot and I left Hebron at ten o'clock this morning to come down to At-Tuwani. As before, we had to come the long way around, west to Dura and then south. The road was open the whole way. The roads have been closed off and on since I left last spring, sometimes with blocks and often with soldiers stopping all traffic.

I got out of the taxi at Karmil. There were a lot of At-Tuwani men at the store. I greeted them and was amazed at the warmth of their hugs and kisses. I sure felt welcomed back. I went with them to the mosque for Friday prayers and got a ride on a tractor and wagon back to At-Tuwani. What a thrill to face the breeze and see all the familiar countryside. Soon we were in At-Tuwani. I felt like I had come home.

I was invited to a home for a lunch of lentil soup, pita bread, olives, dibs, and custard. By the time we finished eating it was time to go to the school for a village demonstration, calling for the freeing of our four CPTers being held in Iraq. There have been demonstrations not only in the West Bank, but all over the world in support of the four hostages, as well as calls from the world Muslim community for their release. This demonstration in At-Tuwani was one expression of the wide support CPT is receiving from the Muslim world.

I stopped by our house and met CPTers Amy Knickrehm, Diane Janzen, Kristin Anderson, and a Dove. They filled me in on our participation in the demonstration. We were not to speak or be the focus of attention. We did not even wear our CPT hats. The team did not want more white Americans speaking to the Iraqi people about the hostages. We think it is better now for Palestinians and Muslims to do that.

People from At-Tuwani and neighboring villages were already gathering at the school when we got there at half past one on this warm, sunny afternoon. I walked around greeting many

Palestinian children in the demonstration supporting the four CPT members who were kidnapped in Iraq.

people, including people from Tuba, Mufakara, and Susiya that I learned to know last year. Some of the Tuba children we accompanied last year were there. Now they had come to support us. I was deeply moved by that.

Before long there must have been more than one hundred people there. They had made many signs and banners in support of CPT. Many people carried pictures of Tom Fox, Jim Loney, Norman Kember, and Harmeet Sooden, the four who were kidnapped. One reason for the outpouring of love and support was that the people here remember Tom Fox from the time he spent here in At-Tuwani last year. I thought of the time we had worked together here.

Soon the march began. It was an impressive sight to see the long procession winding through the village, ending up at the new clinic that is now open when doctors come. The villagers chanted "CPT, CPT, CPT" as they marched. Banners were hung from the roof and second floor of the clinic. Children held signs out the windows. The adults gave speeches. When the men moved to the side, the village women moved into center stage with their signs. Each group of people here expressed their support. All this was done completely at the initiative of the people here in At-Tuwani.

I was moved by the support shown to CPT, but even more impressive for me was the fact that these Muslims were showing so much love and support for a group of Christians. Several Israeli Jews from Ta'ayush also came to express their solidarity. Wow! How exciting it is that in the midst of all the hatred and killing in the world, there are people of good will who are crossing boundaries to give witness to a better way. Too often people rally behind their own religious and political groups rather than stand for truth and justice.

Equally exciting is that Muslim groups around the world are speaking out to condemn the kidnapping of Christians by their fellow Muslims and to demand the release of the four captives. Almost every important Muslim leader in the world has spoken out in support of CPT. Muslims are taking responsibility for the actions of their fellow Muslims. There have been many demonstrations of support by various Palestinian political and Islamic groups in occupied Palestine. The Grand Mufti in Jerusalem, for example, has spoken out in support of CPT. Could we be seeing a breakthrough in Islamic/Christian relations? Will Christians now stand up for Muslims being held by America and Canada in secret prisons, detained without charges, taken to other countries and tortured?

It is important to remember that there are many more hostages held in Iraq than the four CPT volunteers. In addition to the maybe eighteen thousand detainees held by U.S. forces, the whole population of Iraq is being held hostage by Bush's illegal, immoral, and unnecessary war. Add to this the numerous Iraqis kidnapped for money by criminal gangs. Coupled with demands for the release of the four CPTers are demands for an end to the occupation of Iraq.

I spent the evening with Nasser, Keifah, and children, my adopted family here. They have a new baby, Adam. It was so good to be with them again. It seemed like I was never gone.

December 3, 2005, Saturday

It was good to go on school patrol this morning. A Dove and I went up to Khoruba to watch for the children coming from Tuba toward the waiting soldiers. School patrol has changed since last spring. Now, because of attacks on the children from settlers, the children wait near Tuba until they see the soldiers, and only then walk closer to the settlement where they meet the soldiers. The soldiers are now taking the children the short way past the Ma'on settlement.

We now always have two of our team members go up the hill at Khoruba to watch for the children coming from Tuba while two team members wait below the Ma'on settlement for the children to come. When we saw the children going toward the soldiers, we called Kristin and Diane to let them know that the children were on their way. If the soldiers had been late, we would have called the military to remind them to come. We walked back and met the children before they got to school. It was a thrill to see them again as I shook the little hands of each of them.

I learned this morning that the captors in Iraq released a message to Al Jazeera TV demanding that unless all Iraqi detainees are released by next Thursday, they will kill Tom, Jim, Norman, and Harmeet. Hearing that hit me hard. Suddenly it all became more real to me. This is really serious. They really might be killed. I cried inwardly all the way up the hill for school patrol this morning. All sorts of thoughts raced through my mind. After all of CPT's work on the detainee issue, must CPTers also die for the detainees? Is this what it will take? Must CPTers die for Bush's sins? Is this the cross that we must bear?

December 4, 2005, Sunday

We got a call from shepherds in Mufakara this morning saying settlers were grazing their sheep near their village. Two team members went and filmed the settlers. Settlers have been regularly taking their sheep near Palestinian villages to send the message that they still intend to take all the land here, which means continued struggle and confrontation. There were continual problems from settlers since I left last winter.

In October, because of settler threats, our team had sent out an urgent action alert, asking people around the world to contact Israeli military officials to remind them of their legal and moral responsibility to protect all residents in the area. The threats, the refusal of the military to escort the children, and the military saying they were helpless made big news in the Israeli press and became another embarrassment for the military. Because of this international pressure, the Israeli military kept a presence in At-Tuwani Wednesday night and Thursday, and there were no attacks.

This morning we received a call that there were soldiers down on the Israeli road, so we headed down there. Having a presence on the road has become an important part of our work. If possible, whenever we hear that the soldiers have set up a flying (temporary) checkpoint on the road, we head down to have a presence there because the soldiers have caused so many problems there, including beating Palestinians, arresting them, confiscating their car keys, and closing the Palestinian road from At-Tuwani to Yatta.

This morning soldiers stopped Nasser Nowajah as he was transporting Susiya children to the school here. When we got to the road, the soldiers were gone, but Nasser's car was blocking the road to Yatta. We learned that the soldiers had taken Nasser with them. Soon some Palestinians came, and we pushed the car a short way to the side of the road so other cars could pass.

We walked up the hill toward At-Tuwani where about six At-Tuwani men were sitting watching the road. We joined them, drank tea together, and waited. At about quarter past nine, Ezra brought Nasser back. We had called Ezra and Machsom Watch to inform them of Nasser's arrest. Ezra went to the military base at Susya and obtained Nasser's release. Ezra learned from the soldiers that someone had called the military about Nasser's arrest. That call may have helped get him released. We could see the marks on his wrist from the handcuffs which had been very tight and had caused Nasser a lot of pain.

Nasser told us his story. Four soldiers in a jeep stopped him on the main road at half past seven. They didn't say a word to him but made him get out of the car and began pushing him. The children ran crying toward the school. The soldiers took him to Susya. There were no police there, and the soldiers still said nothing but made him kneel with his arms tied behind his back. Two weeks ago Nasser and ten children were detained and held from 1:00 until 4:15 in the afternoon. Soldiers told him he is not allowed on the road. He told us that just this past Thursday, soldiers had detained and beaten him. I asked Nasser if he was afraid. He said, "No, it has happened to me many times." He is no different than most of the Palestinian men here who have had many experiences of harassment from soldiers and settlers. A Dove videotaped him as he described his experience. We wanted to document this and share it with lawyers and human rights groups.

At 12:10 we got a call that soldiers had arrested people across the road. Quickly, cameras in hand, we ran down and found about ten Palestinian men sitting on the ground, guarded by about six Israeli soldiers. The picture was clear. Six men with guns had the power. The Palestinians, including an elderly man, were sitting on the ground, being subjugated, humiliated, and controlled. No matter what had actually happened, the picture did not lie.

The Palestinians told us that they were being detained because they were told that they are not allowed to even be on the Palestinian road. We talked to the soldiers who told us that they had stopped a car and the driver ran away. They said they were only checking the ID's of the men and they would release them. What should we believe? We do know that soldiers are doing a lot of harassment on that road and we did not see the soldiers checking ID's, nor does it take that long to check ID's. About fifteen minutes later, all the Palestinians were released.

A Dove and I left and waited for the children to get out of school. We walked with the children up over the hill to the dirt road leading toward the Ma'on settlement where the children meet the soldiers and below where Kim and Chris were beaten last September 29. We waited for the soldiers to come. We waited some more. I called the military. We waited some more. We called Ezra and Machsom Watch. We called the military. We waited some more.

The eleven children were wonderful. They had so much patience. They did get a bit rowdy at times, but we did a lot of playing, joking, and studying their English books. The children asked us if we are Muslims, if we pray, and if we fast. The questions seemed sincere, and apparently came out not only of curiosity, but also out of a real love and concern for us. At one point one of the boys pulled me aside to a flat rock and invited me to pray with him. He led Muslim prayers. That was really special for me. I felt honored.

Finally, two and a half hours late, the soldiers came. They didn't want to talk and they didn't walk with the children. They rode in their jeep behind the children. I wonder why the soldiers were late. Are they angry with us? Whatever the reason, the children are the ones to suffer.

December 5, 2005, Monday

A Dove and I went to meet the children this morning. I was eager to see them again this morning after that special time with them yesterday. There were fourteen of them with two soldiers walking with them. The soldiers seemed very friendly. We chatted a bit, and they gave each child a container of chocolate pudding. I wondered if this was a peace offering to atone for their irresponsibility yesterday.

After we came back to the house, Nasser from Susiya came by and wanted someone to accompany him to Yatta, for his protection from Israeli soldiers, I think. We decided I should go and check email while in Yatta. It was a joy to read about all of the support coming from around the world. I was in tears as I read the names of people and organizations speaking up for CPT. I also feel this support from everyone here. The man at the Internet café would not accept any money from me.

There are detractors. I read a message that Rush Limbaugh said he was happy to hear that CPTers were kidnapped because maybe that will teach us to not be so naïve. I wondered, who is naïve? Maybe it is naïve to think violence can solve complex problems.

December 6, 2005, Tuesday

There was a demonstration in Hebron this afternoon in support of CPT and the release of the four hostages. About 120 people from the At-Tuwani area went in two buses to join the demonstration. I was practically in tears the whole day because I was so moved by this outpouring of love and support for CPT. It was a great effort on the part of the people here to send so many people to Hebron.

Diana Zimmerman returned. She met us at the demonstration, and came back to At-Tuwani on the bus. She was here last year, was beaten by settlers on October 9, 2004, and was present when settlers attacked Johannes and another Dove on February 16, 2005.

I spent the evening with Nasser and Kiefah's family. I made a big point of thanking them for supporting CPT and for the many women who were at the demonstration. It really is significant that women participated. The women of At-Tuwani will no longer accept being trapped in their homes. Kiefah was part of the demonstration.

December 8, 2005, Thursday

Today is the deadline for our captives in Iraq. The captors said that if the United States does not release detainees by today, our four CPTers will be killed. I have been thinking about what a fantastic victory it would be if they were released today, if all the efforts to free them were successful. It would be wonderful to be able to build upon that. We had a special time of prayer for them last evening. Later this morning we heard that the kidnappers said they were extending the deadline two days until Saturday for all detainees in Iraq to be released. What does that mean? Is it a sign of hope?

Diana and I walked to Qawawis this morning, a village between Mufakara and Susiya. The village had been abandoned, but fifty people from four families moved back to the village in the beginning of March. They had three years earlier abandoned their homes in the village because of settler harassment from the nearby Avigail outpost. Because of the promise of international accompaniment, the villagers decided to take the risk of going back to their homes in the village. ISM volunteers had agreed to live in the village.

On March 5, approximately twenty Israeli settlers invaded the village and occupied the one house in the village. All the other homes are in caves. When the settlers arrived in the village, they threatened to beat an International Solidarity Movement, ISM, volunteer who was there. Israeli soldiers came and removed the settlers but also declared the village a closed military zone. All the Palestinians had to temporarily leave the village except for five landowners who had an order from the Israeli High Court that recognized their right to live there. Our team has had some presence in the village, but we have been unable to accept their request for us to have a permanent presence there. ISM has been there since last March.

We had a fantastic hour and a half hike, walking west past Mufakara and the Avigail settlement outpost, and over mountains and down into valleys. We stopped at a house in the village

of Sh'eb Botom where we had tea with a family. We then continued on our way and visited a farmer in his field. Qawawis is
a beautiful village on a mountainside with big stone walls dividing fields and gardens. We were greeted warmly as we entered
the village and spent time drinking tea with some of the people
there. We met "Ibrahim," the lone ISMer living in the village. He
seemed happy, and it was apparent that the villagers loved this
American Jew.

We left in time to get to Khoruba to watch for the children walking home to Tuba.

December 10, 2005, Saturday

I decided to fast today for our four CPTers held captive in
Iraq, since today is another deadline. I have been praying a lot
for them. But I am at peace. They are in God's hands. Al Jazeera
reported that imams in many mosques in Iraq yesterday, as part
of Friday prayers, demanded the release of the CPTers. I feel so
grateful for all this support. How will God use all this?

Rich Meyer and Dave Corcoran came this afternoon. Rich
led us in thinking about how we are personally dealing with the
hostage situation. We started thinking about our emotions. I
shared that my overwhelming feeling has been gratitude for all
the love and support we are receiving. I have a strong feeling of
trust that our teammates are in God's hands. Even if they are
killed, they are still in God's hands. I thought about all the times
I have given Peggy up to God while she has been in Iraq, including her staying in Baghdad during the "shock and awe" bombing in March 2003, and how each time God has given her back
to me. I feel like that in this situation.

December 11, 2005, Sunday

Rich and I went up to Khoruba for school patrol this
morning. We saw the children coming from Tuba, but it took
a long time before we saw them again coming around the next
hill. It seemed like they were waiting. We saw five settlers

between us and where the children meet the soldiers. We wondered if the children saw the settlers and were afraid to walk farther until they saw the soldiers. When Diana and I were up at Khoruba yesterday afternoon to watch for the children, we saw them running really fast toward home. It looked like they were afraid.

This morning we learned from the children that about seven settlers threatened them yesterday. A settler assaulted one Tuba boy, Tarik, by grabbing him by the throat, and another settler hit him with a stone on the leg, but he was not hurt. This morning there were two jeeps with five soldiers walking with the ten children. Were there more soldiers this morning because of the trouble yesterday? The soldiers gave the children chocolate pudding and chocolate milk this morning.

This afternoon, I asked a soldier what had happened yesterday afternoon. He said that settlers had threatened the children and that the military was filing charges against the settlers for obstructing soldiers doing their duty. I wondered, is there any significance to the military filing charges against the settlers? Will the police follow through on this or ignore the complaint? Has there been any shift in the government's attitude toward the settlements here? But the military today also used a bulldozer to block the road into Qawawis. Like in the American occupation of Iraq, the occasional acts of kindness by occupation soldiers, even if not strategic as they usually are, are overwhelmed by the weight of the destructiveness of the daily enforcement of control over the population.

I learned that on September 21 team members were called to Tuba because settlers and settler security had come to the village to supposedly look for money the settlers claimed was stolen from them. They forced people out of their homes as they went through people's belongings. The settlers left, and a bit later soldiers and settler security came back and threatened to "break their heads open" if the villagers didn't tell everything. When they realized that team members had been called and were on their way, the soldiers left the village. Tuba residents said the settlers had stolen things and damaged a tent.

In our worship today, we focused on the Advent theme of waiting and expecting. We are waiting, waiting for the release of the CPTers, waiting for peace.

December 13, 2005, Tuesday

I came to Hebron yesterday because we have enough team members in At-Tuwani now. I was horrified at the new gates the Israeli military has installed at the entrance to the Old City near the Ibrahimi mosque. There is a narrow passageway made with big plastic roadblocks that herd the Palestinians, like animals, through a corral to turnstiles that are controlled by soldiers. When the soldier presses a button there is a click in the turnstile, which is electronically unlocked, and one person can go through. Sometimes the soldiers let only one person through every two minutes or so.

The soldiers are in complete control of who goes in and out of the Old City. The issues here are domination, control, and dehumanization, in other words, treating people like animals. The old city feels like a prison. Increasingly, the West Bank feels like a prison with more and more people being walled and fenced in or out.

Rich, Dave, Kathie, and I went on school patrol at seven o'clock. Dave and I walked over to Yatta Road, the street on the other side of the Ibrahimi Boys' School, where I was shocked to see a structure similar to a mobile home placed across half the street. Big plastic roadblocks and razor wire block the other half of the street. This is an Israeli military checkpoint, put there last September. The building has two sets of doors that slide open and closed, controlled by a soldier inside. There is a metal detector inside each door, through which everyone must pass. There are guide rails that herd the people to the two doors.

This is an important spot for our morning school patrol, since there has been a lot of conflict there. Many mornings the teachers wait there, refusing to go through the metal detectors. There has now been an agreement with the military that teachers and pregnant women do not need to go through the metal detectors, an agreement that is sometimes respected by the soldiers and sometimes not. Many of the students, especially girls, refuse to go through the metal detectors, some claiming the detectors cause cancer.

I was angry when I saw this. The whole thing has nothing to do with security. The Palestinians can walk a little farther on other streets and avoid the checkpoint. I do not know what to call it other than harassment, control, and dehumanization.

I admired the way the children stood up to the soldiers and refused to go through the metal detectors. The soldiers used various forms of intimidation, such as either taking pictures or pretending to take pictures of the children with a camera. The children would then back off a bit, but almost immediately again move forward toward the soldiers and the roadblocks. Sometimes the soldiers would point their M-16s at the children. There were about twenty-five children there, mostly girls. TIPH people were there, along with two Israeli women from Machsom Watch.

One soldier was upset about a Palestinian boy cursing him. I asked the soldier why he thought the boy would curse him. The soldier acted as if he were clueless. I suggested that maybe it had something to do with the Occupation and the way the soldiers were treating the people here. He seemed to think they were treating the people fine. "Besides, this whole area belongs to the Jews," he said. I asked him how he would feel if Palestinians set up a military checkpoint like this in Tel Aviv and treated Jews in this way. The soldier did not like that.

December 15, 2005, Thursday

I had a strong visceral reaction to going through the cattle line and through the turnstile by the mosque this morning. Then coming back, I had to stand a while at the turnstile until a soldier finally pushed a button to electronically unlock the turnstile to let me through. I decided to just stand there and wait, and not ask for anything. The whole idea of people controlling other people is so offensive to me. People are not animals, and even animals deserve to be treated with respect.

Kathie and I went on school patrol this morning. I stayed on the street between Avraham Avinu and the Gutnick Center, the one small area in Hebron where Palestinians and settlers still share a street. Standing there and greeting settlers as they passed by brought back a lot of memories for me from past years. I had some fear, but more feelings of disgust and revulsion as I watched the settlers with their guns, their refusal to recognize my existence, their hate, and their determination to drive out all the non-Jews. I concluded that to love them I must act respectfully toward them, but I do not need to like them. I greeted each one as they passed by. A few responded positively, but most ignored me. I remembered a few of them from past years. I greeted Moshe Levinger, the founder of the Hebron settlements, but he ignored me.

This afternoon we hosted a group of rabbinical students, mostly from the United States, but also from other countries. These students, who are studying in Jerusalem, had come to Hebron for a tour to meet Palestinians and to understand the Palestinian perspective. They came here to our apartment, partly to meet us, but also because they needed a place for their afternoon prayers. Apparently they did not feel free to pray Jewish prayers anywhere else in Muslim Hebron or with the settlers. If they had gone into the Jewish area here, the soldiers probably would not have permitted them to return to the Palestinian area.

Their prayers had three parts: first, they prayed for release of hostages, including the CPTers in Iraq; second, they prayed for much needed rain here; and third, they prayed for peace and reconciliation. It was all in Hebrew, and I understood little, but the chanting, bowing, and the times of silence touched me deeply. It was so beautiful to have Jewish prayers here. I also silently recited the first chapter of the Qur'an and the Lord's Prayer during the times of silence.

After the prayers, one of the students gave a short sermon based on the story in Genesis 32 and 33 of Jacob meeting Esau after twenty years of separation. Jacob had stolen Esau's birthright by deceit and had left home to escape Esau's wrath. According to the story, Jacob was very fearful of meeting Esau and expected the worse. Instead of conflict, however, they hugged and kissed each other when they met and were reconciled. This story contradicts the traditional concept of tribal rivalry. If there has been a conflict, for example, between my grandfather and your grandfather, for me to reconcile with you would be a betrayal of my grandfather and my whole family. The only way I can be faithful to my family, my heritage, my tradition, is for me to perpetually seek revenge. This continues to be a common theme in our modern world. As we stand here in Hebron, the place of Abraham, Sarah, and Hagar, the place where Jacob and Esau lived, we see reminders everywhere of places where both Palestinians and Israelis have been killed by each other, and the ever-present reminders of the need for bloody revenge.

We were then asked if we are willing to let go of our traditions, our heritage, for the sake of reconciliation and peace. Are we willing to betray our own people for peace? I suggested that in all three Abrahamic faiths, the worst sin is idolatry. Holding on to anything is idolatry and a rejection of the oneness of God. Letting go of revenge is not a betrayal of our heritage. Instead of grasping and clinging to it, we trust God that the heritage can be renewed as we turn it over to God and allow God to give it back to us. How I wish that everyone in Hebron and in this conflicted land could hear this message.

Jews, Christians, and the Muslims who were with us came together in a very deep way through worship and prayer. This was especially healing for me. This was the first time I had participated in Jewish prayer in Hebron.

December 16, 2005, Friday

Sarah MacDonald and Harriet Taylor arrived after I went to bed last evening, so I met them this morning. The whole Hebron team went to At-Tuwani this morning for a joint team meeting. The Hebron team and the At-Tuwani team are now separate teams, with some movement of team members from one team to the other as needed. The plan is to have joint team meetings once each month. I am to be part of the At-Tuwani team, but will be spending some time working with the Hebron team.

We spent most of the meeting talking about how to overcome "isms" in CPT, for example, racism, sexism, ageism, and ableism. We hope to devote part of our Friday team meetings to discussing both the "isms" around us, but more importantly, the "isms" that we carry with us. We want to examine ourselves and also expose discrimination where we see it in our team. This has real possibilities, but will it be safe for us to be honest? We need to show grace to each other by giving each other space to grow.

I wonder, how far will we take this discussion? There is a lot of talk of white privilege and male privilege, things I wrestle with, but will we talk about passport privilege and class/wealth privilege, which demands an unequal share of the world's resources?

How much privilege are CPTers willing to forego? Will racism include prejudice against Arabs, Muslims, and Jews? Sometimes I think some people have a chip on their shoulders and use lofty condemnations of some "ism" to justify themselves and their judgmentalism. The people who talk the loudest about being sensitive toward others often seem to be the ones who are the least sensitive. I do want to take this seriously.

I am especially interested in how racism affects our relationships here. Most North American Christians grew up in a culture with deep fears and suspicions of Jews, Arabs, and Muslims. I know I have had to struggle with my own racist thoughts toward Muslims and Jews.

What does it mean for North American Christians to work in the middle of a deep conflict between Israeli Jews and Palestinian

Muslims? In what unconscious ways do we express our prejudices as we work with these people? Have we gone deep enough in examining our own racism? In what ways do we show disrespect for Muslim culture? In what ways do we see Western culture as superior to Muslim culture? Are our reactions to Israeli settlers and soldiers colored by any deep-seated anti-Jewish bigotry? Is there any truth to the charges made by settlers that we hate Jews?

Sometimes I feel uncomfortable with subtle criticisms of Palestinian culture. Sometimes it sounds disrespectful. Yes, the culture here is sexist and repressive, but do we also criticize American culture to the same degree? Are we just as aware of the repressive, sexist nature of Western culture? To what degree do we unconsciously accept the classist, sexist, and materialistic values inherent in almost all American movies, for example? How uncomfortable are we with watching those movies? Do we accept the values of popular American culture? Have we become desensitized to forms of oppression in our own culture?

There is no question about the deep appreciation of the people of At-Tuwani for the presence of internationals in their village. If we were to suddenly leave, they would be more vulnerable than now. No one actually said this to me, but my impression is that they appreciate our presence so much that they are willing to put up with a lot of cultural insensitivity and arrogance from us internationals. We do so many things that fly in the face of their cultural values.

What does it mean for international men and women to interrelate with few barriers when the lines between genders are more structured in the village? What does it say to the women of the village for international women to relate more to village men than to village women? One team member actually said she did not want to waste her time relating to the women in At-Tuwani. Since the men made the important decisions, she wanted to relate mainly to the men of the village. It has been difficult for the internationals to accept Palestinian cultural norms for cross gender relationships and gender roles within the village. I wonder, is it villagers or internationals that show more flexibility in dealing with cultural differences here?

On our way back to Hebron our van was stopped three times by soldiers checking cars. At the last checkpoint in Hebron, our van turned around and took another street to avoid the soldiers, proving again that the checkpoints have little to do with security, but do cause a lot of inconvenience for Palestinians. After we got back we heard that Yossi Shuk, a settler from Beit Haggai settlement, was killed by someone in a passing car, very close to where we had crossed Route 60, just before we got there. Two others in the car were wounded. Now there will be another round of collective punishment, reprisals, and counter reprisals. It doesn't make sense.

December 17, 2005, Saturday

Sarah and I went on school patrol together on the short stretch between Avraham Avinu and the mosque/synagogue. Saturday is an especially important time since there are a lot more settlers on the street on Sabbath. Often they are more rude and aggressive on Sabbath. As is my habit, I greeted many settlers with "Shabbat Shalom." A few responded in a friendly way, but most ignored me. I expressed sorrow at the killing of a settler yesterday, but that was not acknowledged. I received quite a few curses. One settler that I remember from past years, in a hateful tone of voice, said, "I hear they cut the head off of one of your group in Iraq, and you will be next."

As I think of the closed minds of the settlers and their seeming lack of concern for how they oppress and hurt other people, I think of myself. Do I demand the killing and oppression of other people and the rest of God's creation so I can continue my lifestyle? Do I feel oppressed if I am not consuming more than my fair share of the earth's resources? Do I want the cost of things I buy to be kept unsustainably low through exploitation of other people? Why are some social justice people so blind to the destruction of God's creation? We are all settlers.

A peace activist visited us the other day and was smoking in a room with children. Afterwards, I told him that it bothers me when people smoke in a room with other people, especially with children, because of the harmful effects of secondhand smoke. He said, "I don't want to hear it," and that was the end of our conversation. I wondered, how different are we from the settlers? We also do not want to hear anything about the pain we are causing other people. To what extent am I also closed and in denial?

There is a radical Christian tradition, as exemplified by the Peace Churches out of which CPT emerged, that sees the necessity of one's faith to be expressed as a lifestyle, for there to be a consistency between what one believes and how one lives. To speak about social justice and not be implementing those concerns in our daily lives leaves us empty and sounding phony. For our concerns about oppression, about the poor, about care for God's creation, to be authentic, those concerns must be expressed in our lives. Our witness can have power to the extent that we are living out alternatives to what we oppose.

This tradition also refuses to separate the personal from the political, the social from the spiritual, or prayer from action. A holistic outlook enables us to oppose all oppressions, not just those oppressions that contradict the values of a particular political position or cultural subgroup. Why would we not be concerned about both the millions who are killed each year by tobacco and those killed by war?

At this point I must confess that I am a hypocrite. My words and actions do not always match. Although I try to live simply (some would call me extreme), I am using far more than my fair share of the world's carbon and other resources. So how deep is my concern for God's creation? Do not listen to what I say; look at how I live.

I came back to At-Tuwani this morning. The taxi went to the south of Hebron since the road from Dura to Yatta is closed because of the killing of the settler yesterday. We got out of the

Israeli soldiers block and demolish the only road between At-Tuwani and Karmil.

van and walked across the settler road, across the mounds of dirt and through the mud, to get to the taxis waiting on the other side. At least the road to Yatta from there was open.

I walked to At-Tuwani from Karmil. The road was blocked part way down the hill with a big mound of dirt and a huge boulder. Down the hill the road was blocked by another huge pile of earth. This time the Israeli soldiers used good topsoil from a nearby field that had just been planted. What a waste of good topsoil, something so scarce and precious here. If the Israelis call this the Holy Land, why don't they treat the land as holy?

There was another pile of earth where the Palestinian road meets the new settler road. I soon learned that the Israeli military had closed the roads in many places this morning in response to the killing of the settler yesterday. I wonder, do the Israelis really think that collective punishment will bring peace, or even make Israelis more secure? To punish a whole population for what a few individuals have done is illegal under international law and only increases the anger of that population and makes such attacks more likely.

Blocking roads does not stop the movement of people. It only makes that movement more difficult and more expensive. Now people must walk, drive through fields, or take tractors or donkeys. It obviously has nothing to do with security. It is also a threat to the health of the people living here. If there was an emergency here, it would take a lot of time to get someone to a doctor in Yatta, for example. The cycle of attacks and counter attacks, reprisals and counter reprisals continue. But they do not lead to peace.

It was wonderful to walk back into At-Tuwani. Ezra and a journalist (Tom Segev) from Ha'aretz came and interviewed us for an article about the South Hebron Hills he is writing for Ha'aretz. Tom has been in America and has even visited a Mennonite home in Lancaster County, Pennsylvania, where I grew up. We are all connected.

I spent a delightful evening with Hafez, Aisha, and their family. I played a lot with Hamudi, who is sixteen months. I thought of my granddaughter, Rebecca, who is the same age.

December 18, 2005, Sunday

Diana and I met the children this morning, twelve of them. No soldiers walked with them. The soldiers did wave to us from their jeep. How ironic, I thought. They help the children, they are friendly to us, and then they go to do some really horrible things.

Villagers were working on the road in the village below the school, so I headed there. I love physical work, and I enjoy the fellowship of the people here.

About twenty-five men from At-Tuwani, and also from the neighboring villages of Tuba and Mufakara, were working together leveling the road and building a stone wall on each side of the road. We moved a lot of big rocks to make beautiful stone walls. I again was impressed with the ability of these people to work and make decisions together. Exactly where should the wall go? Which big rocks go where? They kept telling me I am a Palestinian. I felt honored by that.

At one point they told me to call the other team members and head for the road. I noticed that other villagers were also going down toward the road. It turned out that a tractor had gotten stuck trying to cross one of the big earth mounds, and they were afraid soldiers would come before they got the tractor unstuck. They were going to help get the tractor unstuck and wanted us there in case soldiers came. These people understand cooperation and mutual support. The tractor got unstuck before we got there.

The soldiers were a little over an hour late this afternoon, so we had to wait. The children were well behaved. They spent much of the time there on the hillside doing homework together. We made four phone calls to the military to remind them that we were waiting. We also called Hagit from Machsom Watch, who also called the military. We were told the soldiers were busy with the funeral procession for the settler killed on Friday. I expressed my condolences to the soldiers who seemed to appreciate that. I said I wanted the killing to stop on both sides. One of the soldiers expressed agreement. Two soldiers then walked with the children.

Three men from Tuba came to our house at about half past four this afternoon and asked us to accompany them and watch for soldiers as they tried to get their truck onto the Israeli road. When we got down to the road we saw a big truck, loaded with feed for the sheep in Tuba, stuck in the loose dirt mound that blocked an entrance to the settler road. A man from At-Tuwani was there with his tractor. He tried but could not pull the truck up to the road, so he drove down into the field and tried to pull the truck back down the earth mound. I didn't think that was possible, but, with a lot of us pushing, the truck did get unstuck.

Just then four Israeli soldiers pulled up in a Hummer. I was worried. Three of them jumped out with their M-16s drawn. I immediately walked up to them and greeted them with "Shalom, shalom. How are you?" They made no response to me, but at least I let them know internationals were watching them. By this time the tractor was trying to come up the ramp and got stuck where the truck had been stuck. I thought, "Oh no, the tractor driver is in real trouble." But with a little effort, the tractor made it to the road and the soldiers waved him by.

One of the soldiers began talking in Arabic to the Palestinians who were frantically moving dirt with their hands so that the truck could make another try to get to the road and seemed to ignore the soldier. Apparently our presence emboldened the Palestinians. I started talking to the soldier in Arabic, asking him why these people can't get their load of feed to their sheep. I got no answer.

Meanwhile, a Dove, who was videotaping the event, asked another soldier the same questions. The soldier told her this is Israel, the whole area is closed, and Palestinians must stay in their homes and not move around. Then another soldier addressed the maybe eight Palestinians in Hebrew, which I did not understand, after which the soldiers got back in their Hummer and drove off. Wow! I was expecting trouble.

I thought the Palestinians would lay low for a bit, but one of them found another possible opening about a quarter mile down the road, and was moving dirt and rocks as fast as he could and calling for the truck to go and try that opening. The truck tried to get up that ramp, but got stuck again, but was able to back down and try again. The second time, with a lot of spinning of wheels, the truck made it onto the road. Soon, with maybe a dozen Palestinians sitting on the feed on the back of the truck, they were on their way home. The muffler was broken off, but the truck sustained no other damage.

It was an incredible joy to watch that truck go up the road. Maybe the best compliment anyone can give to someone is to ask that person for help. I felt honored to have them come to our house and ask us to face the soldiers with them. I am grateful for the relationships we have established here.

Today was another beautiful day. The past several days were cold and cloudy with the promise of rain. They did get rain north of here, but only a few drops fell in At-Tuwani. There has still been little rain since last spring, except for a little back in November. Now is the time for the rains. The farmers have the grain and lentils planted, but they need rain. Many of the cisterns are empty. The village well is very low. Whenever I mention the need for rain, I get the same response. "Allah karim. God is generous." Muslims do not believe in complaining. They believe in trusting in the goodness of God. They put me to shame. I worry and complain.

December 19, 2005, Monday

The soldiers were a half hour late this morning, but three soldiers walked with the children. When I said to one of the soldiers this morning that I want shalom, he replied that peace is impossible because the Arabs don't want peace. Only the Israelis want peace. He then referred to the settler who was killed on Friday. I told him I was sorry about that. He repeated that the Arabs keep killing Jews. When I suggested that Israelis kill more Palestinians than Palestinians kill Israelis, a ratio of about eight to one, he maintained that Israelis never kill innocent Arabs. The myth of Israeli innocence is common among the soldiers, but could he be that blind to what the Israeli military is doing here? Does he really not understand why he needs to accompany Palestinian school children past the Ma'on settlement?

This reminds me of a conversation I had with a settler in Hebron. When I asked him how we can make peace, his response was that the Arabs do not want peace, that the Arabs only want to kill the Jews. To prove his point, he pointed to a sign on one of the shops remembering a Palestinian martyr. "See," he said, "the Arabs support violence." This martyr was a young Palestinian man who was about to be married. Baruch Goldstein, a Hebron settler, killed him while he was praying in the Ibrahimi Mosque. So who are the terrorists, and who wants to kill whom?

When I told the soldier that I feel safe going anywhere

without a gun, he said that if he would go to Yatta without a gun the people of Yatta would kill him. He did not believe me when I told him that we have Israeli Jews regularly coming to At-Tuwani. I didn't seem able to break through his fears and misconceptions.

Soldiers came again with a front-end loader to rebuild the roadblocks the Palestinians have opened. The military is really serious about this collective punishment for the settler killed last Friday.

December 20, 2005, Tuesday

I helped with building walls again this morning. I was worried when soldiers drove through the village while we were working. Will soldiers come and demolish all our work? It is good that the villagers are acting out of their hopes rather than fears. The improvements people are making here are signs of hope. The people here are not giving up. Repairing those stone walls is an act of resistance.

There are two kinds of walls: walls that separate and divide, and walls that give order and structure to relationships. The Israeli Wall, twenty-eight feet tall, encircling Palestinians, is a wall of fear and hate, and is incredibly ugly. The stone walls around gardens and roads impart beauty and character to the village. Robert Frost, in his poem "Mending Wall," said, "Something there is that doesn't love a wall, that wants it down." Walls of hate do not good neighbors make.

I am taking two days off. I had few plans other than to visit Mirkez and Jinba, about six miles south of At-Tuwani along the Green Line, the 1967 border between Israel and the West Bank. I wanted to visit the people I met there last year and to check on land confiscation for the Apartheid Wall Israel is planning to build there. I did not know how I would get there, or where I would spend the night. I didn't know if I would walk the whole way or get a ride on a tractor. It is a tremendous freedom to give up control and just trust the future to God. I had nothing to worry about. I knew that what God could give me was better than what I could control.

I left At-Tuwani at eleven o'clock this morning and walked south toward Jinba for over two hours, up and down those beautiful mountains. I wondered how anyone could be nasty in the midst of this splendor. Israeli military jets thundered in the sky above me, representing a way of life so different from that of the simple shepherds here, and so different from the message of the Hebrew prophets that so many people have abandoned in favor of the worship of military might. The line of Israeli settlements that stretches to Hebron was quite visible along the way.

The hike brought back lots of memories of walking here with Peggy last year. I spent some time removing big stones from the already rough road, a road the Israeli military forbids anyone to improve. I guess removing those stones was civil disobedience. Apparently doing good is illegal here. An early American Quaker wrote, "I shall pass this way but once. Any good therefore that I can do, any kindness that I can show, let me do it now. Let me not defer or neglect it, for I shall not pass this way again." I believe in leaving things a little better than how I found them.

I greeted many shepherds along the way as they watched their flocks. One group insisted that I walk up the mountain to greet them. I drank tea with three shepherds from Halawa, a village near Mirkez. One of the men said that the Israelis just confiscated five acres of his farmland for the Wall. When I said goodbye they offered me a piece of pita bread. It was delicious.

I walked past fields that, last year, had been torn up by Israeli tanks. The fields have been planted again this year, indicating that the farmers here are not giving up.

All eyes were on me as I walked into Mirkez. Who was this strange-looking American coming into their village? I quickly greeted everyone with "Salaam alykum" to assure them I was not a settler. I was immediately welcomed and invited to sit down in Muhammad Draref's tent, where I will be spending the night. Peggy and I met him here last year. The tent is a Bedouin style tent, ten by fourteen feet, bordered by a three-foot high stone wall, over which the tent is built. They brought me food, and soon I was having intense conversation with some of the villagers about the effects of the Wall, the settlements, and military harassment.

I then helped feed the sheep and take them to water. Muhammad's son gave me his shepherd's staff (actually a piece of black plastic pipe) and told me to lead the sheep to the water. I did pretty well. I did my version of a Palestinian shepherds' call, and the flock of a hundred sheep followed me. What a boost to my ego. When a few sheep started up the hill, I ran up the hill and chased them back. When finished, we put the sheep in a big cave for the night.

Mirkez is a village of about one hundred people. They all live in caves or Bedouin tents, because the Israeli military demolished all the houses in 1978 and 1981, and later demolished the entrances to the caves and destroyed all the trees and cisterns. The Israeli military wanted to drive all the Palestinians out of the area by making life impossible for them so that they could steal all this land.

But it didn't work. The people resisted nonviolently by staying here and enduring the hardships that were imposed on them. Simple survival is an important form of resistance. The population of the village is again growing. The Wall is now the big threat to the village. Since a major purpose of the Wall is land confiscation, it is no surprise that about four hundred acres of the village's best farmland is being confiscated for the Wall.

As I met these simple, friendly people here today, I kept thinking of that soldier who yesterday told me that without his gun, the people here would kill him. He has not seen what I have seen. I wish he could be here with me.

As we were talking this evening after dark, we heard the noise of a tank south of the village. We walked out into the dark and saw what looked like a tank and a bulldozer, with very bright lights, tearing around in fields at the southern end of the village. After about five minutes they were gone. This was a normal evening activity for soldiers, I was told.

We had electricity from a generator for about two hours. Then they lit an oil lamp and everyone began to speak in a softer voice. It was so much more comfortable without the harsh electric lights. I thought of ancient times when people gathered around the fire and told stories.

December 21, 2005, Wednesday

I woke up early this morning and gazed out the open tent toward the Jordanian mountains across the Dead Sea to the east, and watched the sky gradually brighten and turn brilliant hues of yellow, gray, orange, and red. My soul was filled with joy. God was giving us another day.

In the late afternoon yesterday, it began to cloud up, and there was even a bit of drizzle in the air. We hoped for rain, but this morning the sky is clear. The people here are disappointed, but they all said, "Allah karim."

After breakfast I walked over to Jinba and met Musa, and Isa's son, Omar. They were drawing water for their sheep with a bucket from a cistern and then invited me to go with them up on the mountain with their sheep. It was a pleasure to lead the sheep up the mountain. Four of us sat, talked, and drank tea as the sheep nibbled on the shrubbery. There was no grass.

I asked the shepherds about the tanks I heard last evening near Mirkez. Shortly after I asked, I heard tanks south of us. Soon I saw six tanks tearing around on Musa's wheat fields. It hasn't rained, and the land is very dry, so the tanks were stirring up huge clouds of dust. Back and forth they went, round and round. Musa said that big field is about 250 acres. That wheat field is the biggest, most level, best farmland I have seen in this area. Musa said the Israeli military has been using his field for tank practice for the past twelve years, often five days a week. Would it not bother Israelis if they knew their army uses the wheat fields of poor farmers for tank driving practice?

I am so angry I can hardly write this. As a boy, I was taught basic decency and consideration for others. To play with tanks on someone's wheat field is beyond any sense of decency I can imagine. I want to go straight down there and sit in front of those tanks, but my better judgment tells me that would not be wise. I would be acting out of anger. I would be going off half-cocked on my own. I would not have the discernment of either my teammates or the Palestinians who live here. It would not be part of any strategy or have any clear goals. It would only be a release of my anger. I can do better than that.

✳

This is not to reject the need for spontaneity. On January 26, 2003, I saw Israeli soldiers closing a road into Hebron, using a bulldozer to build a large mound of dirt (machsom) in the street. For a minute I stood in front of the bulldozer with my hands in the air. That short action ended with a conversation with an Israeli soldier who wanted to explain that closing roads was a way of ending terrorism. That made no sense to me, but I did decide to not take my protest any further.

Another spontaneous action on my part took place on January 30, 2003, when I saw two Israeli bulldozers and two tanks demolishing the central produce market in Hebron. I was horrified. Produce lay scattered and smashed everywhere in a city where many were hungry. I quickly helped carry boxes of produce out of the way of the bulldozers.

I began confronting soldiers. In a loud voice I asked them if they were proud of what they were doing, if this is peace. I ignored their commands for me to leave. One soldier spat at me, so I walked right up to him and invited him to spit on me. He declined the offer.

Three soldiers aimed their guns at and moved toward a group of Palestinian bystanders. It looked like they might shoot.

I quickly jumped in front of the soldiers, raised my hands in the air, and shouted, "Shoot me, shoot me." The soldiers left immediately.

A tank came roaring toward me, its big gun barrel aimed at me. If the tank had simply gone by me, as many tanks have done, I probably would have let it go by, but I could not ignore the big gun pointed at me. I stood in front of the tank, raised my hands in prayer, and shouted, "Baruch hashem Adonai (Blessed be the name of the Lord)," the only Hebrew I could think of. The tank with its big gun stopped within inches of me. I then knelt in prayer in front of the tank. I felt alone, weak, helpless. I could only cry out to God. I vaguely remember the tank backing up and going around me to continue its destruction.

I hope I was guided by God's Spirit as I responded to the horror around me. I acted without fear. I was sure that that tank would not run over an American. I was right, but six weeks later, on March 16, 2003, an Israeli military bulldozer killed Rachel Corrie, an American college student working with ISM in Gaza, by running over and crushing her, and then backing up and crushing her again. She was standing in front of a Palestinian doctor's house the Israeli military had come to demolish. I had met Rachel a few months earlier when I taught a two-day non-violence training for ISM in which she participated. I may again stand in front of a tank or bulldozer, but I will probably have more fear the next time. I also thought of the man in Tianaman Square who was not as fortunate as I was.

Note: We never know what the consequences of our actions will be. I could not have known that when Peggy was kidnapped four years later in Iraq, she told her kidnappers about our work in Palestine/Israel and showed them a picture of me standing in front of that tank. Her kidnappers were quite impressed, and Peggy believes this was one factor in her being released by the kidnappers. To see the picture, do an Internet search of Art Gish and tank.

✳

Today, here in Jinba, it did not seem to be the time for standing in front of tanks.

I was upset by the destruction caused by those tanks. These simple shepherds, however, were calm and confident. Their faith is so much deeper than mine. They know who holds the future. Theirs is a strength I can hardly comprehend. I wonder how many Americans could endure what the Palestinians have endured and still have a strong faith. African-Americans who endured slavery and years of oppression have displayed this same strength.

The tank practice continued for an hour, after which there was a lot of practice shooting from the soldiers. Then in the afternoon, the tanks continued their games in the wheat field as Israeli jets thundered overhead.

Musa said the Israelis are taking fifteen hundred acres for the Wall from Jinba and Mirkez. They showed me the projected line of the Wall that will snake around to take most of the farmland, including the best fields, from these two villages, but not the villages. The line of the projected Wall has been marked on the rocks, but no bulldozing has started yet. As I stood in Jinba I could look down in the valley and see the road, which is the Green Line, about a mile south of the village. The Wall is expected to come about halfway between the village and the Green Line, just down the mountain from the village, and then go over to right beside the village of Mirkez.

The Israelis want the land, but they do not want to include the Palestinians in the enlarged Israel they are creating with the Wall. The Palestinians are to be separated, encircled, and left in a small area without land, without resources. Israel is the only country in the world that is allowed to keep expanding its borders. Another purpose of the Wall, in addition to stealing the land, is to remove the people by making life so difficult they will leave. So the Wall is also about ethnic cleansing.

✳

I thought back to January 20, 2004, when our Hebron

team watched Israeli bulldozers destroying a strip of Palestinian agricultural land around the Harsina settlement, just east of Hebron. The bulldozers flattened everything. The sight was horrendous. It was difficult to see all the uprooted olive trees and grape vines, the demolished terrace walls. The soldiers destroyed four wells. The Israeli military then brought in truck load after truck load of rock to cover the rich soil and build a road, alongside which they were installing posts to build a fence to separate the Palestinian owners from their land and to expand the Harsina settlement. The Israelis confiscated 250 acres of rich farmland there that week. Distraught farmers asked us how they would now feed their families, which they had supported by farming that prime agricultural land.

We were invited into one of the farmers' homes for tea and spinach cakes. They treated us to a tray of tiny heads of cauliflower. We learned that several days earlier, Israeli soldiers informed the family that if they wanted to harvest anything from their land they needed to do it immediately, because in the future they would not be allowed to return to their land. They harvested lots of the little cauliflower heads, heads that could have grown to twenty pounds. The cauliflower was sweet, tender, and delicious, but it left a bad taste in my mouth. The Palestinians will get no more cauliflower from that land. And I had eaten the last of it.

✳

One of the shepherds here told me that on March 26, 2002, an Israeli saw him grazing his sheep south of Jinba and called the military. Israeli soldiers came and slaughtered his 250 sheep. He then bought two hundred sheep from money raised by other Palestinians in the area. These people survive not only by their faith but also by their cooperation and mutual support.

This afternoon I helped feed the sheep and held a big ram that needed ointment on its feet. The ram really warmed up to me as I scratched its head.

This evening Omar and I visited a family on the other side of Jinba. The two wives were there and seemed to have a warm relationship. The children were very shy, but I started to throw my hat to them and they threw it back to me. They really enjoyed that. The men had lots of questions to ask me. They wanted to know my opinions about Saddam Hussein, Iraq, Bush, and Islam.

We had no electricity this evening because they are out of fuel for the generator and cannot afford to buy more. They would have plenty of money if it were not for all the thievery and destruction by the Israelis. Musa said the Israeli military did not spray herbicides on his crops from an airplane this year as in past years. This year they used a tractor to spray the fields and kill the crops. This year they sprayed about 750 acres in the area. That means a huge economic loss.

During the night I heard tanks and a lot of shooting from the military camp below us.

December 22, 2005, Thursday

Miriam and Omar did a lot of talking and laughing during the night. It brought back memories from last year of Miriam and Hawaida talking all night. I got up early and helped Miriam feed the sheep. I left at about half past seven. Miriam and Omar invited me to come back and told me their cave is my home. They sent some taboon bread and feta cheese with me.

I decided to walk in the field where yesterday we watched the tanks playing. I noticed many new tank tracks on the path I had used yesterday morning. I walked a way south over the 250-acre field, surveyed the path for the Wall, and looked back north to see the caves of Jinba. I thought of all the houses and trees that the Israeli military has destroyed here in the past, and now, the immanent confiscation of this big field and surrounding fields. I looked at the tank tracks and the torn up land and stood there and wept. How can people be so depraved, so callous, so racist? A whole host of feelings rushed through me,

generated by the many experiences of oppression I've witnessed
in this supposedly holy land.

It was an exhilarating hike through the mountains to get to
At-Tuwani. I greeted many people on the way and thought how
fortunate I am. I am free. I can go anywhere. I have no reason
to be afraid. Most people are so bound up in their fears that
they have very little freedom to do anything except within very
narrow, prescribed boundaries. I must ask, however, how much
of my freedom is spiritual, and how much it is a result of being
a white American male.

Since I was in no hurry, I thought it would be nice to visit the
village of Khallet al-Thaba, just south of Mufakara, since I had
never been there. The Israeli military had demolished a house
there back in May. When I got closer to the village, I waved
across the valley and shouted "Salaam alykum" at some people
there. They waved back and yelled, "Come and drink tea." That
was the invitation I wanted, so I walked over to the village and
was greeted by two young men. First I was offered a glass of
water, then a glass of orange juice, and finally tea.

We sat in a beautiful courtyard with stone walls and gardens. I asked about the demolished house and was told I was
sitting right in front of it. The Red Cross had given the family
a tent, under which they are building a beautiful stone house
out of the rubble of the old house. The walls are nearly completed. I could see the Ma'on settlement from where we sat and
heard the noise from construction work going on there. I wondered what the settlers were doing.

When I got to At-Tuwani I learned that Peggy had arrived in
Iraq. Since there were enough team members in At-Tuwani now,
I left to go back to Hebron for four days. I walked down the road
and saw where the military had again dug up the road and made
new mounds of dirt to block the road. But the Palestinians had
already made a new place for cars to go through and had opened
the two other mounds of dirt up the road. That felt good.

The road to Hebron was blocked at Route 60. There was a

mass of people and cars on both sides of the settler road. I had
no trouble walking across the road and immediately got in
another taxi, but it took a long time before we could leave. The
soldiers were allowing one car to leave for Hebron about every
five minutes. They were not searching cars. They just made us
wait. I was furious as I sat and looked out the window. There
stood the soldiers, pointing their guns at people and searching
their bags. I thought, "What terrorist would walk up to those
soldiers with a bomb unless he wanted to kill those soldiers?"

Abdel Hadi Hantash was at the apartment in Hebron when
I got there. He confirmed the figures I got in Jinba, but said that
it is actually twenty-five hundred acres in the greater Jinba area
that are being confiscated, and it was over a thousand acres in
the area that were sprayed with herbicide this year. The whole
issue of land confiscation for the Wall at Jinba is in the courts.
There was to be a hearing on January 9, but that has been
delayed. Abdel Hadi said that postponing a decision is in the
best interests of the Jinba people at this time.

December 23, 2005, Friday

Our team meeting this morning focused on dealing with
oppression. Since I was to lead worship, I decided to focus on
the need for love. I read 1 Corinthians 13 and added two verses
that I composed. I claimed I had discovered them in the archives
in At-Tuwani.

> "You may stand for social justice. You may risk your
> life for peace, but
> if your hearts are not filled with love, you are nothing.
> You may take a
> stand against oppression and be on the right side of
> every issue,
> but if your hearts are not filled with love, you are doing
> more harm than good."

The meeting went well. Sarah led the meeting and had us
focus on three questions. What forms of oppression have you

worked on most, which issues do you feel most insecure discussing, and in what areas do you hope to grow? It felt safe and there was a lot of honest sharing. Racism, sexism, and classism were the primary issues raised.

This afternoon I visited a family in Tel Rumeida. On the way back I decided to walk down Shuhada Street. Walking down that empty street brought back a lot of memories from years past. The street was once the main street through Hebron, each day filled with Palestinians. Now every shop is closed, and only Jews are allowed on that street. The street has been purified.

I turned into the Old City at Gate 5 but was told by soldiers that the gate was closed. The military had just installed a turnstile at Gate 5. A soldier told me I had to go back the way I came. I asked why I had to do that. "Because the gate is closed," he said. That led to a conversation with a soldier from Cleveland, Ohio. I asked him if he thought what he was doing will make peace. He said that unless someone dominates and controls other people, there will be chaos.

I told him that when I was a teenager many years ago, men advised me that when I got married it was essential that I dominate and control my wife, otherwise I would have continual chaos in my marriage. I never accepted that advice. My marriage relationship is based on freedom and trust. We have not experienced chaos. If I were to try to dominate and control my wife there would be chaos, just like when Israeli soldiers try to dominate Palestinians and when American soldiers try to dominate Iraqis. People do not like being dominated. Occupation does not work very well.

This reminded me of another conversation with an Israeli soldier who said to me, "Look, there are a lot of very evil people in the world, and we must kill them. Our job as soldiers is to rid the world of evil. We can and we will." "How naïve," I thought. Evil cannot be crushed or destroyed by guns. The only way to overcome evil is with good. Darkness can be overcome only with light. The ultimate answer to evil is nonviolent, suffering love, the cross. Evil cannot be crushed, but violent situations can be transformed. The real question is what can we do to help make transformation possible?

Soon six of the soldiers, including the one from Cleveland, went into the Old City through Gate 5. I waited a bit and then followed them, ignoring the soldier who told me to stop. I could hear the soldiers ahead of me yelling at Palestinians as they went through the market. I followed them all the way to our street where two Palestinian youth were warming themselves by a fire in front of their chicken shop. Although unprovoked, the soldiers began yelling and became really nasty to the youth. They kicked over the metal can in which the youth had built a fire. I told the soldiers to treat people with respect. I asked them if this will bring peace. They said yes and ordered me to leave. I stayed. Within a few minutes, they left.

December 24, 2005, Saturday

Most of us went to school patrol this morning through Gate 5. After we got through the new turnstile, soldiers saw us and told us to stop and go back the way we came. We just stood there and acted ignorant. I told the soldiers that we have been going through Gate 5 every day and asked them why we couldn't go out to the street. A soldier said, "It is closed." "No, it is not closed, it is open," I replied. He then motioned that we could proceed out to the street.

Harriet Taylor and I stayed there on the street and kept a watch on Gate 5. We later realized that the teachers could not come through Gate 5, and had to go back into the Old City and come out through the Mosque Gate. The teachers were angry about this indignity.

We decided to go back into the Old City through Gate 5 after school patrol. This seemed important to us, because it appeared to us that the soldiers were in the process of closing another entrance and exit to the Old City, thus further tightening the knot around the Old City. We noticed that the soldiers were preventing two female schoolteachers from coming out of the gate. Before we could intervene, the teachers went back into the Old City. We asked the soldiers why the teachers could not go to school. "This gate is closed and they can go another way." We said the gate was obviously not closed and that teachers have always come out that gate.

The soldiers then told us we could not go back into the Old City through Gate 5. We said we could, that the gate was open. Before we could continue this conversation, a group of six soldiers arrived, headed by someone of much higher rank. He walked up to us and in perfect English asked if there was a problem. "Yes, there is a problem," I said. "These soldiers have prevented teachers from going to school and now are preventing us from returning home." The officer didn't say much, except to say that we could go through Gate 5 and that tomorrow the teachers can go through Gate 5. Our persistence seemed to pay off.

The other Hebron CPTers went to Bethlehem for Christmas Eve services. I decided to spend the night with a family in Halhoul, just north of Hebron. This family took in Peggy for three days back in 2002 because she could not get to Hebron due to shooting across the bridge into Hebron. Abdel Hai told me that recently he was going home when Israeli soldiers stopped him about a quarter mile from home and told him he could not go home, that he needed to go back to Hebron. He just stood there for a half hour before the soldiers let him go home.

December 25, 2005, Sunday

A joyous Christmas. I went to the East Jerusalem Baptist Church and was deeply moved by the singing and Scripture readings that brought me back to my Christian roots. I do believe in the incarnation and the importance of the revelation in Jesus. We had a special time of prayer for CPT and all captives in Iraq, including the eighteen thousand prisoners the Americans are holding. I deeply appreciated that.

December 26, 2005, Monday

Sarah and I came back to At-Tuwani. The road was still blocked at Route 60, so we had to walk across the bypass road to get another taxi to Yatta. Team members were still out on school patrol when Sarah and I got to At-Tuwani this morning. No one went up to Khoruba because it was very foggy, and they could not have seen the children. The soldiers were late. At 9:05, the team called Omar in Tuba. He said the children saw soldiers, but they left without the children. With Omar's permission, two team members decided to walk up the road past the Ma'on settlement where Chris and Kim were beaten, and walk with the children themselves. They called Hagit and the military to inform them that they were walking with the children.

They walked up the hill and met the children. Settlers saw them on the way back. Soon Gdalia, the settler security man from South Africa whom we met so often last year, came and threatened the children in Hebrew (We have it on tape) and told team members that if they walked with the children again, there would be no more military escorts for the children. At ten o'clock, soldiers came and reminded the team that internationals may not escort children past the settlement.

A lot of things happened while I was gone. Team members accompanied the reopening of the road to Karmil to protect a Palestinian bulldozer that was brought to reopen the road. There were continual problems with soldiers not allowing Palestinians to cross the settler road and making them stand in the cold rain. Military harassment of the people here has definitely increased during the past two weeks.

At half past ten last Wednesday night, team members heard loud music down on the road. They went to investigate and learned that settlers were having a party on the road for the soldiers who had set up a flying checkpoint there. Team members watched and got into a conversation with some of the soldiers. In the course of the conversation and answering questions about our work here, they told the soldiers about the beatings our team has experienced here. Team members taped this conversation and later learned from a Hebrew speaker who listened to the tape that one of the soldiers said in Hebrew to his commander, "I hope the next time the settlers kill the CPTers."

Yesterday, on Christmas Day, settlers had a 9K run on the settler road to remember the settler who was killed recently. The military closed the road and brought a bulldozer to close more entrances to the road, including the road that comes up into At-Tuwani. The military had not bulldozed this road for over a year. As soon as the race was over, the soldiers reopened the road to At-Tuwani and said they had made a mistake in closing the road to At-Tuwani. Did they make a mistake? Why would they use a bulldozer to close a road for an hour or two? There are easier ways to temporarily close a road. All I know is that road now is a muddy mess.

Sarah and I walked to Mufakara this afternoon. A shepherd invited us to his cave. At first all the women and children were very shy, but gradually they came closer to us and by the time we ate, we were all sitting around the fire in the cave. We ate a soup made with yogurt, lentils, and noodles. I got to hold a little girl, help a boy with his English homework, and laugh a lot with everyone. This shepherd lost a lot of sheep last spring when settlers scattered pellets of rat poison in grazing areas.

December 27, 2005, Tuesday

The two Doves walked to Tuba this morning for school patrol. Sarah and I met the eight children. One little girl was late and left behind, so the Doves decided to walk with her past the settlement. They called the police, who now do the accompanying on Tuesdays and Wednesdays, and informed them that they were walking with the one girl. They also called us to tell us and told us to inform the police in the jeep that they were coming.

I tried to talk with the police when they came, but the driver was very hostile. He would not listen. He kept repeating that he is not the children's mother, that he is not responsible for the children getting here, and that he only drives. I said I understood that. He finally did hear that the Doves were walking with the girl but seemed to pay no attention. I also informed him that because the children were having exams today, the children would be getting out at half past ten.

Sarah and I left at quarter past ten to go up to Khoruba to wait for the children. The police didn't show up until after noon. We were concerned when we saw the children were running toward home, while two men were in that area.

We were all invited to a village home for supper. Two other families were also there. What a wonderful time we had. Not only was the machlube delicious, but the whole time of sharing was so peaceful. We all sat around on mats on the floor (they have no furniture) and ate out of a common platter. There was little serious talk, just a lot of joking, laughing, playing with the little children, and telling stories. It was a cold evening, but we kept warm by huddling around a tray of hot coals and covering ourselves with blankets we shared with the people sitting next to us. We were warm and cozy. How different from sitting in a centrally heated room, separated from each other by tables and stuffed chairs.

December 28, 2005, Wednesday

Rich and I left early enough to meet the children in Tuba before they left home. I suggested to Rich that we take a short cut to get there, instead of the hour-and-a-half walk on the long path. There has been some feeling on the team that since this way is not very far from the Ma'on outpost and we are more visible, it is somewhat risky. It seemed to me if we do this early in the morning, and not do it regularly, the risk is small. Rich felt good about us trying this way.

What a joy to meet the children in Tuba and then walk with them toward the Ma'on settlement where a police jeep was waiting for them. I learned that the children were running just for fun yesterday afternoon, and that the two men we saw were Bedouins, not people the children feared.

We walked up to the construction site south of the Ma'on settlement. It didn't feel safe to me to go farther. We saw people there who looked like settlers. Omar, who walked with us, didn't feel safe to go that far. We watched two jackhammers breaking up rocks at the construction site we have been observing from a distance for the past weeks. Rich took some pictures. "How horrible," I thought, "tearing up and building on Palestinian land, on stolen land." This construction is a clear violation of international law, the Oslo agreement, and the more recent Road Map, in addition to the Israeli law forbidding construction in agricultural areas.

We started to walk back toward Tuba when a man I assumed to be a settler walked toward us and called for us to stop. My mind went into crisis mode. I told Rich I would feel much safer walking toward the man and in no way expressing fear or playing the victim role. He agreed. I walked toward the man and greeted him in Hebrew. Rich stayed back, ready to use the video camera if I got beat up. The man was a construction worker, and friendly. He spoke broken English. He said that he watches the children and us every day and feels sorry for what the children have to endure. He said he wants us to stop and drink tea with him. I asked him what they were doing. He said they were building another huge chicken house, in addition to the three big chicken houses the settlers already have. I wished him a happy Hanukkah.

We walked back to Omar. With disgust in his voice, he told us that the man was not Jewish but an Israeli Arab. That surprised me, although the man in one of the bulldozers looked as if he were wearing a kafieh. I did ask the man if he spoke another language other than Hebrew, and he said no.

We were invited to Omar's cave for breakfast. He has lost much of his good farmland to the settlers. Life is doubly hard for him since settlers closed the road to At-Tuwani. He can walk the long path, or take a rugged mountain road east to the Bedouin area, and then go back west on the settler road if that is allowed. Then there always is the question of whether the road to Karmil and Yatta will be open or closed.

When it was time to leave, Rich and I had to decide how we would get back home. I had planned to come back the long path because I considered it too dangerous to be seen by settlers near the settlement. Rich wanted to either come back the way we went or walk the short path past the Ma'on settlement, the way the children now walk. We have learned that the short path is no longer considered by the military to be a closed military zone, although we are still not permitted to accompany the children on this road. The only issue was our safety. We may be allowed to walk on that road, but settlers may also attack us if we walk on what they consider their turf. Rich believed that we should be pushing back these boundaries. I agreed but felt we needed to consult with villagers to do this. We decided to come back the way we went to Tuba.

After we got out of sight of the settlements, we stopped and decided to wait there until the children went home from school since they would be getting out at 10:00 this morning. We sat on some rocks and continued our conversation. Before long we saw a maybe twenty-five-year-old settler with a guitar on his back approaching us from the valley below. He was almost past us before he saw us. He immediately got out his cell phone, obviously calling other settlers, and walked toward us. I walked toward him and greeted him in Hebrew. He was cautious, neither friendly nor hostile.

He asked us what we were doing there and then told us to leave the area. I said we were waiting for the children returning to Tuba. He said, "You are allowed to watch from the next hill where you usually watch, but not from here." He then passed his cell phone to me, saying someone wanted to talk with me. I took the phone and greeted the man in Hebrew.

I think it was Gdalia. He asked me what I was doing there. I repeated that we were waiting to watch for the children. He repeated that we can only wait on the next hill and that we need to leave immediately, otherwise he would call the police.

It felt to me that this was not the right time for a confrontation, so I sort of agreed to leave. I wished him a happy Hanukkah. Rich had some uneasiness about us leaving. He felt that since we were on Palestinian land, it was important that we not back down and not accept orders from settlers. The young settler kept telling us to leave, or other settlers would come. Rich and I continued our conversation with the settler. The settler again handed his phone to me. The man on the phone asked me why we had not left and warned me again that we had to leave. I said OK and again wished him a happy Hanukkah.

We continued the conversation with the young settler. I suggested that I would like to be invited into the settlement and have a conversation with him and his friends. He evaded that question and said that we support the Arabs who every day attack and kill Jews. I told him I was sorry about the death of Dov and Nati. He said Dov was his friend and pointed to where Dov's house had been demolished by the Israeli military. Rich told him we have a lot of concern about demolition of houses and asked him who demolished Dov's house. After Rich asked several times, he reluctantly said the Israeli government demolished Dov's house.

He continued telling us to leave. I asked him several more times if I could visit him in the settlement. He said he could not invite us because we are friends with the Arabs and that our presence with the Arabs gives them more strength and courage to fight the Jews. "Before you came," he said, "there were no problems here." We then decided to go and wished him a happy Hanukkah.

I was elated. This was my first conversation with a Ma'on settler. I felt we met in some small way on a human level. It didn't end in a negative way. Rich had some concerns about the conversation. Is it right to remain silent when a settler gives us such a warped picture of reality? Should we have reminded him of how settlers are attacking children? Should we have challenged his claim of ownership of that land? I felt that the first step with him needed to be just listening to him. He already knew something of our views. Rich and I had an exciting discussion of the creative possibilities that lie before us, about where and when to push, when to back off, and when to take risks.

Rich suggested we walk back to Tuba and meet the children there. That felt really unsafe to me. I felt there was a good chance we could be attacked by a gang of settlers. Rich was sensitive to my fears. I also had some uneasiness about us acting without consulting other team members or the Palestinians. We ended up agreeing to head back to At-Tuwani rather than wait on Khoruba hill where the settler suggested we go.

January 2, 2006, Monday

Sarah and I went on school patrol this morning in Hebron. The soldiers at the cabin checkpoint seemed really grumpy. We recognized each other from previous encounters. When I informed the soldiers that some children were waiting to get through the metal detectors in the cabin, one of them cursed me in English. Some of the girls were waiting to be allowed to go around the metal detectors. I then saw one of the soldiers spitting at the schoolgirls. That was too much for me.

I was incensed at this racist disrespect for those beautiful schoolgirls. I kept my strong feelings under control, and tried to act respectfully toward the soldier, but I confronted him quite directly. I said, "Let's treat everyone with respect. Spitting at those girls is not respectful." Then I upped the ante a bit and asked him, "Didn't your mother teach you how to act respectfully?" He screamed at me. "Shut up your… Get out of here." Another soldier ordered me to leave the area. I replied, "Let's be respectful. We want shalom." I refused to leave.

On the way back to our apartment, Sarah and I talked

about the confrontation. How could I have responded better? Should I have been less confrontational? Maybe I should have just asked probing questions like, "Why did you spit at the girls? Why are you angry at these schoolgirls?" I do not know how to reach the hearts of these soldiers who live in so much fear, who seldom have positive relationships with the Palestinians here. Maybe they need to be jolted and assertively confronted with the inappropriateness of their conduct.

Maybe they need a more subtle confrontation. I really want to be loving and peaceful, to not make things worse. I also do not want to seek tranquility in the face of oppression. My gut tells me it is better to err on the side of confronting the soldiers too assertively than to passively accept their oppressive, racist behavior. An Israeli friend told us that Israeli society is a very brash, confrontational society, and assertive confrontation feels normal for Israelis.

As we approached Gate Five, one of the soldiers yelled something to us. When I turned toward him, he yelled, "Go home. Get out of here." He seemed very angry, and closed to any conversation, so we headed toward the gate. The soldiers have put big pieces of sheet metal near the gate to let them know when someone is approaching, because it makes a lot of noise to walk over the metal. Sarah acted out some of her feelings by stomping on the metal as we walked over it, making extra noise. The soldier came charging toward us with a big rock. By the time he approached the turnstile, we were fifty feet beyond the gate. He threw the rock into the fence beside the turnstile.

I did a lot of thinking about the meaning of these checkpoints as I stood there this morning. They feel like international borders between Israel and the Palestinian areas. People passing through these checkpoints are leaving one country and entering another. Soon Palestinians may need a visa to enter the area of Hebron controlled by Israelis. The control the soldiers are exercising here has nothing to do with security. These checkpoints are setting a precedent. They are preliminary border crossings.

Although this all looks rather ridiculous to us, it does follow a logic in the Israeli process of taking more and more, and cutting the West Bank into separate enclaves. The plan is that no one will be able to go from one area to another without going through Israeli checkpoints, in other words, without the permission of the Israelis.

January 3, 2006, Tuesday

This afternoon Lorin and I went to a Palestine People's Party election campaign rally at the Temporary International Presence in Hebron (TIPH) park in the Old City. There were several hundred people there. Several candidates spoke. I met some of the leaders who expressed support for our four captives in Iraq. Suddenly, near the end of the rally, six Israeli soldiers entered the park with their M-16s half drawn. They looked very tense and afraid. We sprang into action. Lorin and I moved toward the soldiers and stood between them and the Palestinians. Three of the soldiers ventured partway into the crowd. They never said anything.

I wanted to let them know that Americans were watching them, so I asked them in English if there was a problem. I got no answer. Lorin moved away and began taking pictures. It felt pretty scary because I didn't know what would happen. Were the soldiers going to disrupt the rally? Would anyone throw stones at the soldiers? Would the soldiers start shooting? Why had they come? Within a few minutes the soldiers left.

January 4, 2006, Wednesday

John and I had a momentous morning on school patrol. When we got to the checkpoint with the metal detectors, we encountered the same soldiers that I confronted two days ago. They were in a surly mood. We decided to stand a little farther away and not be as confrontational. Soon some of the soldiers started chanting, "Kill CPT, kill CPT." I thought, "This should be interesting." I was glad that they were expressing their anger so directly. They talked rudely to a Palestinian man who walked past us.

But then, after venting their anger, they wanted to talk. They were still being rude, but almost in a friendly way. They acted like they were curious and wanted to know more about us. I told them a bit about our work here and in Iraq, and that my wife was in Iraq. We talked about the possibilities for peace and nonviolence. The one who had spit at the girls two days ago joined the conversation. The conversation felt like a breakthrough.

Then on the way back, the six soldiers at Gate 5 wanted to talk to us. These were the same soldiers who invaded the park yesterday and the same soldiers who had raided our apartment last week. There was a mixture of skepticism and curiosity in their attitude. We learned that today was the last day for these soldiers to be in Hebron. I am so thankful that I got to interact with them again today, and in a better way. I have done a lot of thinking the past two days about how confrontational we should be. I now have less doubt that being so assertive in the past few days was what was needed. It ended with both reconciliation and a serious time of sharing together.

As we talked, a settler drove up, cursed us, and yelled at the soldiers not to talk with us. Within a few minutes another settler drove up, greeted me, and invited me to visit him in Kiryat Arba. I have known this settler for ten years and have had many conversations with him. John said the soldiers were quite amazed that the settler and I were relating as old friends, which we are.

January 5, 2006, Thursday

We went to a birthday party for Hani and Rima abu Heikel's one-year-old girl. We tried to walk to their house, but when we passed the Tel Rumaida settlement, a settler stopped us and talked to a soldier who then decided not to allow us to go to Hani's house. I felt bad for the soldier who believed he had to do what the settler told him to do. He seemed embarrassed that he couldn't let us go to a birthday party. I told him this is not shalom. We then walked around Palestinian homes below the settlement and went to Hani's house from the other side.

I remember Hani and his family from my first trip here in 1995. He has been a close friend of the team and has suffered greatly from the settlers. Hani told a lot of stories about troubles their family has had from settlers, even though their family saved the lives of Hebron Jews in 1929. Hani saved the life of a settler child a few years ago and got only hostility in return. Soldiers would not allow Hani and Rima to go to the hospital the evening their baby was born, so they had to walk in the dark the back way over rocks and rough terrain, with Hani carrying Rima part of the way. The baby was born ten minutes after they got to the hospital. Hani's father had a stroke, and the soldiers made him wait three hours before he was allowed to go to the hospital. He didn't survive the stroke.

When we left, Hani accompanied us as we walked the long way back over a hill and rough terrain in the dark to get to the street in front of his house. We decided to take a shortcut from there and walk on Shuhada Street past the Beit Hadassah settlement. Our logic was that we should do what we can to keep that street open to us. Why can't we go the most direct route? Also, the U.S. government put millions of dollars into that street after the Israeli government promised the street would be open.

As soon as we got to Beit Hadassah, we saw more than a dozen settler boys, ages maybe eight to twelve. I immediately felt a lot of fear. I knew how aggressive those boys can be. When they saw us they started cursing. A soldier tried to calm them down, but did nothing more. It wasn't long before they were pelting us with stones. Adult settlers watched. The boys kept throwing stones for the whole two blocks until we went out the gate at the Beit Romano checkpoint. I yelled, "Stop it, stop it," very loudly to attract the attention of other soldiers, but apparently the soldiers had taken no notice. None of us were hurt. I

did find it amusing that some of the stones ended up hitting settler cars.

January 6, 2006, Friday

We left at eight o'clock this morning for a joint team meeting in At-Tuwani. As we walked down the road toward At-
Tuwani, we noticed military vehicles on the road and a group
of maybe fifty people, including team members, standing in a
field across the road from At-Tuwani. I wondered what this
was all about, and then to my horror, as we rounded the bend
in the road, we saw that a large grove of a hundred olive trees
had been cut down during the night. The big branches were
laying on the ground: a horrible, disgusting sight.

This is nothing new. More than two thousand Palestinian
olive trees were cut down in 2005 alone. This is a major economic loss for the people here. My mind immediately went to
the settlers, but then I remembered that the Israeli military has
destroyed a million Palestinian trees during the Occupation.
The soldiers said they had not had any patrols on the road last
night. Whoever did this, it was a dastardly act, a terrorist act
against the people here. It was also an act against God. Both

Grove of demolished olive trees.

the Jewish scriptures and the Qur'an forbid the destruction of trees during warfare.

We all stood there, like at a funeral wake, mourning the loss of those thirty-year-old trees. I walked over to the trees and cried. There were a few Israeli soldiers there, but they kept a low profile. Police came a little after half past ten. The At-Tuwani team was busy making phone calls to media, peace and human rights groups, and governmental organizations. People from the UN and news media came.

Then an unfortunate thing happened. Some Palestinians got into an argument over money and land, and in the end there was a fight between maybe six people. What impressed me was not only the small amount of violence, but also the skillful way most of the other villagers intervened by separating the antagonists, nonviolently restraining people, and trying to reason with those involved. Two Israeli police also intervened in a helpful way by separating a few people. The anger Palestinians feel sometimes gets directed toward other Palestinians.

As we left to come back to Hebron, we noticed that a military backhoe was re-closing the road to Karmil. A group of soldiers were guarding the backhoe. I was angry. After these people had their trees destroyed, now they also have their road closed again. What arrogance on the part of the Israeli military.

January 9, 2006, Monday

It was a joy to come back to At-Tuwani again today after three days in Hebron. I stopped and talked with some of the men at the store. I looked down in the valley across the road and saw the olive grove with every tree cut. How disgusting. I asked some of the men about the loss. They said at this stage, each tree was producing about twenty-five dollars worth of olives a year. That means a $2,500 loss for the next number of years before the trees grow back. Olive trees grow very slowly. I read in the news yesterday that Shaul Mofaz, the head of the

Israeli military, said that there have been two thousand trees cut recently, and that he will investigate and compensate the farmers who lost trees. That sounds good, but I do not believe the farmers will get one shekel.

I was invited up to Nasser and Kiefah's house this afternoon. Nasser was helping scoop out zucchinis in preparation for stuffing them. I made a big deal of complimenting him for doing what is supposed to be women's work. But I wonder, what right do I have to try to influence the culture here? My complimenting and supporting Nasser for doing what I, a Westerner, think is right, was a brazen attempt to change male/female roles in At-Tuwani. What right do I have to do that? On the other hand, Kiefah appreciated this support.

January 10, 2006, Tuesday

Today is Eid al Adha, the Muslim feast commemorating Abraham's willingness to sacrifice his son. I went with others to the mosque in Karmil for the Eid prayer. I came back on a tractor but was not sure even the tractor could make it up over the big hump of earth that blocked the entrance to the Israeli road. We did make it. But then I saw what must have been a miracle. A villager tried to get up over that hump with his car. He got stuck so some of us helped push, and he got up over that steep hump. I still do not think that was possible.

Christy told me that she and Kim watched the Israeli bulldozer close the road again last Friday as I left. Within only a few minutes, a Palestinian tractor came and reopened that entrance to the Israeli road. Christy said that apparently most soldiers do nothing more than follow the orders they have been given. The soldiers who were accompanying the bulldozer were there only to accompany that bulldozer. As soon as the Palestinian tractor reopened the road, a Palestinian truck drove out into the Israeli road. Other soldiers saw the truck go on the road and did nothing. The game goes on.

At quarter past twelve we were told there were soldiers

down on the road. They were gone by the time we got there, but a man said the soldiers had taken his identity card and car keys. He was supposed to wait there four hours before getting them back, as punishment for having tried to drive out on the settler road. He told us he was going back to Yatta and would not wait for the soldiers. Apparently he had other keys because he drove off in his truck. Many vehicles went across the road today. It seems like the strategy now for the Israeli military is to harass just a few people each day.

This evening our team was invited to eat with the extended Adara family. We had a lot of fun joking and laughing. Since our Dove team members are Italian, we were comparing the Arabic words for a lot of things with the Italian words for those things. There were lots of similar words. We did a lot of laughing which was healing for me. When we left I said, "It has been a happy Eid. *Insh'allah* it will also be a blessed Eid."

January 11, 2006, Wednesday

I went down to the road at seven o'clock this morning to monitor the movement of people across the road. We plan to spend four days counting people, vehicles, modes of transportation of Palestinians crossing the settler road, and the number of vehicles using the Israeli road. Today is the first day. We also want to do it on Friday, and on a regular work and school day.

This is a first step in beginning a campaign to stop the Israeli military from building a fence or wall along the other side of the settler road, all the way from the Green Line to north of the Karmel settlement, about twenty miles. This is an extremely serious threat to the future of the people here. First, this would be different from fences and walls that separate people from their land. This fence would cut the people here off from almost everything, isolating them into a small island. They would be cut off from schools, hospitals, doctors, work, extended family and friends, land, shops, government and social services, pretty much everything.

A quick review of how Israel developed closures may be helpful. Before the Oslo Agreement, there were no checkpoints or closures. Palestinians were free to travel in Israel. With the Oslo agreement came implementation of a program of apartheid, the gradual separation of Palestinians and Israelis. After the Oslo Agreements, military checkpoints were set up, and the movement of Palestinians began to be restricted. First, Palestinian men needed permits to be in Israel. Next, permits were needed to take Palestinian cars into Israel, and then Palestinian women also needed permits to enter Israel. Finally, all Palestinian cars from the West Bank and Gaza were banned from Israel. Any travel of people into Israel from the occupied territories gradually became more difficult.

Israeli military law was then imposed on the Palestinians, under which Palestinians have few rights. Following this, movement of Palestinians within the West Bank itself became restricted and continues to become more restricted as we now see every day here in At-Tuwani. It is important that we see events in At-Tuwani as a small part of a bigger picture. Essentially, military checkpoints became de facto international borders where one needs a permit (visa?) to cross. Under Israeli law, Palestinians have no legal rights to go through checkpoints.

All this is a gross violation of international law. International human rights law requires that occupied people be able to move freely, as in Article 13 of the Universal Declaration of Human Rights, and in Article 12 of the International Covenant on Civil and Political Rights, and in the International Covenant on Economic, Social and Cultural Rights. Israel is entitled to restrict movement in order to keep order, but general and prolonged restrictions that produce grave harm to the occupied people are illegal. The fact that these restrictions apply to only Palestinians and not Jewish residents makes these actions doubly illegal. Instead of rectifying the problem, every year Israel makes travel more difficult than the year before.

Building a fence or wall along this road is part of the goal of the Israeli government to cut up the West Bank into small segments: some people say fifteen separate areas, divided by walls, fences, settlement blocks, and roads, leaving possibly as little as 28 percent of the West Bank for the Palestinians. Eight major Palestinian population centers would be cut off by roads and gates that Israelis can close at any time. The Hebron District would be divided into two parts. The Palestinian people in each of these areas would be fenced in and walled in, making each area effectively a prison. The gates in the Old City in Hebron are examples of this.

Jeff Halper points out that in prisons, prisoners control 90 percent of the prison space. That does not mean the prisoners are free. They do not control the walls, the gates, etc. Slowly but surely, the infrastructure is being built to separate and imprison the Palestinian people, while stealing their land. The issue here is not sharing the land. The land here has always been shared. The issue is that the Israelis want exclusive use of the land and have a clear strategy for removing the Palestinians and taking all the land.

We want to have concrete data to show how important it is for Palestinians in the South Hebron Hills to cross Highway 317 at At-Tuwani. This information will both be given to lawyers who are fighting this fence and be used in a public campaign to stop the Israeli military from building the fence.

It was a good day for me, greeting people as they were passing by and sharing a bit of the holiday spirit. But it was also sad to watch the cars and tractors coming over the huge hump of dirt where the old Palestinian road crosses the new settler road, thinking how difficult the Israeli military has made life for the people here. Some of the cars didn't make it over the hump. Some people parked their cars and walked over the hump and walked to At-Tuwani to visit family. But these hardships are nothing compared to the problems they will face if that fence or wall is built.

This evening we tabulated the results of our survey. I was

somewhat surprised at how many people crossed that road today. It is a very important crossing, too important to be closed. We counted 316 people traveling across the road today from 7:00 until 5:00. There were 157 people going from At-Tuwani and surrounding areas toward Yatta (66 walking and 20 cars), and 159 people coming from the Yatta side of the road toward At-Tuwani (51 walking and 28 cars). There were also people traveling by donkeys and tractors. We counted 580 vehicles on the settler road.

I have some uneasiness that this data could be used as an argument for a gate in the fence here. We must be clear that there be no fence separating people, period. If there was a gate, the Israelis could argue that it would be opened during the hours of peak traffic. Not only would this be horribly oppressive, but the gate could be locked any days the Israelis felt like it. If the Israelis will go to all the effort to sometimes almost daily re-close the roads with a bulldozer, it would be so much easier to just keep the gates locked for days or even weeks at a time. In no way should the Israeli military be given that kind of control over the people here, a severe violation of international law and basic human rights.

We spent much of our team meeting this evening talking about our roles in the upcoming grazing season. The grazing season has not yet started because of the lack of rain and grass. There seems to be general agreement among the shepherds that we will be pushing boundaries again this year. We talked about technical things like keeping phones and cameras charged and being careful with cameras, for they can be used both to reduce violence and aggravate a situation. We talked about when to leave an area rather than take the chance of getting beat up by settlers and when to face the settlers. We want to stay together in tense situations, although at times one person might stay at a distance to film the incident. We take our cues from the Palestinians. It is important that we build trust among ourselves and with the shepherds. We also need to deal with our fears.

January 12, 2006, Thursday

Three of us went to Tuba this morning because we heard there were problems there yesterday. We had a breakfast of bread, yogurt, and scrambled eggs with Omar's family and learned that settlers came Tuesday night with a tractor and plowed up one of Ibrahim's lentil fields. After a delightful time of talking and joking together with the family in their cave, we went out to see the field below where the settlers are building a new chicken house.

The whole three-quarter-acre field was plowed up, tearing up all the tender young lentil plants. My heart ached to see yet another scene of vicious destruction. How much more will these people have to endure? Omar said he fears this is just the beginning. Just below this field, Ibrahim has other fields planted with barley. Will the settlers also destroy these fields? The strategy is not difficult to understand. First the settlers destroy the crops, then the military orders the farmers to not use their land, and then the settlers take the land.

Omar and his brother Ibrahim have already lost fertile land to the Ma'on settlers. While standing in the middle of the plowed-up crop, Omar, with pain in his voice, explained, "The money and support from America keeps coming to the settlers, and the Palestinians keep being pushed further into the dirt." Amazingly, he said this without any bitterness in his voice. He told us, "Our faith is in God."

Omar told us that last Friday when he was on his donkey going to Friday prayers, a settler, whom he can identify, approached him as he passed the cow barn at the Karmel settlement, knocked him off his donkey, pointed a gun at his stomach, and threatened to kill him if he ever sees Omar there again. What can Omar do? He could go to the Israeli police station and file a complaint, but that will not do much good, and he could end up getting harassed or even arrested, as has happened to so many Palestinians here in the past. The Israeli government wants the people here to be quiet and submissive, to accept their status of powerlessness with docility. The people here are not accepting that status. They choose when and how to resist, instead of just reacting.

I feel a lot of responsibility to do something about this most recent destruction, and will see that these stories get out to our worldwide networks. We will also contact Palestinian and Israeli human rights groups, the UN representatives here, and the U.S. consulate to inform them of yet more human rights abuses. I will also pray that some good can come out of this suffering, that we will be given vision and strength to do what needs to be done.

January 13, 2006, Friday

I walked to Karmil for Friday prayer and got a ride back in a car. As we were about to cross the settler road into At-Tuwani, soldiers in a Hummer stopped and two of them, with guns drawn, walked toward us and the ten or so other Palestinians on foot. It was 12:50. I immediately walked toward the soldiers and asked them if there is a problem. I did this both to let them know an American was present and to divert their attention from the Palestinians. A soldier responded, "Yes, there is a problem. These people are not allowed to cross the road." "Why are they not allowed to cross the road and go home?" I asked. "There is another road to the north that they can use." The soldiers were referring to the checkpoint at Zif, probably ten miles to the northeast. That would make the few mile trip to Yatta a very long trip. Also, that road at Zif is closed and has been closed for a long time.

The soldiers told me there is no road here. I pointed out to them that this road has been here a long time and that the Israeli road is the new road. "No," they said, "this is not a road." I guess the Israeli military can construct or deconstruct reality as they please. The two soldiers were snotty and condescending. I could sense their distain for the Palestinians as they sought to further humiliate and oppress them. I asked, "Why can't they go to Karmil and Yatta to buy food and go to Friday prayers?"

Earth mounds blocking access to the settler road.

"Because it is forbidden." I pointed to the big mounds of dirt blocking the road. "Is this shalom? Do you think this will bring peace?" They responded by referring to suicide bombings. I said, "Oh, I understand. So you will also be blocking the road to the Ma'on settlement because of the nearby olive grove that was cut down a week ago?"

They asked me what I was doing here. I said, "I live here." They seemed shocked. "What are you doing here?" they asked. "I am here to document human rights abuses by the military and the violence of the settlers." I quickly made a phone call to Diana to inform her of what was happening. Soon she and Sarah arrived with cameras. We made phone calls to our Israeli support network.

The soldiers demanded the identity cards of all the Palestinians and took the driver's car keys. I insisted that they take my passport too. I didn't want any special privilege, although I well knew I cannot get rid of my privilege. When they gave back my passport, I thought they were giving back everyone's ID but then realized that they were leaving with the Palestinians' IDs and car keys. The soldiers said they would return in about four hours.

Diana started arguing with the soldiers, and asking them why they are taking the IDs. "Because we want to and because we can," was the response. Diana told them that they are cutting these people off from their sources of commerce, hospitals, family, religious services, etc. The soldier said, "I don't care." Diana informed him that what they were doing was illegal. Again the soldier said, "I don't care."

We had encountered this group of soldiers before. Last Saturday, Christy asked this soldier, "Are you not the soldier we filmed pushing little school girls in Hebron?" The soldier said,

"Yes, I am. Sometimes we have to hit little girls." This group of soldiers is particularly nasty and has been causing a lot of problems in the area.

At around two o'clock all the Palestinians decided to leave. The driver got another set of car keys and drove his car home. Apparently it is becoming common practice now for the soldiers to simply confiscate IDs and car keys. We were told that they probably will be able to get their IDs back at a military office in Hebron. The villagers opened a new and better entrance to the settler road while we waited, making good use of a shovel and rolling away big rocks.

After everyone had gone, Diana, Sarah, and I decided to walk to Karmil to visit a family where soldiers spent two nights this week in their new house. We saw where the soldiers broke off a key in an outside metal door and damaged the lock. Inside, we examined two bedroom doors and a bathroom door that were badly damaged, along with the doorframes. It looked like someone had broken into these rooms. Things were scattered in the rooms, indicating there had been a search of the rooms. We drank tea with the family and gave them a military phone number where Palestinians can make complaints about soldier abuse. We also took pictures and videotape of the damage.

January 14, 2006, Saturday

This morning about thirty Israelis associated with Ta'ayush came to work in the olive grove that was destroyed last Thursday night. Including Palestinians, there were about a hundred people all working together. We drug out all the branches to be used as firewood and loaded them on a big wagon. The Israelis brought two chain saws and were busy cutting off all the broken limbs so that the trees would have a clean cut to heal. I asked to borrow a chain saw so I could prune one of the trees. We gathered the cut limbs in a big pile. We also gathered stones and put them on a wall around the olive grove.

I had mixed feelings as I worked. It was so pathetic that we had to clean up after the despicable act, but my heart also was filled with joy as Jews, Muslims, and Christians worked together, demonstrating that peace and reconciliation are possible. What a beautiful demonstration of peace this was. I was deeply moved by the willingness of these Israelis to come and work with the people who are supposed to be their enemies, people they are told to fear, and the willingness of these Palestinian Muslims to accept these Jews, especially since it was Jews who had destroyed their trees.

This was not only a moving act of solidarity on the part of the Israelis, but also an act of repentance for what their people, their culture have become. These Israelis are resisting the degradation of their culture and religion. They are building bridges instead of walls. They are creating possibilities of peace for the future, sowing seeds of compassion, mutuality, and community. It is inspiring to work with people who have integrity and enough spiritual maturity to recognize the sins of their own community, who are able to identify with the victims of their own nation's actions, who can love those who are called their enemies.

As a striking contrast, Israeli soldiers drove up in a Hummer and began to harass some of the Palestinians. The soldiers, with their semi-automatic rifles at the ready, seemed so out of place. There in that field this morning were two very different choices for the future: one of peace and cooperation, and one of domination and control. I know which future I choose.

Then began the second part of today's action. Shortly after eleven o'clock, the Ta'ayush group went over to At-Tuwani where we gathered and prepared to walk to Tuba to meet Omar and Ibrahim in order to see the destroyed lentil field, and for an opportunity for the Israelis to offer their condolences for the destructive actions of their fellow Jews. We walked around the hill where the settler outpost is located in the trees, on the road where last year the school children made their daily walk to and from school. Soldiers in a Hummer followed us, just like they follow the children everyday. I had never been on that road before. I could see a few settler shacks in the trees. When we saw two settlers in the trees, I wondered if there would be trouble. Settler children yelled curses at us.

It was a moving time as Ibrahim and Omar stood in the lentil field and shared their pain and suffering with this group of Israelis. Omar also told the story of the settler threatening to kill him last week. The Israelis expressed their sorrow for what fellow Jews were doing to Palestinians. There in the middle of that destroyed lentil field, there were no enemies. We were all part of a common humanity.

As we headed back toward At-Tuwani, I could see about fifteen or twenty young settlers on the road near the Ma'on settlement. I was worried. The soldiers accompanying us seemed worried too. Another group of soldiers arrived in a jeep. We approached the settlers and walked right by them. I was nervous. The settlers were disciplined and quiet, but I could feel their hatred for us. One middle-aged settler walked with us, talking with a mixture of friendliness and cynicism. He mocked us as he talked about peace and love in a degrading way. Gdalia, the South African settler security person, acted very hostile while taking pictures of us. The settlers followed us as we walked the short path to At-Tuwani, the path now used by the Tuba school children and past where Chris and Kim were beaten on September 29, 2004. I had also not walked this way before today. So I got to walk the whole way around the wooded hill between At-Tuwani and Ma'on where the Havot Ma'on illegal outpost is located. Now I have a better picture of this area, particularly what the children see each day.

We got to the hill above At-Tuwani without incident, but the settlers followed us. I thought we were going back to the village, but then the Israelis turned back toward the settlers, resulting in a standoff between the Israeli peace activists and the settlers. About twenty villagers joined us. There was a bit of shouting back and forth, but everyone was under control. Soldiers were both with the settlers and between us. It was clear that the soldiers were most concerned about what the settlers might do.

I thought about how dangerous these settlers are for the future of Israel. What does it mean to raise up a generation of children and youth who are taught to hate, whose hearts are filled with so much fear? What will they be doing twenty years from now? I fear for them. I fear for the future of Israel. These settler youths think of themselves as victims, an unhealthy and uncreative way to approach life. How are they victims? What is the root of settler children chanting, "Kill the Arabs," and calling for revenge?

After an hour, we all left, but I am worried about what the settlers might do tonight. I heard they made a threat to cut more olive trees tonight.

January 15, 2006, Sunday

I got a ride with some of the activists to the Beqa'a yesterday and ended up spending the night with the Jabers. As we were approaching Dura on the way to At-Tuwani this morning, we got caught in a traffic jam with lots of people on the road ahead. I, at first, thought it was a political rally but then noticed that the Palestinians were carrying clubs and walking toward Hebron. I began to get worried. When we stopped, men with clubs opened the side door of our van and looked us over. I said "Salaam alykum" but got no response. We soon learned that they were looking for someone from Hebron. Men with clubs opened the side door of our van several more times. Each time our driver argued with them. After about ten minutes, we were past the mob.

This is troubling. I sensed the same spirit I have seen in the settlers. Is there a difference between settlers or Palestinians carrying clubs? I would guess that if they kill the person they were looking for, they will pray to God, feeling just and righteous in having enforced God's justice and revenge, just like settlers praying before or after they enact their vengeance on Palestinians.

There is a false spirituality that justifies me and my sin, that creates god in my image, a god who is my errand boy, a god I can control. That is the opposite of humble confession and seeking to hear the voice of the One who is greater than we are.

This is not unique to the Middle East. Americans also enact vengeance. Usually Americans do it in more formal ways by using American power structures to enact their vengeance. George Bush initially had wide support for his massive acts of vengeance in God's name after the September 11 attacks, with the support of many so-called Christians.

These Palestinians feel powerless. Today, I would guess, these men saw a small opening where they could exercise a bit of power and make a difference. Here was a small opportunity for them to act out a bit of the anger that has been building up in them for years. This anger was misdirected, as is most of the anger in the world.

Salman and Hathra came back this morning from their pilgrimage to Mecca. The next days will be filled with celebrations. I went over to their house and greeted Salman this afternoon. I watched the villagers kill three sheep for the next days of feasting. I thought of biblical images of killing the fatted calf for special occasions. This evening we all went over to their house for feasting and visiting.

I asked villagers how they felt about the action yesterday. One had mixed feelings. He said it was good, but then the Israelis left and the local people must deal with the consequences. One was more positive, saying that the settlers must be confronted and shown that we are not afraid. Another said the action made it on Israeli news, and he was grateful for that attention on the problems here but was concerned that the Israeli activists had consulted with Omar, but not with people in At-Tuwani before their action.

I learned that a Ta'ayush member negotiated during the standoff yesterday with the soldiers in the Hummer who then gave back the car keys and IDs taken from villagers on Friday.

Apparently the soldiers had kept them in their Hummer for twenty-four hours.

January 22, 2006, Sunday

I came back today after a few days in Hebron. I sat in the back of a van on the way back to Yatta with women and children. Beside me was an eight-year-old boy who thought I was Jewish and was extremely afraid of me. All my attempts to break through his fear failed. I don't want people to be afraid of Jews. I don't want people to be afraid of anyone.

The taxi driver on the way back from Yatta was very concerned about the possibility of encountering soldiers along the road. He kept phoning people and also stopping to check with people in oncoming cars as to whether there were soldiers on the road ahead. What a way to live, always living in fear of what the soldiers might do. I was delighted to notice that the soldiers had not re-closed the roads. They are having lots of flying checkpoints on the roads. Apparently the soldiers are looking for someone. There were eight soldiers hiding behind rocks across the road this morning while two soldiers checked IDs on the road.

This afternoon Limor Yehuda, an Israeli human rights lawyer with the Association for Civil Rights in Israel (ACRI) was in At-Tuwani to inform people about the status of the court case to stop the wall along the road here. Up to now, we were told that it was to be a fence. Now the military says that they want to build a twenty-mile-long wall from the Karmel settlement to the Green Line. The wall supposedly would be thirty-two inches high, only high enough to stop vehicles and animals, not pedestrians. There would be seven gates that, of course, would be controlled by the Israeli military. How much the gates would be open is anyone's guess. And the wall could be made higher at any time. Limor wants us to write a report on the effects this wall would have on the people in the South Hebron Hills, which Limor will use in her appeal to the Israeli High

Court. We asked Matt to write the report, since he was the author of an important 2004 CPT report documenting seventy-two cases of detainee abuse in Iraq.

At quarter past four this afternoon we saw eight Israeli soldiers walking up the hill toward the village. It looked threatening. We didn't know what to expect. We decided that I should hide in case they were coming to remove us internationals. Soon I was called and told the soldiers were only checking IDs and not the IDs of team members. They went all around the village checking IDs, and did a few brief house searches. Two team members followed them around the village and filmed everything they were doing. They told the soldiers that they could not go into certain houses because there were only women present in those houses at the time. The soldiers did not go into those houses. When they came to our house, I greeted them in Hebrew. They were friendly. They said they also want peace. I said we don't get peace with guns. They said there were guns in the village. We are puzzled. They didn't do a careful search, either of houses or people. Anyone they might have been looking for could have easily eluded them. By quarter past five they were gone.

Team members briefed me on things that happened while I was in Hebron. Rabbis for Human Rights came last Friday, January 20, and planted olive trees up the hill to the south and also west of the village. The villagers then provided a meal for them.

Three people from the U.S. consulate also came that day. They met with team members and village leaders to learn what has been happening in the area. People in the U.S. consulate have consistently shown interest in the problems we regularly report to them.

Then in the afternoon, soldiers blocked the road into At-Tuwani. Ten to fifteen villagers went down to the road to challenge the soldiers. Soldiers told one villager that if he went the whole way to Hebron, more than an hour's drive, and came back, then he could pass by on the road. The people from

Rabbis for Human Rights went down to the road and also challenged the soldiers, after which the soldiers allowed everyone to pass. However, the soldiers continued the checkpoint.

The next morning, January 21, soldiers again set up a checkpoint and would not allow people to come into the village. Again, villagers went down to the road to challenge the soldiers. Then fifteen Ta'ayush people came. After a short confrontation, the soldiers, led by "Mister Three Bars," declared the area a closed military zone for the next three days. Because he refused to give us his name, we gave him the nickname, "Mister Three Bars" because of the three bars on his uniform indicating he had the rank of captain. Mister Three Bars is a reservist and a lawyer, and recently came here for his yearly month of military duty. We learned that his name is Moshe.

Since the map outlining the boundary of the closed military zone that Mister Three Bars showed them did not include the Khoruba area, the Ta'ayush people left and went there to accompany villagers who wanted to do some plowing near the Havot Ma'on outpost. There were three tractors doing the plowing. Settlers came and talked to the soldiers, including Mister Three Bars, after which Mister Three Bars ordered the Palestinians to stop plowing their fields. The Palestinians complied with his orders. He then ordered everyone to leave the area.

Our team members argued with him, and at one point, Matt was close to being arrested because, although he showed his passport, he refused to hand it over to Mister Three Bars, who became very angry and then called the police. Matt then left the area. Villagers suggested that the other team members also leave the area because of fear that Mister Three Bars might want to remove all internationals from the village. After the soldiers left, team members came back into the village.

We have on tape Mister Three Bars telling the Israeli activists in Hebrew that the reason he was removing everyone from the area was because Gdalia told him to remove everyone. What an admission of settler control over the Israeli military!

January 23, 2006, Monday

We counted the number of people and vehicles going back and forth from here to Yatta again today. I went down at seven o'clock this morning. There were four soldiers across the road, so I decided to stay on this side to do my counting. The soldiers stopped all cars but not pedestrians or tractors. They allowed cars to go toward Yatta but no cars from Yatta toward At-Tuwani.

We had a strange experience this afternoon while counting. Soldiers would not allow a Palestinian to drive his car onto the settler road even though he had a special permit to drive on the road. He said he needed to pick up workers returning to Yatta. We volunteered that two of us would ride with him for his protection if he wanted that. Mister Three Bars was there and was being really nasty. We asked him why the man could not go on the road. "Because it is closed." "No, it isn't closed. Many people have been driving here as you can see." Mister Three Bars said that the man could drive back to Yatta, and then back east to Zif (maybe fifteen miles) and get on the Israeli road there. We told him the road is closed at Zif. He said it wasn't closed. We checked later, and we were right: that road is still closed.

After the soldiers left, we made a few phone calls. We learned that the Palestinian man who was not allowed on the road was actually a contractor who is hired to help build the Wall, and was going to transport Palestinians who were working on the Wall back to their homes in the Yatta area. Israelis treat like dirt even those who sell their souls to the Israelis. How ironic. But even more ironic, the Palestinian driver decided he would risk it, and since we promised we would help him, two of us went with him and brought back eight workers. So we helped people building the Wall evade Israeli restrictions on them. Fiction could never be this weird.

January 24, 2006, Tuesday

Two European election observers from Germany and

Slovenia stopped in to visit us. They are here for the election of a new Palestinian government tomorrow. Villagers want us to watch soldier activity down by the road and for some of us to be around the school where the voting will take place. Their main concern is disruption of the election by either settlers or soldiers. The school is the voting place for all of the villages south of here, and for many people living in Yatta whose roots are here. The list of voters here includes 360 names.

Two Palestinian policemen are spending the night in the village in preparation for the election. Team members were down by the road this afternoon when Israeli soldiers for a time would not allow these policemen to come into the village. The Palestinian police expressed a lot of fear about settlers attacking during the night. We joked with them about that.

January 25, 2006, Wednesday

The same four soldiers who have maintained a checkpoint down at the road for the past week or so were there at seven o'clock this morning when the polls opened. They had stopped a number of people from coming to the election. I immediately called the election observers, who I assume called the military. Before long, the soldiers let the people pass, but they continued to stop people and check their IDs. That looked like intimidation to me.

I had a long talk with one of the soldiers. He said they were there because a terrorist might come and disrupt the election. I readily agreed and suggested that the most likely place from which a terrorist might come to disrupt the election was the Ma'on settlement. I suggested that they might want to monitor the settlers. That caught him off guard.

These four soldiers seem to be kind people. They said they want peace. They are reservists and would rather be home with their wives and children. But they are afraid, and they accept the myth of Israeli innocence. They do not see what I see. Maybe I don't see what they see.

I went up to the school at half past eight after other team members came down to observe the soldiers. I had a great time at the school. The election served as an important social occasion, bringing together people from the whole area. At least a fourth of the voters were women. I met lots of people from Yatta and the outlying villages that I had not seen since last year. It all reminded me of the biblical story of Mary and Joseph going to their ancestral home in Bethlehem for the census during the Roman occupation. Israeli military jets thundered overhead, reminding us of who are the present occupiers.

There was lots of joking. Some of the joking was about me voting. In jest, I said I should be able to vote since I live in At-Tuwani and my adopted name is Jaber Adara. One villager gave me his identity card and told me to go vote. I kept telling the two policemen that I thought settlers were coming. I was impressed with how much respect the two policemen received. And they had no guns.

I went back down to the road at half past three. The same group of soldiers was there. Now they were hardly stopping anyone. Campaign workers drove back and forth, taking voters to and from Yatta. I wondered what the soldiers were thinking as a car with a Hamas flag went back and forth past them. The soldiers left at quarter of five so I went back to the school. For some time I sat outside around the fire with Jinba people. I felt right at home with them. It was a cold, windy day, and the fire felt good.

We wondered what the effects of our presence today might have been. Did we make a difference? We don't know. I am not sure my presence at the school made much difference, but it was very important in building and maintaining relationships with people in the area. It increased the visibility of our team. It seemed the people appreciated that we felt it important for us to be there with them. Would the soldiers have acted differently if we had not been there with them? Did the soldiers allow the people to pass this morning because of our presence? Would the soldiers have made more ID checks if we had not been there?

I do believe the perceptions of the voters going through the checkpoint would have been different if we had not been there. Seeing us watching the soldiers must have given them some reassurance. We are not sure what effect the presence of the soldiers had on voters. We saw a few vans turn around and not attempt to go through the checkpoint. Were they voters who decided not to vote? People who could be wanted by the soldiers would not have passed there.

January 26, 2006, Thursday

We learned that Hamas won the election by a big margin. What a blow to Fatah and U.S. interests. It is ironic that one of the effects of U.S. policy is to promote Islamist movements around the world. I was told that many nonreligious Palestinians voted for Hamas as a protest against Fatah corruption. The vote in the At-Tuwani area was around 130 for Hamas and a hundred for Fatah. How will the United States and Israel respond to this voice of the Palestinian people? Will this vote be respected?

January 28, 2006, Saturday

I could hardly wait to meet the children this morning, the first day of school after three weeks of vacation. But the soldiers didn't come. We waited and waited. Soldiers in a Hummer came by at half past seven, but they said they knew nothing about school children. They made some calls and left. Matt and Sarah, who were watching up at Khoruba, called and said they had repeatedly called the military and were told the soldiers were on their way. We finally decided that we would just accompany the children ourselves. At 8:50, a Dove and I started walking up toward the Ma'on settlement. It felt scary, but it also felt like it was the right thing to do. We had Omar's permission to walk with the children. I called the military to inform them that we were walking toward the children. I learned that the soldiers were there with the children as we spoke, so we stopped. At nine o'clock, the fifteen children came walking toward us, singing and acting happy to go back to school, even though they had stood in the cold wind for an hour and a half.

When I talked with the soldiers, they acted like they knew nothing of what was expected of them. Apparently they were a new group of soldiers, but it still seemed impossible to me that they would be so uninformed of their responsibilities. Various people had repeatedly informed the military that school began again today. Surely their superiors should know what is expected of them. Then they asked us if we knew the combination to the lock on the gate on the settler road. That sounded weird. I asked them how they got through the gate this morning. They said the children knew the combination. The soldiers were a half hour late this afternoon. I again reminded them of the times they are to be there, and they said they knew.

I am impressed with how inept the Israeli military is. How could they ever fight and win a war? They are unable to even remember to escort the children. I have no doubt of the ability of the Israeli military to destroy and kill, but their ability to coordinate and do their jobs seems somewhat limited.

Two settler youths were over on the next hill by the Ma'on settlement this afternoon and began to yell at us as we waited with the children. At first the settlers asked us to come over to them. They then yelled obscenities at us. There was also Hebrew that we did not understand. We decided to ignore them.

I left at three o'clock to come to Hebron where I will have a few days off. I learned that the kidnappers released a video of our four CPTers in Iraq to Al Jazeera. So we know they are still alive. That is encouraging.

January 29, 2006, Sunday

I met this morning with my settler friend from Kiryat Arba who I have known for eleven years. He expects the Israeli government to evacuate many of the settlements in the Hebron area, including Kiryat Arba and the Hebron settlements. He expects that to be brutal and asked if CPT would be willing to protect the settlers from abuse from the police and military. "What a Christian witness that would be," he said, "for CPT to protect Jewish settlers." I found his suggestions quite intriguing.

I shared the idea with the team. Everyone was pretty skeptical. They did wrestle with the idea of protecting settlers. We are about protecting people. We want to protect life and oppose all brutality. Two serious concerns were raised. The settlers didn't invite us, and they are not committed to nonviolence. This led to a team meeting to discuss how we relate to groups that use violence. It is a complex issue because repeatedly we are thrust with groups that are not committed to nonviolence. We neither want to compromise our commitment to nonviolence nor cut ourselves off from the struggle. We do want to make it clear that we do not engage in violent actions.

I spent some time in the Beqa'a visiting friends and learned that one evening, about two weeks ago, soldiers shot out the windows of my friend's car, which was parked across the settler road from his house. The family watched it happen. The problems they are having now come from soldiers, not settlers.

February 1, 2006, Wednesday

I left Hebron at noon to return to At-Tuwani. I was glad to see the roads were still open. Everything has been quiet. Soldiers have not been setting up checkpoints on the roads, and the Palestinians are still able to get through the roads they reopened.

Four shepherds went to court in Be'er Sheva this past Monday to testify about the incident last February 16, when a settler attacked Johannes and others. This hearing was not a trial but was held for the purpose of taking testimony from witnesses. Four settlers and their lawyer were present. The settlers insulted the shepherds and tried to prevent them from entering the courtroom. Hagit, our Israeli friend from Machsom Watch, got the attention of a court security guard who told the settlers, "This is not Havot Ma'on. This is a court of law." A settler got angry and threatened to throw Hagit out the window. Hagit replied, "I will throw you in jail."

February 3, 2006, Friday

We were planning to join Rabbis for Human Rights in planting olive trees today at Maghair al-Abeed, a small village just south of Tuba. Some of the children we accompany each day come from this village. In addition to the Israeli activists who gathered in At-Tuwani, including Arik Asherman, there were three young German conscientious objectors, three CPTers, and maybe fifteen Palestinians. About twenty-eight Israeli soldiers and police arrived. I was amazed at the amount of energy and effort the Israeli military was putting into stopping this planting of olive trees. Nothing, it seems, threatens the Israeli authorities the way peace threatens them.

Jonathan, one of the Israeli activists and a former Israeli Air Force pilot who is now a peace activist, said, "The soldiers are not worried about us. They know we have no guns. They are concerned about the settlers who will get angry if the military allows us to plant those olive trees. They take their orders from the settlers." Gdalia was present and was clearly exercising influence with his repeated conversations with the soldiers and police.

I thought of Romans 13, where Paul says that the governing authorities have been ordered by God to protect the innocent and punish the guilty. Sometimes authorities rebel against these orders and punish the innocent and protect the criminals. That is what I saw happening this morning: Israeli military rebellion against God's order.

There was a big discussion between police, military people, Israeli activists, and Hussein Daoud Shadi Salaami Mahamri, the owner of the land where we had planned to plant the olive trees. We learned that a settler had shot at Shadi yesterday while Shadi was on his land.

Amir Mullah from the DCO was the spokesman for the

military. The Palestinians do not trust Amir, a Druze, whose people live at the bottom of Israeli society, and are often seen as doing the Israelis' dirty work for them in hope of getting a few crumbs from the Israelis. Being a Druze, Amir speaks fluent Arabic. Amir took Shadi in his military jeep to survey the land where we were to plant the olive trees, and to check once again if the land really belonged to Shadi. They came back after a half hour. There were more intense conversations. We could see both police and Amir repeatedly talking on their phones. We then learned that the whole area was declared a closed military zone "because the issue of who owned the land had to be settled before any olive trees could be planted," something rather absurd. Shadi has the papers for his land and has repeatedly shown these papers to authorities.

At ten o'clock, Mister Three Bars told us we had five minutes to leave the area, even though we were still in the village. Everyone ignored him at first, but by half past ten the soldiers had pushed all of us a short way down the hill in the village. They detained one German who didn't leave fast enough, put him in a military jeep, and dropped him off down by the road below the village. This was a big show of military force with Gdalia standing in the middle with his gun, looking pleased. None of us felt this was the time to resist. We mainly observed. The Israelis and Palestinians did not need our help. We did film the whole event.

This was a sad day. Again, the Israeli military prevented Israelis and Palestinians from coming together. Why would they not encourage steps toward peace instead of blocking those steps? The answer, of course, is obvious. If the Israelis want peace, their actions make no sense. But if their real purpose is to take more and more land and gradually push out the Palestinians, then their actions do make sense. The goal of the Israeli military here is not peace but to remove the people and take all the land. How sad. We could have had a wonderful day of fellowship, working, talking, and eating together. But all is not lost. This tragedy also was a significant event, for it was a graphic picture of the reality of the Israeli occupation.

About three weeks ago the Israeli High Court ruled that the Israeli military, DCO, and police were interfering with the rights of Palestinians to access their land. The court ruled that the military, DCO, and police must protect Palestinians on their land, especially when the Palestinians try to coordinate with the DCO and the military. By law, the military is charged with protecting all the people under its control, including the Palestinians. The court will reconvene around February 19 to evaluate the progress, and, if military behavior has not improved, the court will mandate actions for the military and DCO to take to improve the situation.

The Palestinians here have decided to concentrate, with our help, on documenting abuses for this court case. They will inform the DCO when and where they are going out on their land. They will only inform, not negotiate. Therefore, what happened today is an excellent example for the Palestinians to use in their court case. The rabbis did inform the military, and the military abused their power. This should help the Palestinians. I wrote up a summary of what happened today to give to the lawyers to be used in this court case.

I approached one of the soldiers who has been nasty in the past, greeted him in Hebrew, and told him what is happening here is not shalom, that olive trees are a symbol of peace and not a threat to anyone who wants peace. He responded by saying, "I know, I know, but there is nothing I can do. I am in uniform and have to take orders. It is a complex situation, a deep personal dilemma for me." I told him, "Maybe you can do something to change things. I am old and you are young. My generation failed. I hope your generation does better." He said, "I hope so too, but I can do nothing while I am in uniform," and walked away.

The soldier saying that it is a deep personal dilemma for him touched me. Questioning him or confronting him further seemed out of place. But it is not true that he has to follow orders. That is his choice and his responsibility. Yes, it might be costly for him to refuse to cooperate, but maybe in the long run it will be more costly for Israel and the future of Judaism if he doesn't do what he knows is right. He also could ask himself if he would lose more than what the Israelis are taking from the people here, what the cost is for the people here. He does have a choice. He can refuse.

Jonathan, the former Israeli Air Force pilot, said, "It doesn't sound good for Israeli soldiers to say they are only following orders. That is what Eichman said." I thought it was ironic that there were three German conscientious objectors, who have refused military duty, standing there listening to an Israeli say he had to follow orders.

I told Jonathan the story of a recent encounter I had with an Israeli soldier in Hebron. The soldier asked me, "Do you know Santa Claus?" Apparently my bushy beard reminds Israeli soldiers of Santa Claus because they often refer to me as Santa. "Yes, Santa is my brother," I told him. I asked him if Santa brings him good things. "No, Santa doesn't bring me anything because I am a soldier and I do bad things. Soldiers do bad things." "Yes, I know," I said and tried to show some warmth to him. He greeted me in Arabic and left. Jonathan said, "He will have to live for a long time with what he has done." Victims can forgive, but what can these soldiers do to heal from the horrible things they have done?

How can we reach these soldiers? I heard a story of how an Israeli soldier became a refusenik. He was part of a group of soldiers who stormed into a Palestinian home to occupy it. The soldiers herded all the family into one room. In accordance with Palestinian hospitality, the family made tea and offered it to the soldiers. That act of kindness was too much for this young soldier. Something in him cracked, and he decided to refuse military duty.

February 4, 2006, Saturday

The soldiers didn't show up this morning so two team members walked with the school children past Ma'on. I walked part way up the road to meet them in case there were problems from settlers. It felt scary, but there were no problems. We have a clear impression that the military is trying to back out of their commitment. They said this morning that they didn't know there was school on Saturday. How many times are we to believe them when they tell us they didn't know? The children got to school an hour late.

The soldiers were late again this afternoon so we called them. When, they finally came, I saw Mister Three Bars in the jeep. I greeted him really friendly with "Shabbat shalom" even though he has been so nasty. I believe each new encounter offers the possibility for something new to break into a relationship. I believe in always giving people another chance, in trying to appeal to what is best in people. He was very friendly and greeted the children in Arabic. Soon they were on their way.

Team members who were watching from the other side of the mountain at Khoruba noticed that the children ran really fast toward Tuba. They also saw the soldiers running. We then got a phone call from Omar, saying settlers had attacked the children. Ezra was in At-Tuwani, so he decided to go to Tuba to investigate and took the two Doves with him. After they got to Tuba, Israeli police came. Ezra had called them. The police took statements from the children, something unheard of here. The police took the children seriously and did not demand that they go to the Kiryat Arba police station to make the complaint.

We learned that around six masked settlers had hidden behind rocks and ambushed the children after they left the protection of the soldiers. The settlers used slingshots to hurl stones at the children. No one was hurt. The soldiers tried to intervene, but the settlers got away. I thought of Mister Three Bars and wondered what he was thinking. I also thought of the irony of these Orthodox Jews attacking people on Shabbat, something forbidden in Jewish law, not to mention the cowardice of attacking little children.

We wondered if this attack was in reaction to our walking with the children this morning. We can't know the answer, but we concluded that the question is not important. The settlers were attacking the children before we internationals ever came here. They attack the children when no one else is present, and they attack the children even when soldiers are present. We must continue our task of accompanying, monitoring, and reporting to the world what is happening here. The attack could also have been a response to the Israeli military evacuating the Amona settlement outpost in the northern West Bank on Wednesday, which was quite violent. The settlers are feeling angry at the Israeli government and military. They feel betrayed by their government, which they say has totally surrendered to the Palestinians.

We checked again with Omar and Zahreia about whether we should walk with the children if the soldiers do not come. They made it clear that we should walk with the children if soldiers don't come, that it is important to them that the children get to school.

So why would Israelis attack Palestinian children? I remember a confrontation with an Israeli soldier during school patrol in Hebron. The soldier said to me, "It is better if the children do not go to school since the children are trained in the schools to be terrorists." Not only is this not true, but also it masks the real training Palestinian children receive every day to hate Israelis: namely their daily negative experiences of oppression from Israelis.

There is actually some twisted, rational basis for Israelis fearing Palestinian children. These children are growing up and will also want to live here and have children. These children are a real obstacle to the Israeli goal of taking everything. One Israeli soldier said to me, "If you were an Israeli, you would want all of these children dead. Keeping children from going to school is one way to make peace."

February 5, 2006, Sunday

There were sixteen children this morning. The soldiers were

on time, and two walked with the children. It has been a while
since we last saw soldiers walking with the children. What a joy
it was to see all those happy faces on the children eagerly running to get to school. The horror of yesterday didn't seem to
dampen their spirits at all. It seems like God is protecting them.
We talked a bit about yesterday, but they didn't seem to need to
dwell on it.

I greeted the two soldiers who were walking and then walked
over to the jeep and greeted Mister Three Bars in Hebrew. In jest,
I told him it was important that he walk too because he needed
the exercise. We did a bit of light-hearted chatting, and then I
asked him what happened yesterday. He asked me how I had
heard about it. "The father of some of the children called us," I
replied. I then again asked him what happened. He said, "Some
settlers were hiding behind rocks, waiting for the children. The
soldiers tried to catch them, but they got away. The authorities
will be watching for them and try to catch them today because
we know who they are." I am grateful for this human exchange
between us.

Four soldiers who had a checkpoint down by the road this
morning were allowing passage of foot traffic and cars going
toward Yatta but no cars coming toward At-Tuwani. Even the
woman who works at the school was not allowed to drive to the
school. Because of a leg injury, she could not walk that distance,
maybe a mile, so she went back home and lost a day of work. The
soldiers said the road was closed, that Palestinians could go the
extra ten miles around by Zif, which is and has been closed.

This afternoon, soldiers in a Hummer drove to where we
were waiting with the children. They waited until other soldiers
came to accompany the children. Gdalia came, talked, and joked
with the children, and even had a conversation with one of our
Doves. He asked her what happened yesterday, that he had heard
rumors of problems. He wanted to know what the children told
us about the incident. He said he also heard that someone tried
to attack the children yesterday. Did he really not know? This is

interesting. Gdalia is never friendly with us. We conjectured that he might be concerned about the bad publicity for the Ma'on settlement resulting from yet another settler attack on school children and was trying to patch things up. Ezra told us yesterday that the Israeli government is planning to evacuate all the settlements in this area. We do not know if this is true, but certainly the settlers here must be worried.

Before the children started walking, the soldiers in the Hummer went on ahead, probably to look for settlers. Two soldiers walked with the children. The military is taking this seriously. When the children left the soldiers, they ran until they got to Omar who was waiting for them.

February 6, 2006, Monday

Two soldiers were walking with the children this morning and interacting very positively with them. I greeted Mister Three Bars, who was friendly. I asked the children why they were running yesterday afternoon. They said even though they had not seen any settlers, they were still afraid.

Sarah and I went with the children this afternoon. It was a beautiful, warm day, and the seventeen children were in a playful mood. Two soldiers walked with the children. I again talked with Mister Three Bars and again reminded him that he needed exercise. I even dared to tell him that if he had had more exercise he might have been able to catch those settlers two days ago. The driver of the jeep really laughed, and Mister Three Bars seemed to like the joke.

He then asked me how long I have been here before saying he found the place boring. I told him that I come only three months each winter since I am a farmer in America, and that I was here three months last year and again this year. He responded in a friendly way. "So you come here and cause a lot of trouble and then leave?" I replied, "I hope I don't cause a lot of trouble. I don't want to do that." He said, "Maybe you don't cause trouble, but some of your group does."

He spent some time talking to the children in Arabic, in what I thought was a warm, non-condescending way. In spite of his nastiness, Mister Three Bars revealed something good in his heart.

February 7, 2006, Tuesday

I talked to soldiers who had set up a flying checkpoint down on the road. One told me that they were expecting a terrorist act and were trying to find the people involved. He readily agreed that what they were doing was not very effective, that anyone with a bomb can simply go around their position. "But we have to do something," he said. That makes no sense at all. Doing the wrong thing is worse than doing nothing.

Recently I encountered some Israeli soldiers who had closed a street in Hebron's old city. They threatened children by pointing their M-16s at their heads. I told the soldiers to treat everyone with respect. In return, I got cursed with some of the most disgusting language I have heard for a long time. I told one of the soldiers he needed to have his mouth washed out with soap. He didn't like that. He said he would treat Arabs with respect only after they stop suicide bombings in Tel Aviv. He probably did not even know that there were no suicide bombings until after many years of continual humiliation and oppression resulting from the Occupation. The first suicide bombing in Israel was on April 16, 1993, twenty-six years after the beginning of the Occupation, and forty-five years after the creation of the state of Israel. How his actions will prevent suicide bombings is not self-evident. Political leaders use the violence of others as justification for their murderous policies. I think violence is another proof of the foolishness of their policies.

I got a ride at noon today with Nasser Nowajah to Susiya where I plan to spend the night. Nasser drives a group of children to the school in At-Tuwani every day and waits around until school is over. He has been a good friend and keeps asking me when I will come and spend a night in Susiya. I have felt bad about continually putting him off, so since I had a day off today, I decided to use it in this way.

Susiya is a village about five miles southwest of At-Tuwani, beside which the Israeli settlement of Susya has been built on Susiya land. I remember being in Susiya a year ago on Christmas Day, 2004. In the past, Susiya was an important Jewish and Byzantine town, the ruins of which are still here, including a Byzantine church building, a mosque, and a synagogue with impressive mosaic floors built in the second or third century. A network of old Roman roads is still visible. The ancient village of Susiya was located in the area of what is now an archaeological site. In 1985, the Israeli military removed thirty families, one thousand people, from the old village and demolished their houses and caves. The soldiers deposited the people at Zif, about ten miles away. Some of these families then moved to their land about half a mile east, where they now live in tents.

After removing the Palestinian families from the old village, the Israeli government declared the area a national park because of the important archaeological site there. In the early 1990s, settlers took over the site and now charge admission for anyone to enter the site. Palestinians, even those whose homes were there, are prohibited from entering the site. There is now a settler outpost on one side of the archaeological site and an army base on the other side.

Beginning in 1985, Israelis inflicted upon the people of Susiya a devastating period of destruction and oppression, destroying Palestinian houses, caves, cisterns, wells, fruit trees, and grapes. Every house and cave in the village was demolished. Everyone now lives in Bedouin style tents. Any building of houses is strictly prohibited by the Israeli military. The Israeli military burned all the people's tents in 1990, but they still refused to leave and continued living on their land.

The residents of Susiya have experienced repeated attacks from the settlers, including a settler killing one villager, and another time a settler beat a villager on the head, leaving him severely mentally disabled. When settlers attacked Susiya on August 6, 2005, two team members rushed there with Ezra and saw Palestinians trying to chase the settlers away. A settler shot at Nasser as he was filming them. Police and soldiers came and took statements. Some team members and Ta'ayush people then slept in the village for a few nights after the attacks and have continued to visit regularly. Operation Dove had a continual presence in the village last October during a time of repeated threats from settlers. Ta'ayush kept a presence in Susiya on Saturdays.

The first thing that struck me was the vast area covered by the settlement, which dominates the area in a much larger way than the Ma'on settlement dominates the area near At-Tuwani. The settlement itself is around twenty-five hundred acres, plus a vast area around it that is prohibited for local Palestinians to enter. Everything to the south and west of the Palestinian village has been taken by the settlement. The road from Jinba in the south used to pass through Susiya on the way to Yatta. The Israeli military demolished that road farther to the south. Part of that road is for Jews only, so the residents of Susiya and Jinba have to go many extra miles to go the short distance to Yatta.

It was a difficult time for me as Nasser and his neighbor, Yusef, took me on a tour of the village. I was filled with grief as I looked at the rubble of the demolished caves, houses, and wells. I have experienced the cozy warmth of so many caves in the South Hebron Hills and could easily picture intimate family gatherings and happy times in these caves. Now the collapsed roofs of the caves were piles of rubble, monuments to human depravity. It is amazing how Israeli soldiers leave the evidence of their cruelty and sadism behind for everyone to see.

While we were visiting one family, seven Israeli soldiers walked toward us. Three soldiers came to the tent, while four soldiers stayed up the hill with their M-16s at the ready. The soldiers were friendly, spoke Arabic, shook hands with everyone, but refused the tea that the family offered them. They explained they were searching the village. Their search was barely a search. What were they doing? Were they just familiarizing themselves with the village, or was this yet another not-so-subtle reminder of who has the power? I greeted the soldiers but stayed in the background. I was not asked to help. How ironic, I thought. Settlers threaten these people, yet they are the ones to have their homes searched.

My time was not all depressing. We ate and joked together. I helped Nasser with some jobs, distributed animal feed in the village with the tractor, visited every home in the village, and helped with milking and feeding the sheep. I got to bottle-feed one little lamb. That was fun. We developed an immediate friendship.

I was especially impressed with Imam and Wadah, two of Nasser's sisters. The family has a house in Yatta, but the two young women said they would much rather be in the village caring for the sheep. Their love for those sheep was obvious.

February 8, 2006, Wednesday

I slept well, got up, and helped with feeding and milking the sheep. That was wonderful, but I continued to feel the deep spiritual heaviness I felt the whole time I was in Susiya. The rubble of the family's demolished cave is right in front of the tent in which I slept. When I looked out last night from the tent across the valley, I saw the Susya settlement full of bright lights contrasted against the family's land across the valley which now is forbidden to them. How does one live with so many constant reminders of oppression?

I also thought of the settlers and their dreams. How exciting it must be to start a new life in the desert, to build new towns, develop new lifestyles, create community, feel like pioneers, live a simple, primitive lifestyle, struggle against many adversities, and do it with like minded people. That sounds exciting to me. How sad that their dreams are rooted in racism, hate, and fear, and built on the oppression of others.

After a breakfast of taboon bread, sheep milk, olive oil, and feta cheese, Nasser and I were on our way. We picked up twelve children in his little car. They were joyful and friendly, just like the Tuba children. We met no soldiers as we drove down the settler road. Soon we were in At-Tuwani, the children eager to get to school, and I ready to get back to work after a day off.

February 9, 2006, Thursday

There were only four children this morning because it was so cold and windy. Since school let out early, the children came to our house to wait for an hour and a half. It was fun to play and laugh together.

We all went to Juma's house this morning to tell him we discovered that some of the olive trees that Rabbis for Human Rights planted on his land on January 20 have been damaged and that his fields just below Khoruba were plowed up. Yesterday afternoon, while we were there, we saw no problems. It must have happened last night. Word soon spread, and quite a few people, men and women, gathered at Juma's house to drink tea and wait for the Israeli police to come. It felt somewhat like a funeral wake with everyone again reminded of the constant danger and threats they have to live with. What will they have to suffer tomorrow?

The police came and other team members went along up the hill to view the damage. Some olive trees were broken off, with about a dozen olive trees apparently stolen. About three acres of wheat and barley were plowed up. The police took pictures and then took Juma to the Kiryat Arba police station to make a statement and file a complaint, before, surprisingly, bringing him back.

Juma told us that the police took him seriously, although he doesn't expect anything to come of this from the police. Apparently the police are getting frustrated with the settlers due to the many settler attacks on police recently. Juma said that when Gdalia, the settler security man, arrived on the scene this morning, the police ordered him to leave the area immediately because he is not allowed to be on Palestinian land. He left. I can hardly believe this.

February 10, 2006, Friday

I went to Karmil for Friday prayers. It was fun walking back with a group of At-Tuwani men. After I got back, all of our team went to the hill over toward the Ma'on settlement because we were told there might be some problems there. Children were taking care of their sheep there, and had seen settlers and soldiers over by the settlement. Sarah and I stayed with the children as they made tea with a little fire from dried thistles they collected. It was a joy to watch as they happily worked so hard to boil the water for that tea, which we then all enjoyed together. There are so many positive things about the life they have: connected to nature, caring for sheep, feeling useful and happy. How many American children can say the same?

A neighbor boy came running to our house just before seven o'clock this evening and in an urgent tone of voice told us there were settlers near Juma's house. It sounded serious so we quickly headed toward Juma's house. We had just left our house when we heard rapid automatic weapon fire coming from the direction of Juma's house. I kept walking. Soon there were two or three more shots.

I thought, "Am I ready to die now?" I felt at peace. Within two minutes, there were four or five powerful shots coming from real close, just up the hill to my left. I felt some of what soldiers must feel when going into battle. I felt an adrenaline rush, excitement, and a feeling that I was invincible. I also felt fear. The whole time I was walking toward the gunfire, I knew that I didn't have to do this. I could turn back to the house. To act with courage involves a choice, a choice to run, to become violent, or a choice to face and accept our fears, and then act nonviolently. I was as afraid as anyone. I am not courageous. I am a weak coward. I accepted my weakness, asked God for strength, and went to face the violence.

A group of about twenty village men headed toward where the shooting had come from. I thought, how brave these people are to go out unarmed and face the guns, and how cowardly it is to hide behind guns. At first glance, it seems rather ridiculous for villagers to face those heavily armed Israelis with stones. I wish they had not picked up those stones, but the important thing that was happening was the villagers communicating that they would not be intimidated, that they would not play the victim role, that they were ready to die before letting the settlers drive them out. Gandhi said it is better to use violence than to act as a coward.

I started to follow the men, but Matt, who had just talked to the Israeli police on the phone, asked Sarah and me to go down to the road to meet the police and direct them to Juma's house. He said the police would be expecting to see us there. Matt and Diana also called the army, Israeli friends, and the U.S. consulate, who expressed deep concern and will make a protest to Israeli authorities because someone fired guns in a village where Americans were present.

By 7:24, Sarah and I were waiting down by the road. We didn't know how to respond to a car that stopped near us in the dark. Was it settlers looking to attack someone? Was it plainclothes police? Should I greet them in Hebrew or Arabic? I didn't want to make a mistake. I greeted them in Hebrew, but it turned out they were Palestinians looking for the road to Yatta, to which I directed them.

We waited a long time for the police. Diana called us to tell us that the police were claiming that Israeli soldiers did the shooting, that there was no problem, and that the police would not come. Diana and Matt kept insisting that the police must come. Soldiers stopped in a jeep at 7:50 and told us they were the ones who did the shooting and that there was no problem. They said they were patrolling the area above the village on foot when stone-throwing villagers attacked them. They shot in the air only to scare away the villagers. They repeated that there was no problem, and the police did not need to come.

In a few minutes three police arrived. I greeted them in Hebrew, and they said they spoke only Hebrew and Russian. My little bit of Russian was not helpful. It was clear they did not want to go into the village. I soon learned that the policewoman in the jeep did speak English and the driver spoke Arabic. I insisted that they go to Juma's house, which they did. Sarah and I had to walk back up the hill.

Matt, Juma, and Ghanam went with one policeman to the cistern above Hafez's house and showed the policeman where villagers found bullet casings. The policeman picked them up with his hands, did not document where he had found them, and acted very unprofessional. He was clearly not interested in doing any serious investigation.

Matt was really frustrated. He called the police office again and told them that the police here were refusing to investigate. He handed his cell phone to the police for them to talk to someone back at the office. The police were offended by Matt's mistrust, but Matt would not back down. Soldiers came in a jeep and also did nothing.

Matt told the police that the soldiers' story did not make sense. The shots fired were attack shots, not warning shots. The shooters were really close to the village. The attackers had yelled curses at the villagers. Why did it take an hour for the police and soldiers to get here? If the villagers had attacked soldiers, would the soldiers do nothing but run? If it was soldiers, why would they not want an investigation? What are they hiding, or who are they covering for? If it was a mistake, why didn't the soldiers immediately come to the village to explain what happened and remove all this suspicion? If the villagers are correct in saying they saw both soldiers and settlers, is the army covering for the settlers? Did a soldier get scared and lose it, and are the authorities covering for him? Soldiers are not known for running. Why then were they seen running toward the settler outpost? The villagers claim they never heard anyone identify themselves as soldiers and that they had not thrown stones at anyone.

We did about two hours of debriefing after we got back to our house. We had a time of prayer and a time of sharing feelings and rehashing what happened. It was helpful to talk about what we had just been through.

February 11, 2006, Saturday

Matt and I met seventeen children this morning. We talked with the military captain with whom I talked down by the road last evening. He again said that they were on foot patrol near the village, the villagers thought they were settlers, they fired warning shots, and there was no problem. We didn't ask him any probing questions, but we still wonder what did happen. This soldier is a captain and apparently replaces Mister Three Bars. I keep thinking about Mister Three Bars. How will God continue to work in his heart?

Sarah and I, along with two village men, walked down to the road to get a ride with an older Israeli man who stopped to take us to a Ta'ayush action. Just before we pulled away, soldiers in a Hummer stopped and asked for the villagers' IDs. I gave them my passport, even though they had not asked for it. They questioned the driver about where we were going. Soon soldiers in a jeep stopped. There were eight soldiers there to check on us. In about ten minutes we were on our way without any trouble.

We went to Libwib, a Palestinian village of about one thousand people, just south of the Peni Hever settlement, southeast of Hebron. About ten days ago, settlers from Peni Hever beat a shepherd from the village. Our action was in response to that beating and to assist the right of shepherds there to graze their sheep on their own land. After meeting people in the village, we drove north, down a narrow road to the base of a high, steep mountain and then up the next mountain to a new road and fence that marked the expanded border of the settlement. It felt a little scary being so close to the settlement. What if settlers attacked us? There were flocks of sheep grazing nearby on Palestinian land that is now forbidden for the shepherds to use.

After about half an hour we saw soldiers in a Hummer turn into the settlement, apparently to get the settlers' perspective before approaching us. It seemed like the soldiers didn't know what to do when they did approach us. They were dealing with Israelis and internationals, not just with Palestinian shepherds, all the while being filmed. We greeted them in a friendly way, and Ezra talked with them. The situation was relaxed, although three soldiers did stand around with their M-16s ready.

A young settler, maybe thirty years old, who the shepherds said did the beating, walked down from the settlement and talked to the soldiers. After that the soldiers became more assertive. Soldiers then demanded IDs from the Palestinians, but for about ten minutes everyone refused to show them. I tried to start a conversation with the settler, but the only response I got was, "F— you." I replied, "What? You say you want to have sex with me? Really? I don't believe it." Everyone laughed, and the soldiers became more relaxed.

The settler then started walking toward the sheep. A Dove, who had come with Ezra, followed him very closely, with Sarah a little way back with the video camera. Two soldiers followed them. The settler tried to chase the sheep, and to my amazement, the Dove followed the settler, keeping herself between him and the sheep, preventing him from chasing the sheep. The soldiers did nothing.

Soon another young settler, also about thirty years old, arrived. When I saw him heading toward the other settler, I followed him. He cursed a Palestinian in Arabic and then turned to me. "I want to burn you in Auschwitz. The Arabs want to finish what the Nazis didn't finish. They want to kill all the Jews, and you are helping them." I felt a lot of compassion for him. I am sure he believed what he said. What would it mean to live with so much fear and hate? I had no chance to reply because he headed toward the sheep.

I followed him and soon I was following the Dove's example. I tried to stay between him and the sheep, which was quite a challenge. He moved fast, but every time he tried to get to the sheep, I stood in front of him and blocked him with my body. I was careful not to use my hands because I am sure he would have interpreted that as an assault and given him an excuse to strike me. I felt pretty safe because we were being videotaped, and there were lots of witnesses, including soldiers.

Soon some of the shepherds were following our example and nonviolently blocking the settlers. I was proud of them. Several did use their hands a few times but immediately backed off. When things got tense, several shepherds picked up rocks, but they restrained themselves, and no rocks were thrown.

I kept repeating the Shema in Hebrew, "Hear O Israel, the Lord your God is one," and telling the settlers that there is one God who created us all. These few words of the Shema encapsulate the heart of the Jewish faith. I kept reminding them that it was shabbat, and that they were violating the Sabbath by their aggressive actions. I kept repeating, "Shabbat shalom," and some of the time just chanted, "Shabbat, shabbat, shabbat."

At one point the second settler said to me, "We love everybody on the knife." Then he said, "First the Arabs will kill all the Jews, and then they will kill all the Christians. The Qur'an commands them to kill us all." That was too much for the Muslim shepherds, who began a discussion of the Qur'an with him, some of it in Hebrew, and some of it in Arabic. They tried to talk to the settler about the Qur'an commanding tolerance and respect for the People of the Book (Jews and Christians). They offered to sit down and drink tea with him. The settler refused.

I was impressed with how focused and disciplined the two settlers were. Their one goal was to move the sheep farther away from the Peni Hever settlement, and bit-by-bit they succeeded. In spite of our best efforts, they did manage to move the sheep away. Inch by inch, the two of them moved us back maybe a hundred feet. Had the shepherds changed from being totally on the defense, the shepherds could have moved their sheep toward the settlement.

I was really frustrated with the soldiers, who did nothing. They just stood there and watched. They half-heartedly asked us to move, but our Ta'ayush friends stood up to the soldiers. Police also came and did nothing. The settlers were free to do as they liked. We were always on Palestinian land, but the soldiers and police never stood up for the Palestinians. They seemed to be accountable mainly to the settlers.

At about noon, the two settlers left. Did they succeed in their mission? They did move the sheep and shepherds back, but the Palestinians reaffirmed their right to be on their land, the soldiers did not remove them, and the whole issue of Palestinians being able to be on their land was raised again in a way that the Israeli authorities will not be able to ignore.

Before we left, I prayed the noon prayer with the shepherds. I was told the soldiers who were standing nearby looked astonished. As soon as I finished, I walked over to the ten soldiers standing there and told them I also wanted to pray with them. They didn't seem to know how to respond. They probably had not been trained for this. I explained to them that I attend worship regularly in the synagogue back home and believe there is but one God. I felt it was important to make that clear to them. One of the soldiers offered me his Hebrew prayer book, but I told him that I do not read Hebrew. I would have read a Hebrew prayer to the soldiers if I had been able to read Hebrew. I did repeat the Shema to them in Hebrew.

We then went back to Libwib and had a feast of rice and a sheep that they killed for us. We ate sitting on the grass just below the school, where we could look straight ahead to Jordan and the Dead Sea, see the Peni Hever settlement on our left, and the Karmel and Ma'on settlements on our right.

February 13, 2006, Monday

Sarah and I went with the children this afternoon. They got out a little early and the soldiers were a little late. Some of the girls were trying to convert Sarah to Islam, and the boys were playing soldiers and Palestinians, something similar to cowboys and Indians.

Nasser came by this by afternoon and reported that settlers had planted olive trees on Susiya land where Ta'ayush is planning to plant olive trees this Saturday. Matt and Sally Hunsberger went with Nasser to document the problem. People there called the police and the DCO to come. Finally the police did arrive but left immediately. The DCO came and said they would meet the Palestinians on the land but then left before the Palestinians could get there. The villagers will probably not get any cooperation from the Israeli authorities, so they will have to work through their lawyer.

I ate supper with a family whose husband just got back from working in Israel for ten days. To get home, he had to go a long way around east through Bedouin country. It is becoming increasingly difficult for villagers to get back and forth to Israel to work. The economy of the village is partly dependant on villagers doing some work in Israel.

February 15, 2006, Wednesday

It has been raining the past two days. Finally we are getting a little rain. Ilhamdililah. Allah karim. See, we can trust the future to God. Why is my faith so weak?

I went alone with the children in the cold rain this afternoon. They had first come to our house to wait because they got out of school early. It was really cold with freezing wind, rain, and sleet. The children were not adequately dressed. We waited in the cold for forty-five minutes before the police finally came. I called them twice. How disgusting. The Ma'on settlers threaten the children, and the children end up being the ones to suffer. The police do nothing and even come late.

February 16, 2006, Thursday

I went alone to meet the children this morning, but none came because of the cold and rain.

We started a new monitoring and counting of traffic to and from Yatta today for another Israeli human rights lawyer. Soldiers stopped by while I was helping with the counting and asked if they needed to accompany school children at noon. I told them I didn't think there would be anyone, but to be sure I would go up to the school and check and then call them. It turned out that there was no school today because the teachers didn't come. I then called the soldiers to let them know that they didn't need to come today. They thanked me. It felt good to have that positive interaction with the military. So much of my relationship with them is adversarial and confrontational.

It seems that recently most of the soldiers have been reservists who are doing their yearly one month stint with the army. By the time we establish a relationship with them, they are gone and we have to "train" a new group. I still miss Mister Three Bars. We seem to have a good group of soldiers here now. Sometimes we have more right-wing groups who tend to be more rude and aggressive. One of the soldiers this afternoon had lots of good questions about organic farming.

February 18, 2006, Saturday

Matt woke me up in the night to tell me that Rich called saying my visa to get into Iraq has been approved, and I am to go immediately to Amman, Jordan. I didn't get much sleep the rest of the night. I am amazed at how my attitude has changed. It has been hard thinking about leaving At-Tuwani early. I really didn't want to go. But when I heard that I am to leave now, I felt a deep sense of joy and excitement. All of a sudden I was ready to leave.

I said my goodbyes to the Tuba children this morning. What a joy they have been to me.

Sally and I then went with some villagers to Susiya for a tree planting action with Ta'ayush people. I was glad that I had spent that time a week ago in Susiya, because I immediately connected with the people there and had some understanding of the context for today's action. About 100 Ta'ayush people came and planted olive trees in three different villages. We got to Susiya early and waited. Police arrived at 9:30, along with a special unit of about eight police, something like a SWAT team. They drove around and surveyed the situation. Soon there were about twenty soldiers and police. Were they there to protect us from the settlers or to prevent our action? By 10:30 there were maybe thirty-five Israelis and forty Palestinians ready to work together. There were lots of warm greetings exchanged as we all drank tea together. I was excited.

We loaded about one hundred olive trees on a trailer and walked together through the valley to the top of the next hill, near the edge of the Susya settlement. It felt like a religious procession to me.

Soon we were digging holes in the soil and planting olive trees. Israeli men and women, along with Palestinian women and men, were all working together, each putting some sacred soil around the sacred roots of the olive trees. What a picture of peace: people who are supposed to be enemies planting olive trees together. Don't tell me peace is not possible between Palestinians and Israelis. I saw it with my own eyes again today.

Many people are concerned about terrorism. I am too. I also am concerned about state terrorism. Today we experienced the true antidote to terrorism: working together in peace instead of oppressing and dominating. Because of what we experienced today, those young Palestinians who planted olive trees with Israelis will be less likely to become suicide bombers, and those Israelis will be less likely to support the terrorist actions of their government. This, not repressive actions, will lead to peace and security. "There is no way to peace, peace is the way."

Settlers were watching us and engaging in conversation with the soldiers and police near the edge of the settlement. By eleven o'clock, Tarik, another Druze who works for the DCO, came. I saw him and the police studying their maps. I was not surprised when they soon ordered us all to leave the area, but

I was angry. We continued planting the olive trees as fast as we could. Then the police became more threatening and ordered us to leave immediately.

One of the police said to one of the Ta'ayush people, "Why plant these trees when you know they will soon be uprooted by the settlers?" He didn't get it. Yes, the policeman was right, but that is not the point. By all of us working together, Israelis, Palestinians, and internationals, we proclaimed, demonstrated, and acted out the message that peace is possible, that there is another way. We enacted a vision of hope. That witness was given to the Palestinians, to the Israelis, to the soldiers and police, and to the settlers. Seeds of peace were planted today. I trust that both Israelis and Palestinians were changed today.

It was also a prayer to God, telling God that we are ready for and will work together for peace. I believe that prayer was heard in the highest places in heaven. Prayer is not magic, but prayer can create the openings through which it becomes possible for God to work. We created some new openings today.

The soldiers and police started getting nasty and began forcing everyone to leave. I asked Tarik why he was afraid of olive trees, why he found people working together for peace so threatening. No response. What could he say?

I am not as naïve as I sounded. I know that it is not the olive trees that are threatening. What is threatening is for Israelis and Palestinians to be planting olive trees together. That coming together threatens the whole apartheid goal of the Israeli government to separate the Israeli and Palestinian people. Another threatening aspect of planting olive trees is that olive trees symbolize ownership and permanence, a threat to the Israeli goal of stealing all this land and removing the Palestinians. So we made a profound political statement in addition to our affirmation of peace. Planting olive trees is an act of resistance to the Israeli government's vision of domination, conquest, and ethnic cleansing.

We all headed back to the village. I was angry, but the Palestinians held their heads high. Their faith is so much stronger than mine. As we sat together in the village we could see settlers uprooting some of the olive trees we had just planted, as Israeli authorities stood by and watched. I thought of the hope of the resurrection. Authorities believe they can crush and kill hope, but hope rises again. God bless those olive trees. Their story has not ended.

There were a few speeches, both by Palestinians and Israelis, but mostly there were many conversations in Hebrew and Arabic. Many Palestinians speak Hebrew and some Israelis speak Arabic. A group of Israeli and Palestinian women sat in a circle talking together. What a beautiful sight. It was so beautiful I had to cry. I have seen and experienced so much ugliness here, but also incredible beauty.

One of the Israelis said to me, "We are all Iraqis." I think that he meant that as children of Abraham, an Iraqi Bedouin, we are all Iraqis, or he might have meant that since civilization began in Iraq, we are all Iraqis. Either way, yes, yes, yes.

I got a ride on the Ta'ayush bus and got off at the entrance to Kiryat Arba at the edge of the Beqa'a Valley to begin my journey to Iraq. What a beautiful way to end my time in At-Tuwani this winter. As I looked north and surveyed the Beqa'a Valley and thought of all my relationships in this valley, I burst into tears and sobs. An avalanche of feelings poured out, both negative and positive. I have experienced so much more than I can contain within myself. I let my feelings pour out. Then I was ready to walk into Hebron to begin the next part of my journey, a trip to Iraq to see Peggy, to experience a bit of what the Iraqi people experience under occupation and be part of CPT work there.

December 14, 2006-January 27, 2007

December 14, 2006 Thursday

I am one happy person. This afternoon I came back to At-Tuwani for my third winter here after spending two weeks working with our team in Hebron. I walked here from Karmil with one of the young village men. I kept my eyes focused on At-Tuwani in the distance as we walked, with many memories and thoughts rushing through my mind.

It was sobering to walk through the narrow opening, just wide enough for one car, in the thirty-two-inch-high wall which the Israeli military built this summer along the settler road below At-Tuwani, in spite of much opposition. The ability of Palestinians to cross the settler road has been a major issue since last winter.

It was a great joy to be back in At-Tuwani and greet people. I felt warmly welcomed. The second floor above the clinic is finished, and a new mosque is being built on the ruins of the demolished mosque. I met CPTers John Funk from British Columbia and Heidi Schramm from Illinois, and two Doves, all wonderful people. This evening I met with the extended Adara family. That was wonderful. They certainly made me feel part of the family.

December 15, 2006, Friday

I was awakened at half past one this morning and told there were soldiers up at Juma's house. I quickly got dressed and joined the others in rushing up the hill. We could see the soldiers shining their spotlight around the area. Before we got up the hill, the soldiers drove down the hill past us. We continued walking up the hill and met about six villagers who were out on the road.

Israeli soldiers and Palestinians during a demonstration.

The soldiers had not caused any problems except to awaken some of us. I learned that the other team members had gotten up about two hours earlier because soldiers were here.

Soldiers have been causing a lot of problems here recently. The past month here has been horrendous. Team members have been getting up almost every night. Soldiers have been repeatedly coming into At-Tuwani at night and raiding homes. On December 4, soldiers attacked a villager, held a gun to his head, and threatened to kill him if they see him again. This past Tuesday night at ten o'clock, soldiers came into the village and broke three windows in a villager's car. A year ago soldiers broke out all the windows in this villager's car. The soldiers then went to a village house, sprayed a white powder on the house, and threw rocks through one window in the house, just missing two men sleeping in the room. Five minutes later, two army jeeps arrived. The soldiers said none of the above could have happened since there were no other army jeeps in the area that evening. The police refused to come.

I got stopped in Karmil yesterday on my way here and was invited to drink tea with a group of Palestinian men there. They told me that soldiers had entered Karmil on both November 29 and December 7 and did a lot of seemingly random destruction, especially to glass: car windows, door windows, and glass inside people's homes that they invaded, using both rocks and bullets. I saw two of the broken windows.

I wonder if the war between the Israeli military and Hezbollah in Lebanon this past summer is a factor in what is happening here now. Each day Hezbollah rained rockets on northern Israel, and Israel did major bombing of the infrastructure of Lebanon. Sadly, the U.S. government did all they could to prevent a ceasefire and rushed more bombs to Israel. In the last seventy-two hours, when they knew a ceasefire was near, the Israeli military dropped four million cluster bombs, made in the USA. These bombs, which then served as landmines, are shiny, interesting-looking objects that were then picked up by Lebanese children in whose hands they exploded.

UN peacekeepers in Lebanon have also been killed by these cluster bombs. Team members in Hebron noticed increased military activity and overall increase in violent behavior by Israeli soldiers in the Hebron area. Team members heard several reports of Israeli soldiers threatening Palestinians, saying they would do to the Palestinians what they did to the people in Lebanon.

Maybe we just have an especially bad group of soldiers here now. The Israeli military is organized along ideological lines. When an Israeli is drafted into the military, the person can choose what kind of brigade one wants to join. It can be leftist or rightist, religious or secular. That helps explain why some groups of soldiers are kind and some very bad.

Since it is Friday, everything was quiet today. I went to Friday prayers in Karmil. It was a joy to worship again with the simple people of the South Hebron Hills. When I got back, the team was invited to have lunch with the extended Adara family. Some of us visited another family in the afternoon. Both of these families had

weddings in the past few months, so I got to do some congratu-
lating. I went to sunset prayers in the new, partially completed
mosque here in At-Tuwani being built on the ruins of the old
mosque that was demolished in 1987. I appreciated being able to
pray with the villagers again.

December 16, 2006, Saturday

Soldiers came into the village again last night around midnight. The soldiers made a lot of noise with their jeep but didn't
cause any other trouble. They seemed upset that our team members were right there watching them.

John and I went over to the gate toward Ma'on to meet
the seventeen children this morning. It turned cold and windy
last night, so it was cold standing out there waiting for the children. What a joy to see those children again. And they seemed
glad to see me. They immediately asked me if I had prayed this
morning. What a blessing! What a deep concern they have for
me. No soldiers walked with the children, and the soldiers
ignored us. This is not a friendly group of soldiers.

I learned there were continual problems for the school children while I was gone. Soldiers repeatedly were late, sometimes
as much as three hours. The settlers increased their attacks on
the children, soldiers, and police. A settler once blocked the road
with his vehicle and would not allow soldiers to pass with the
children. The soldiers complied with the settler's demands and
turned back. Even when settlers broke a window in a police jeep
on April 27, the police took no action. In May, the settlers
blocked the road to Tuba with large rocks to prevent soldiers
from accompanying the children. Instead of removing the roadblock, two different groups of soldiers and police accompanied
the children each day on either side of the roadblock. On many
days settlers stood by the road and yelled at and frightened the
children. One day, a settler woman tried to drag a seven-year-old
schoolboy away. Even when a group of thirty-five settlers threw
eggs and rocks at the children, the soldiers and police took no

action against the settlers. One day one of the young children asked an Israeli police officer, "Are you afraid of the settlers too?"

On Saturday (Sabbath), May 6, about thirty settlers threw rocks at the soldiers and the children. Several children were injured by being kicked and punched by settlers. Three required medical attention. At the same time as three soldiers tried to deal with the thirty settlers, there was a massive presence of soldiers and police in At-Tuwani throughout the day to prevent Israeli peace activists from visiting the village. On Saturday, November 11, Israeli soldiers were busy preventing Palestinians farmers from plowing Palestinian land near the Havot Ma'on outpost. After this standoff ended, settlers left and attacked fourteen school children as they walked home toward Tuba after being escorted by Israeli soldiers. Recently, soldiers have been making the school children run, are not walking with them, and even have called the school girls Sharmuta (whores).

John and I went up to Khoruba to watch for the children this afternoon. It was cold and windy. I saw the two huge new chicken barns over by Ma'on that they started to build last year. The soldiers now meet the children at the chicken barns.

Soldiers were briefly up at the edge of the village this morning and came into the village at four o'clock this afternoon. Basically they just drove around in the village, and left. But they drove at a very high rate of speed as they left, leaving behind a big cloud of dust. I was worried they would crash because of all the stones and fine, loose dirt on the road.

I was exhausted, so I went to bed at seven o'clock. I was awakened at half past eight because soldiers were back in the village. We rushed up to where the soldiers had stopped. I waited half way up the hill as the jeep slowly came down the hill with its spotlight on me. I assumed they had their guns pointed at me. That was a bit scary. I was sure they would not shoot me, but I did think about the possibility. Then, slowly, they backed up the hill to where about twenty villagers were gathered around a burning tire. The soldiers verbally harassed the men in Hebrew, using various sexual terms to degrade the Palestinians. Some of the village men wanted to throw stones at the soldiers. I can understand that. The daily harassment the villagers are experiencing is disgusting. We all feel a lot of anger.

Throwing stones at the soldiers may feel like an attractive response, but that would bring more repression. The wiser men in the village are making a strong case for continuing their non-violent response. The people of At-Tuwani and the surrounding area have fine-tuned a creative response to the repression they experience every day. Unlike in some villages, the people here do not hide, withdraw, or buckle under attacks. Every time the soldiers or settlers do something bad, the villagers are out there confronting the soldiers and settlers. The soldiers do not know how to fight this battle. If the villagers used violence, the soldiers would know how to respond. But the villagers have chosen another battle plan, an approach that must be quite frustrating for the military, an approach by which the villagers keep winning. It is a constant struggle here in the village over whether the villagers will remain nonviolent. The temptation to use violence is strong. Violence sounds like a quick fix, but there are no quick fixes. Most of the villagers understand that we are engaged in a long, serious struggle.

The idea that violence can overcome evil is a lie. Watch any violent scene in any film and watch the lie being repeated again. Chaos threatens, and the only possible solution is violence. It seems so simple. After a little violence, maybe five minutes, like magic, peace and tranquility return. Those who believe this lie think nonviolence is incredibly naïve. I understand that. In every violent film I have seen, I have seldom seen any way that nonviolence could be relevant or effective. The scenario is always set up to make it seem that violence is the only solution. One can never reason with the enemy. The only answer seems to be massive retaliatory violence, and magically, yes magically, peace and order instantly return.

But all this is a lie. We do not live by magic. Life is not that simple. Violence does not magically save and bring peace. Violence is not redemptive. Those films are lies. In those films the power of evil is given mythical status, its power greatly exaggerated. Those violent films do not portray reality any more than do our politicians who exaggerate the power and evil of the enemy and promise peace and tranquility after a brief volley of violence.

In reality, the power of evil is actually extremely fragile. Dictators are never as strong as they appear. In fact, dictators seem to realize this since they put so much energy into preserving their power. Oppressive structures are unstable and have within them the seeds of their own destruction. In nonviolent actions we seek the weak spots in those oppressive structures, unmask, and reveal those weaknesses. Dictators prefer violent resistance because they have the means to repress violent opposition. They realize that the power of nonviolence is a much deeper threat to their power.

Christians express a profound truth when they say that in the cross the powers of evil were broken and defeated. The Muslims are right when after every tragedy they repeat, "Allah karim (God is generous, God is good)." The Jewish, Christian, and Islamic scriptures are correct in affirming that it is the love and mercy of God, not evil, that is the ultimate power in the universe. The myth of redemptive violence is a lie. Only love can overcome evil. It is nonviolent action that is based in reality. There are no easy answers. We must struggle, pray, and love.

We tried to talk to the soldiers, but they were horribly arrogant and resisted any rational conversation. The soldiers are playing a game, but it seems to me that we are playing along with their game. What could we do to interrupt this game? We have become too involved. When we argue with the soldiers, we are buying into their game. I am thinking we need to be less involved, and just by our presence let the soldiers know they are being watched. It is a big question. At what point do we only observe, and at what point do we jump in to confront or interrupt oppressive behavior?

One morning back in February 2002, we witnessed a soldier beating a Palestinian on the street in Hebron. Attempts to get him to stop failed, so I decided to physically stop the soldier. I knew I could not use my hands, for certainly he had been well trained to handle attacks, and he could have had me laying on the street in seconds. Instead, I put my hands behind my back in order not to in any way threaten him. Without saying anything, I then stuck my ugly face in front of the soldier with my nose practically touching his nose. The soldier was furious with me, but I had accomplished my goal. He forgot about the Palestinian and was angry with me. Since I had not threatened him, I am sure he never thought of using his M-16. He was not going to shoot an American. What could he do? He was almost helpless.

He radioed his commander, and within a few minutes six Israeli soldiers marched toward us. This was the same six soldiers with whom just an hour earlier I had had an extended discussion of nonviolence. One of the soldiers was considering becoming a refusenik and dropping out of the military. They knew me. The commander said, "Art, you cannot interfere with soldiers." "Yes, I can," I replied. "I just did." I described to the commander what had happened, whereupon the commander reprimanded the young soldier who was practically in tears. At that point, we team members left. About an hour later I saw the young soldier I had confronted and told him, "I am sorry for what happened this morning." He said he was sorry too and apologized to me for the way he had acted.

Another time, two days later, on a cold evening in Hebron, we saw a young Palestinian, lightly dressed, sitting on the sidewalk, obviously very cold. I asked the soldier guarding him what the problem was. The soldier said there was no problem, that they were only checking his ID. I asked the young man who told me he had been sitting there for three hours. I confronted the soldier, told him this was torture, and demanded the young man be released. That didn't work. I then decided to take matters into my own hands. I gave my coat and hat to the Palestinian. I took off my sweater and shirt. I did not take off my tee shirt, since that would have been culturally inappropriate in conservative Hebron. I told the soldier I was not leaving until the young man was released and sat down beside the Palestinian and started shivering with him. I am very stubborn, and if necessary, I would have sat there all night. In about ten minutes the soldier gave back the man's ID, and I was invited to his home to help celebrate his release.

In these two cases, intervention seemed appropriate.

December 17, 2006, Sunday

Ezra and two other Ta'ayush people came and spent last night in the village to be here in case soldiers came into the village again during night. What a wonderful witness these Israelis make. Soldiers came back to the village twice last night, at eleven o'clock and again at half past two. The Ta'ayush people stayed in the house and did not go outside, but the soldiers certainly saw Ezra's truck. I think it was smart that they didn't go out. I think we have been overreacting by going out and playing into their hands. Maybe we need to relax. Our role is first to observe and document what happens. In some cases we need to intervene, to get in the way, but that is not usually the first thing for us to do. The villagers know we are here and the soldiers need to know we are here, but further action on our part needs careful thought.

December 18, 2006, Monday

Two Israelis slept in the village last night. Apparently no soldiers came into the village.

There were nineteen children this morning, along with three soldiers walking, even though lately the soldiers have not been walking with the children. Actually the soldiers today were quite friendly, even though one of them was the one who threatened to kill a villager the other night.

Soldiers came into the village at quarter of one today on the way to meet the children. Because a villager didn't move away fast enough, a soldier jumped out of the jeep and pushed him away. John talked with the soldiers about what happened and suggested they use another way, since where they were is a private driveway and children are often playing there.

December 19, 2006, Tuesday

Apparently there were no problems last night. Two Israelis were here until two o'clock this morning.

John and I went up to Khoruba this morning. What a joy it was to see the children coming across the distant hill. I think one of the most beautiful sights I have ever seen is watching the silhouettes of the children walking across the horizon in the morning sky. I love those children. We got back in time to meet the children below the school. They said two settlers came to Tuba last evening around sunset and threw stones. Again the children asked if I had done my prayers this morning. That really touches me.

After worship this morning, I led an Arabic class for our team. That felt good. It is interesting how we are speaking English, Italian, German, and Arabic here now.

December 20, 2006, Wednesday

Two Israeli activists were here again last night, but there were no problems from soldiers.

John left for two days and Amy Peters and Allan Slater arrived. Allan is a Canadian dairy farmer who spent considerable time in Iraq with our team. He plans to be here for a month. Amy is a Canadian college student. I took Amy and Allan up to Khoruba and did a lot of orientation for them along the way.

I was invited to go to Mufakara and meet with two At-Tuwani men and some Mufakara men, including Maher, a sensitive activist who was recently released after being arrested because a settler accused him of attacking the settler. Ta'ayush people got him released. I had lunch there in a tent and listened as they talked. They then invited me to pray with them in the beautiful new mosque they just built there. That was special. I hope the Israeli military will not demolish that mosque.

At 4:40 this afternoon, a military jeep tore through the village. It went up the hill, came back, went up to the school, and then came back down to the Israeli road, leaving a cloud of dust behind. I suggested only two of us respond, so Allan and I started up the hill, but they were gone before we got far. What were the soldiers doing? Did they speed because they were afraid? Was it to send an aggressive message? I don't know. It felt really aggressive and hostile to me.

December 21, 2006, Thursday

Everything was quiet last night. Amy, a Dove, and I went to meet the nineteen children this morning. No soldiers walked with the children. The soldier who opened the gate would not respond when I greeted him. The driver did wave back to me.

I then got a phone call from Allan and a Dove, saying there were settlers in Mufakara, so I hurried up the hill and met them at Khoruba. When we got to Mufakara, one settler and a dog had taken off toward the Avi Gail outpost. We were invited into one of the caves for tea. We joked together for a while and then came back.

December 23, 2006, Saturday

I went with the Hebron team to Beit Ummar and met with the Hamas mayor, abu Musa, who was elected a year ago. The Israeli military has repeatedly arrested him as part of the larger repression of Hamas leadership. I was deeply impressed with abu Mussa, a gentle intellectual with obvious spiritual depth. He had pictures of Gandhi, Martin Luther King Jr., and Nelson Mandela in this office. Our conversation helped me understand the Hamas perspective.

After Hamas won the election last January, the U.S. and

Israeli governments decided to prevent the newly elected Hamas government from governing. One tool was to arrest and detain many of the Hamas legislators. Another tool was to cut off funding for the new Palestinian government. That meant no paychecks since February for police, teachers, and other government employees. School reopened on September 2 in At-Tuwani, but the teachers decided to honor the teachers' strike and dismissed school early. School reopened in November after a two-month-long teachers' strike. The teachers have now received some of their salaries. The Palestinians are being punished for choosing democracy.

Abu Musa said there is no way to survive except to trust in God. God wants a beautiful life for us. He expressed deep appreciation for internationals coming to stand with the people here, people who recognize that the Palestinians are human beings and give the people here hope that there can be a better future. He was very clear that God does not want us to kill or harm another human being, the highest of God's creation. He spoke very highly of Christianity and how the Qu'ran calls Christianity the closest religion to Islam. He studied at Bethlehem University, a Christian school, and has Christian friends with whom he visits regularly.

One of his arrests came the day work began to expand the nearby Karme Tzur settlement. He was released when the bulldozing was finished. He explained that the main source of conflict between Hamas and Fatah is coming from the outside. For example, there is a lot of pressure from the outside to annul the last election and cut off of all funds to the Palestinian Authority in order to make Hamas fail. "The way to end the conflict between Palestinians is to end the external pressures. Is it poor children who are causing the problems here? Is it poor farmers who are confiscating the land? Is it unpaid teachers who are building walls to separate people? It is not Hamas that is creating these problems." The people of Beit Ummar depend on agriculture, yet their land is being confiscated or they are not allowed on their land. Often they are prohibited from marketing their produce. I could sense it was painful for him to describe the suffering of the Palestinian people.

"Why don't you just say you recognize Israel?" he was asked. He replied, "Lying is not a solution. Arafat recognized Israel. What did he get in return? He was held hostage. Don't give anything for nothing. The question is, when will Israel recognize Palestine? Does Israel recognize any borders? Will Israel recognize the borders of 1948? What borders do you want us to recognize? Israel is the only expanding state in the world. The world is asking the victim to recognize the criminal. It is the Palestinians who need to be recognized."

After that we joined a demonstration against the Wall and a new Israeli bypass road that will take a lot of Palestinian land around Beit Ummar. We marched in the rain to the agricultural school at Aroub. There were several hundred Palestinians and about twenty-five Israeli activists, many of them Ta'ayush. There were speeches by Palestinians and Israelis. In spite of the worsening conditions and the increasing separation of Israelis from Palestinians, Israelis and Palestinians are still coming together in moments like these. How profound. I was especially impressed with Rami Elhannan from Bereaved Families. He spoke about when his daughter was killed by a suicide bomber he had the choice to either seek revenge or seek peace. He chose peace. What a witness this Jew made to that large gathering of Palestinians, Israelis, and internationals. The Palestinians applauded him.

December 24, 2006, Sunday

A Dove and I met the children this morning, but the soldiers refused to recognize our presence. I tried to tell them there will be no school tomorrow because of Christmas but was ignored. The children then told us that one of the soldiers threw a stone at them this morning. It was a light toss that did not endanger anyone, but it clearly was an act of hostility toward the children. The spirit behind the act is dangerous and destructive. This afternoon we videotaped the children telling about the soldier throwing the stone this morning. The same soldiers came this afternoon, so we got them on videotape. This is the same group of soldiers who have recently called the schoolgirls bad names and have been harassing the village at night. We hope to give this tape to the lawyer. I again tried to be friendly with the soldiers, but they ignored me. When I told them again that there would be no school tomorrow because of Christmas, I added that Santa Claus is my brother. That actually got a few small smiles from them.

December 25, 2006, Monday

Yesterday, since it was Christmas Eve, we read the Christmas story from Luke for our worship. That led to a time of sharing about occupation, be it Roman, Israeli, or American, and how during times of occupation, signs of hope and new life are given. Can we see those signs of hope? This morning, we all went up to the cave above the school for our time of worship. Our Christmas theme was liberation for the oppressed. We then explored around the top of the hill. We had a quiet day. Various people wished us a happy Christmas.

December 27, 2006, Wednesday

We got over a half-inch of rain during the night. Ilhamdililah. This should get all the crops germinated and give some relief to the trees that are suffering from the drought. There was also wind and thunder. It rained all day today. In all, we got about two inches of rain. That should mean the end of the drought.

There was only a small amount of rain this past winter, so the summer was a time of drought; some say the worst drought in fifty years. Even water is affected by the Occupation since, except for the rain, all water resources are controlled by the Israelis. Israeli public water is denied to Palestinians in the area. In contradiction to international law that states that any occupying power is responsible for the welfare of the people they occupy, the Israeli government does not accept responsibility. Instead, the UN and Oxfam took responsibility for the water needs and helped supply water and animal feed to the area. On September 12, a truck hired by Oxfam was disabled near Susiya by metal spikes someone spread on the road, damaging five tires on the water truck.

Because of the small amount of rain, shepherds began grazing their sheep only after I left last winter. There were problems from both settlers and soldiers for the rest of the summer. Repeatedly, settlers would confront the shepherds. Soldiers would then come and order the shepherds to leave the land until someone from the DCO could come and determine whether the shepherds were, in fact, allowed on that land. Repeatedly, the DCO would come and declare that the land was open to the Palestinians. After a few days settlers would again challenge the shepherds, and the cycle was repeated.

On June 17, after first talking with settlers, soldiers came to shepherds and said they were not allowed to graze their sheep in that area. When shepherds told the soldiers that just the day before, soldiers said they could graze in that area, a soldier looked at the settlers and responded, "I know they are a little crazy, but they don't want you here, so you must leave. After all, they are still Israelis." On July 22 and 27, Israeli soldiers tried to remove Palestinian shepherds from their land when settlers came on the land. This was in defiance of a high court ruling on June 26, reaffirming that Israeli soldiers have an obligation to protect Palestinians on their land, and may not remove Palestinians from their land as a means of pacifying settlers or protecting Palestinians from settlers.

We got a call this afternoon saying there was trouble at the La Safer checkpoint at the Green Line and that a man would come by and pick us up. John, Allen, and I went with him. It didn't take us long to figure things out. We immediately saw about thirty Palestinian men standing behind razor wire. It was really cold on top of that hill and the wind was blowing hard. Thankfully for all of us, the rain had temporarily stopped. I walked up to the men and greeted them. They said they had been standing there in the rain for five hours. They were wet and cold.

Allen and John talked to the soldiers who said these men were coming home from working illegally in Israel. The soldiers were making the men stand in the cold rain and snow for hours to punish them for their illegal activity. "This is how we control the situation," the soldier said. The soldier did not mention that extrajudicial punishment also is illegal, or that mistreating people causes resentment and anger, hardly the way to build peace. The soldier did not mention that Israel needs these "illegals" to do their dirty work for low wages in the same way American businesses need "illegal" Mexicans to do their dirty work at low wages while both the Israeli and American governments look the other way. The only difference here is that the Israeli military adds on punishment by making the workers stand in the cold rain for hours.

Soon after we arrived, the soldiers began giving the men back their IDs, and they headed toward cars waiting to take them home. Within ten minutes, all of them were released.

We walked back to the small Palestinian village of Beit Yatir, sleet stinging our faces as we walked. We drank tea with some men in Beit Yatir, a small Palestinian village near the Green Line. Five times over the years, they told us, the Israeli military has come into the village to demolish their houses and caves. Now all of them live in tents. Soon we saw Israeli soldiers stopping two men in a field below the village. We talked to the two men a few minutes later as they walked up toward the checkpoint. They explained that the soldiers had taken their IDs. They were walking up to stand in the cold rain at the checkpoint until the Israeli soldiers were ready to return their ID's. The men said they were not workers coming from Israel, but local men tending their sheep.

I thought of my friend in At-Tuwani who has been leaving his family to work in Israel to pay off a hospital bill. He is simply trying to be a responsible father, but is in danger of being punished for trying to do what is right. The man is working on a twenty-story building in Eskalon where there are fifty Chinese workers. No way is the Israeli government going to punish rich Israeli capitalists for hiring illegal workers. But someone must be punished for breaking the law, so the Palestinians are the preferred scapegoats.

December 28, 2006, Thursday

John, a Dove, and I went over to the gate to meet the children. We waited a long time, but soldiers did not come. We then decided that the three of us would walk up past the settlement, meet the children, and accompany them ourselves. One settler tried to run us down with his car as we walked up the hill, but other than that, we reached the children on the other end of the chicken barns without any trouble. Wow! Those chicken barns are huge.

Gdalia, the settler security man, was at the end of the chicken barns and told us we had to wait there while he called the army. The army had not heeded our calls, but after about fifteen minutes, they came. We walked with the children on the narrow path outside the fence around the chicken barns. I had not realized that the two new chicken barns and that fence cut off access to and from the road to Tuba. The Palestinian road is no longer there.

I wondered what would happen when we met the soldiers after we got around the chicken barns. I hoped we could either just walk along with the children or wait a bit and then walk down the road. Gdalia was there, giving orders to the soldiers, who then prevented us from proceeding. Both Gdalia and the soldiers said we could not walk back the way we came, that we had to go back to Tuba. I argued a bit with them by telling them that the Israeli High Court a year ago had ruled that the road past Ma'on was not part of the Ma'on settlement and was open to anyone, but they ignored me. Gdalia threatened to call the police if we did not leave. I told him I wanted to talk with the police, but I do not know if he actually did call the police. I told him we did not want to cause any trouble, that it was his people who beat up little children. I told him that the Dove with us had heart problems and should not do a lot of extra walking. Gdalia said he wished a happy life for him and for all of us, but we cannot walk on the road past the settlement. It seemed to me that Gdalia was not as gruff as I had remembered him. However, we were in a standoff. Gdalia was not going to back down, the soldiers were not going to disobey Gdalia, and we did not want to back down either. The soldiers stayed, but refused to talk with us. I wanted to talk with Gdalia, but this was not the time for that.

We then got a call saying there was no school and that the children wanted to go home. I tried to tell this to the soldiers, but they would not listen to me. We decided to call back and have them send the children, and we would call the army to tell them the children were coming. We then informed everyone of this and said we would wait for the children at the end of the chicken barns. This seemed like a face saving way out for all of us.

We met the children and then cut across the hills for a short cut home. Soldiers and settlers watched us from the top of one of the ridges. When we approached the Khoruba hill, soldiers drove near us and wanted to talk. We waved at them and pretended not to understand their calling us. My guess was that they wanted to inform us that we are not allowed to be anywhere in that area, something we did not want to hear. That area belongs to the Palestinians, not to the settlers. We got back with no trouble.

December 30, 2006, Saturday

Today is the first day of Eid al Adha. I got up at five o'clock and walked into Karmil for the Eid prayers. I listened to the call to prayer and the chanting from the mosque as I walked. I could hardly wait to get there. The antiphonal chanting was inspiring. "God is great, God is great, there is no God but God." How true.

The sermon mentioned Saddam Hussein being executed this morning, on one of the most important Muslims days of the year, while two million Muslim pilgrims are in Mecca. Just the execution of an Arab leader is being taken as a slap in the face and doing it during the Eid adds insult to injury. I sat there in the packed mosque, the only American there among the maybe four hundred Muslims listening to a harsh criticism of America, but I never felt uncomfortable or unsafe. There was no hostility in any way shown toward me as an American. In fact, people greeted me warmly after the prayers, with all of us wishing each other a blessed Eid.

Saddam has been an important subject of conversation during the day today. A common theme has been that Saddam was a bad man, but no worse than Bush or Israeli leaders. I wonder why today was chosen for the execution. Was this another attempt to increase the hostility between Sunni and Shia?

Our team was invited to eat lunch with the Adara family. I did some translating for the other team members, which resulted in a discussion of nonviolence. Someone made a comment about the continuing violence and oppression in the world and expressed doubt that anything can be done about it. I disagreed, saying that people in At-Tuwani are building an alternative to violence. Everyone seemed to agree with that. I then made a comment about the need for Muslim Peacemaker Teams. One of the villagers corrected me and said there already is a Muslim Peacemaker Team in At-Tuwani, the villagers here. I was a bit taken back by that. How could I have been so blind? Of course there is a Muslim Peacemaker Team here. We need to start thinking in those terms.

I then talked a bit about the Muslim Peacemaker Team in Iraq, a group of people who went through a week of nonviolence training and identify themselves as MPT, and pointed out that Allan had been in Iraq for eight months.

About ten days ago, a camel showed up in the village, a gift from a Bedouin to all the people of At-Tuwani. This afternoon the villagers butchered the camel. I felt very sad for the camel. We have been joking about bringing all the CPTers from Hebron to protect the camel. It again was exciting to see almost the whole village working together. It has been a blessed Eid.

John, Allan, a Dove, and I went for a walk up the hill to see the olive tree Hafez's mother planted in memory of Tom Fox. This past March 11, team members received word that Tom Fox's body had been found in Iraq. Many villagers stopped by our house to offer condolences. On March 23, the team learned that CPTers Jim Loney, Norman Kember, and Harmeet Sooden were freed in Baghdad. The people of At-Tuwani rejoiced with team members. Forty days after Tom's death, Hajji Fatima planted an olive tree in At-Tuwani in memory of Tom. Today we stood around the olive tree thinking about Tom.

December 31, 2006, Sunday

We learned that Ha'aretz ran a story about the recent soldier harassment here, which the Israeli military apparently has now stopped. People coming together from across national and religious barriers to stand up to the harassment achieved this little victory. The Israelis sleeping in the village and all the publicity the village generated seem to have had an effect.

So, the Israeli soldiers are not a law unto themselves, even though they sometimes act as though they are. There is some accountability in the system. By getting the stories of what soldiers and settlers are doing here into the Israeli media, we put pressure on the Israeli government to do what is right. The Occupation is built on very shaky grounds and full of contradictions. Israeli officials understand that actions like harassing villagers in the night undermine the legitimacy of the Occupation. If Israeli control were secure, the Israeli government would be able to ignore media criticism.

There is no unified Jewish state. There is no agreement on

what "Jewish" means. The divide between religious and secular is deep. Jews are only one of the ethnic and religious groups here. The Jewish state is propped up by U.S. aid, by ideologies rooted in the Holocaust, by perpetuation of fear of Arabs, and by military repression. The Israeli state is not secure.

It is important to recognize that insecure states do not act rationally. Suicide bombings, in addition to being immoral, make Israel less secure, and, thus, are counterproductive for Palestinian goals. So how can Palestinians take actions that will undermine the ability of Israelis to oppress them while not increasing Israeli insecurity? The people of At-Tuwani are involved in an exciting journey, learning how to win struggles for their rights without threatening the Israeli military.

January 1, 2007, Monday

Happy New Year.

I had an extended conversation about Islam with a former resident of At-Tuwani. It was interesting how he described something very close to non-resistance. He quoted a Hadith saying it would be better to destroy the Kabah in Mecca than to kill one person. We cannot kill for any political purpose. It is better to let people kill us than for us to kill anyone. We can only trust the future to God. There is something important in totally trusting the future to God, but we do not need to understand this as fatalism. Because we can totally trust the future to God, we can have the faith and confidence to struggle non-violently for a better future instead of feeling a need to kill.

It was great having lots of children from Yatta in the village for the Eid. I joked with them about At-Tuwani being much better than Yatta. As I sit outside trying to write my journal, about a dozen of them are on the flat roof next door, looking down on me, trying to get my attention. Sometimes they speak to me in Arabic and sometimes in English. Right now they are asking me if I am writing about the Eid here. I tell them, "Yes." They just told me they want to go with me to America. I said I would take them with me in my suitcase. They are having a great time talking to this weird foreigner. Now they are asking me about Saddam Hussein. I just told them that anyone who kills other people, be it Saddam, Bill Clinton, or George Bush, they are doing something very bad. The children seemed to understand.

I then decided this was the time to distribute the balloons Nancy Beres from back in Athens had sent with me. I gave one to each of the children on the roof. I then went to every house in the village and gave out balloons. Ghanam said he was a boy too, so I gave him one. I suddenly became quite popular with everyone.

January 3, 2007, Wednesday

When we got to Hebron for our joint team meeting, we learned that soldiers had detained John Lynes and Dianne Roe on Shuhada Street. The team has regularly been trying to walk on Shuhada Street, sometimes successfully and sometimes not. Jan Benvie, John Funk, and I went there and met Dianne and TIPH people, and some ISMers. John Lynes was down the street on the other side of Beit Hadassah. A soldier said Dianne and John had to stay where they were and wait for the police to come because they tried to walk on Shuhada Street, even though the Israeli High Court recently ruled that Shuhada Street must be opened. The soldier said that the reason we could not walk on Shuhada Street was because the settlers did not want us to be there. The soldiers did nothing about a settler woman who assaulted Dianne.

As we stood there and waited, I saw Noam Arnon, a Hebron settler leader, leading a tour group. I immediately decided to greet him in front of the tour group, where he had no choice but to be polite. I ignored the soldier who ordered me to stay where I was. When Noam came closer, I walked up to him, said "Shalom, shalom," and told him he has been in my prayers. He replied, "Why can't Jews go anywhere they want in Hebron? Why are

there fences and walls to keep us Jews fenced in? Will CPT publicly stand up for Jews to be free to go anywhere in Hebron?" I
replied, "Yes, I believe Jews should be free to go and live anywhere. I have always said that. Maybe we could get together and
talk about this." He did not respond.

If I could have a conversation with Noam, I would want to
ask him what steps he thinks Hebron settlers could take to
make it more possible for them to freely go anywhere in
Hebron. What could settlers do to help end this conflict? I
would want to ask him if he believed Palestinians should be free
to go and live anywhere they want, including Tel Aviv and
Jerusalem. It would be difficult, almost impossible, but I believe
that if there were true repentance and humility on the part of
the settlers, reconciliation and peace with the Palestinians in
Hebron and At-Tuwani could still be possible. It would take a
miracle, but miracles are possible. Some people may question
why all the responsibility for repentance is put on Israelis. The
reason is that they have the power. They are the ones who are
doing the confiscations, demolitions, and most of the killing.

At that point members of Noam's tour group became curious about us CPTers. I was sure they had already been briefed
about us, because at one point in their tour all of them looked at
us. I greeted them in Hebrew and shook hands with a number of
them. One of the women introduced herself as having come from
Iraq. She said that in the past Jews had had good relations with
their Iraqi neighbors. She portrayed herself as a liberal, cosmo-
politan person who longs for an open, free society. A local settler
kept trying to quiet her, telling her she was wasting her time talking with me. She would not listen to him, saying, "This man
seems open and I want him to understand."

She said she had nothing against Arabs, but then very quickly the liberal veneer melted away, and she talked about how terrible the Arabs are. "Arabs are emotional and easily excitable.
They are very violent people. They kill Jewish children. Look at
Iraq. See how savage those people are." Then she said, "The

Arabs here just need to recognize the reality that this is Israel and move on with their lives. They have twenty-two other Arab countries they can go to. Why do they keep hanging on to the idea that they can stay here? The Arabs are unable to accept reality."

I wanted to provide historical context for what she said, how outside powers have instigated the violence in the Middle East, that Israelis are not innocent, that most of the children who have been killed here have been killed by Israelis. She seemed totally unable to see any way Israelis might be responsible for some of the turmoil here, so I did not try to change her perspective. I just listened.

Other team members said the conversation seemed to have an effect on some of the Israeli youth in the tour group. One of them said, "You people are awesome." We never know how we influence others.

Eventually John and Dianne were released, we came back to the apartment, and we had our joint team meeting. Each team reported on what they had been experiencing. We worked on schedules and how to coordinate activities, especially the upcoming CPT delegation. I am grateful for the positive relationships we all have with each other.

January 4, 2007, Thursday

I am wrestling with the meaning of Saddam Hussein's death and the growing Shia/Sunni split. I am deeply troubled by all the anti-Shia bigotry I am hearing from the Palestinians. It is clear to me that the West is working to split and divide Muslims and get them to fight and kill each other. It is called "divide and conquer." I wonder what role CPT could have in this. Should we be sending people to Iran? How could we stand in the middle? One CPT response to threats of violence is for us to go live with people who are being demonized and expose the lies told about those people.

Although it is true that the United States and Israel have

done much to create the strife in the Muslim world, it is important not to slip into a victim mentality and blame our problems on some outside group or force, a perspective that is disempowering and immobilizing. Whatever the problems we face, we need to take responsibility for those problems and find solutions. We are not helpless victims.

January 6, 2007, Saturday

It rained during the night. Because of the fog, we did not go up to Khoruba this morning, this first day of school since the Eid. I called Omar who said a few children were on their way, so John and I went over and met the seven children. Two soldiers walked down the hill with the children and seemed friendly. Because of the mud, the jeep stayed up on the top of the hill.

I went up to the school this morning to check if there would be school tomorrow, Orthodox Christmas. They told me no school tomorrow. I ended up staying over two hours talking with the principal and some of the teachers. We got into a big discussion of Islam, which they said is not being practiced by most Muslims. We talked about Islam demanding equality, for we are all equal when we prostrate ourselves before God. It is an affront to Islam when some people are rich while others are poor and some people live in mansions while others have nothing. Islam demands that we all share.

That led to a discussion of nonviolence. I told them I had refused to be a soldier, did two years of alternative service in a home for crippled teenagers in Germany and that war is contrary to God's will for us (haram). They agreed and told the story of Omar Kittab who was found sleeping under a tree in Mecca by a visiting dignitary. The visiting dignitary could not believe that this man was the leader of the Islamic empire, since he had no soldiers to protect him. Omar replied, "If one rules justly, one needs no body guards." They then noted how Muslim leaders today need lots of armed protection.

I told them that I often tell soldiers that with their guns they are neither safe nor free, but that I, with no weapons, feel safe and free to go anywhere. I mentioned that American soldiers in Iraq are shocked to meet Peggy in many places in Iraq. They say, "Are you crazy? Don't you know how dangerous it is here? You do not even have a gun or armed guards." Peggy replies, "Without guns, I am safer than you are."

January 8, 2007, Monday

It rained all night. We now have close to five inches of rain, the average yearly rainfall. And it has been coming slowly, so there has been little runoff or erosion. The cisterns are filling up.

After John and I watched for the children at Khoruba, we then walked over to Khallet al-Thaba, the little village just south of Mufakara that I visited on December 22, 2005, on my way back from Jinba. We drank tea with Ali abu Jaber, a simple sixty-year-old shepherd who was eager to talk. He told us that all people are equal because we are all descendants of Adam. It makes no difference whether we are Israeli, American, Iraqi, Palestinian, Muslim, or whatever, because there is one God. No one is better than anyone else. What an incredibly profound worldview he has. This shepherd understands the starting point for building a stable, peaceful society, something most of the world leaders do not understand. His worldview leads to respect, dignity, and human rights.

He showed us another house the Israeli military demolished on May 31, 2006. This came without any warning. We saw little evidence of the demolished house. What we saw were four beautiful, well-crafted walls for a new house. The villagers had taken all the stones from the demolished house and rebuilt the walls for another house on the same site.

He then led us up the hill to where, on the same day, the Israeli military demolished their outhouse. I was amazed at how the soldiers broke up that concrete structure into very small pieces. The soldiers must have put a lot of effort into doing such a thorough job of breaking up that outhouse. I joked with Ali that maybe there had been terrorists hiding in that outhouse. Are Palestinian bodily functions now also to be prohibited? How much further will the Israeli government go in denying the humanity of these simple shepherds? I do not know how to express my deep feelings of revulsion and disgust.

January 9, 2007, Tuesday

A Dove and I went up to Khoruba this morning. On the way up the road we met Ali, who we met yesterday, riding on a donkey. He jumped off his donkey to hug and kiss me. What a gift it is to be able to walk these hills and meet both friends and strangers, feeling welcomed and accepted.

The soldiers were an hour and a half late this very cold afternoon. We called the soldiers three times. The children were just starting to walk the long way home when the soldiers finally came. The soldiers didn't want to talk with us, and they didn't walk with the seventeen children.

January 10, 2007, Wednesday

There was a checkpoint down on the road, the first in a number of weeks. It has been very quiet the past few weeks. I talked with one of the soldiers. It was interesting that he asked about the last group of soldiers. I told him that they had caused a lot of problems, such as breaking car and house windows, and harassing villagers in the middle of the night. He told me that I do not understand. When soldiers do something, they always have a good reason for doing what they are doing, even if we do not understand the reason. I just need to trust that soldiers are always doing the right thing. I told him that when someone does bad things, it does not matter who does it, it is still bad. I think he heard that.

The leaders of the domination system tell us that we do not know enough to have informed opinions about the big issues, and so need to trust those in power. We may not know everything, but we know enough to know that we are being lied to, manipulated, and deceived. We know enough. We have no excuse to not resist the evil around us.

January 11, 2007, Thursday

Allan, John and I left at six o'clock this morning to spend the day in Tuba. We took a shortcut on Palestinian land below the outpost. We got to Tuba about seven o'clock and waited for the children to arrive from their homes. We then walked with them to the end of the chicken barns. The soldiers were late, so we called them.

We walked back to Tuba and visited with Omar and his family in their cave. We learned that their family has three caves in the wooded hill where the settler outpost now is. They used to live in those caves. I felt a deep peace as we talked together.

We then walked over to Omar's brother, Ibrahim's tent. He was not home, but we visited with some of his older children. They all remembered how I slept on the mat outside their tent when I visited them last year.

We then walked over to a cave at the east end of the village and visited with Issa Ali Muhamri and his family. Three of their girls go to school in At-Tuwani. It was a very cold and windy day, but we were quite warm as we sat in the sun on top of the new entrance to their cave on the south side of some big rocks. Israeli soldiers demolished the entrance to their cave in 2000. The family has rebuilt the entrance. We had a spectacular view over the mountains south into Israel and East over the Dead Sea into Jordan. Shepherds moved with their flocks across the landscape. We talked about our families, laughed together, and talked about the goodness of God and God's creation. If only the world leaders could understand this goodness. I was deeply moved by this simple sharing of our common faith in God.

We then walked to the south end of the village and talked with three women who came out to greet us. They were mothers of some of the Tuba school children. Since there were no men at home, we did not feel free to visit their homes, but we did have a short conversation about their children and school. I gave them enough balloons for all their children, as I did everywhere today.

We headed back toward the chicken barns and had a pleasant rest in the sun as we waited half an hour for the children to come. Omar joined us. It was fun greeting the children as they came running toward us. They were in no hurry to get home, however, so we walked quite slowly.

Our plan was to walk home with the Maghair al-Abeed children, but they walked the long path to school today instead of walking to Tuba. We walked down the long steep path toward Maghair al-Abeed and were greeted by Shadi's children as we approached their cave carved into the steep hillside. We saw a nine-year-old girl doing laundry by hand in a scrub tub. I wondered, what do American children do when they get home from school these days? The parents were not there, so the two little girls, with help from their two brothers, quickly made a lunch of bread, scrambled eggs, sheep milk curds, dibs and tahini. First, they gathered firewood, started a fire, and then began cooking. It was touching to watch those little girls work so hard to make a meal for us.

Last year, on February 3, 2006, we had hoped to plant olive trees on Shadi's land but were stopped by soldiers and police. Police came to At-Tuwani this summer after three settlers attacked a shepherd from Maghair al-Abeed, injuring his son and two sheep. They said they refused to go to Maghair al-Abeed saying, "We need a whole army to go in there. The settlers will break our windows." Later the police told the victim the same thing, that they are afraid of the settlers. The victim asked the police, "If you are afraid of the settlers, how do you think I feel?"

The parents never arrived, so we left after an hour. I forgot that one of the reasons I wanted to visit there was to see the outhouse the Israeli military demolished last March. We walked home on the long path back to At-Tuwani. It took us over an hour to climb those steep mountains and get home.

It was a wonderful day for me connecting with the families of the children we accompany each day. That makes my connection with each of those children even more special.

There was a downside to our special day with the gracious people of Tuba and Maghair al-Abeed. All day there was the pounding of bombing and tank fire from near Jinba. Omar said the bombing was not far from Garateen, their home village in Israel. How ironic. Some people are practicing and training for war and killing, while the victims of those forces are harassed and continue to have their land stolen from them by those forces. The people of Tuba have suffered greatly in the past year. The racket of the guns and bombs put all our wonderful experiences into a larger context.

Children came down to our house at about half past seven and wanted us to take our computer up to their house so they could watch a video of Saddam Hussein's execution. I was exhausted and fighting a cold, so I went to bed. I did want to watch the video with the villagers. The video shows Saddam being cursed and berated, and then dropped to his death by hanging before he could finish repeating the Shuhada, the Muslim confession of faith. I heard that while everyone in the house grew quiet and subdued, the older women in the house covered their eyes so as not to see the end.

January 12, 2007, Friday

When I got to Hebron, I caught up on my email and read several emails describing a new Israeli military order prohibiting any Israeli or international from having any Palestinian passengers in their cars. Wow! This is another major step in imposing an apartheid system on the people of Israel/Palestine. It means another loss of freedom for both Israelis and Palestinians. Palestinian travel is already severely restricted. Now it will be even more so. I keep being surprised at how unjust and racist Israeli policy can become.

I then headed out to the Beqa'a. When I got to the top of

the hill above Kiryat Arba, I saw an older settler walking up toward the big towers. That surprised me. I asked a Palestinian there why the settler was walking up the hill. The man told me settlers are living up on the hill, and also down to the right. So Kiryat Arba settlers are expanding their reach. Later a friend told me that the man I saw may have been Dov Driven's father who lives there.

January 13, 2007, Saturday

John Lynes, Bill Baldwin, Rich Meyer, and I joined a Canadian film crew for a ride to Susiya to participate in a big event there in support of the villagers' land rights. We got to Susiya just as five Israeli buses were arriving, bringing over two hundred Israeli activists who joined about two hundred local Palestinians. I was overwhelmed with joy as I joined all those Israelis and Palestinians intermingling and greeting each other in Hebrew, Arabic, and English. I must have greeted over half of the people there, many of whom I already knew. There were speeches in Arabic and Hebrew.

The purpose of the gathering was to build support for the people of Susiya, combining a legal strategy with a public campaign. There is to be a very important hearing before the Israeli High Court on January 29 to hear the case of the Israeli military's plans to demolish all the tents of the Susiya village. The Israeli military already has demolished all the houses and caves. A number of Israeli lawyers are working on litigation in support of the land rights of the Susiya people. The High Court has already ruled in favor of the Susiya people, but the Israeli military really wants to get rid of these people and has appealed the court ruling. As a result the villagers face another round of anguish and turmoil. With conduct such as this it is difficult to have much respect for the Israeli military, which, since 1948, has never stopped its policy of ethnic cleansing.

Today, Palestinians, Israelis, and internationals joined together to say that these simple shepherds should not be removed from their land, and neither should the Susya settlement be allowed to expand and confiscate additional land. In addition to presenting a lot of history and facts in order to place the struggle in historical context, speaker after speaker articulated a clear vision of peace. An Israeli speaker said he dreams of a peace between Palestinians and Israelis that does not need to be defended by weapons. "Beat those weapons of war into agricultural implements," he said. A Palestinian speaker quoted the Prophet Mohammad, saying "God did not create you to be enemies."

At around half past two, we saw six teenage settler girls and one boy walking from the Susya settlement toward the village. Camera crews quickly went to get some interesting footage. Before long, police went toward the young settlers, who immediately went back to their settlement. There were lots of police present, but they caused no trouble for us today.

I learned that settlers destroyed all the olive trees we planted a year ago on the hill between the village and the settlement. That, however, was the least of the trouble. On March 25, about ten settlers wearing masks attacked Susiya residents as they slept in their tents. One villager awoke as settlers beat him on his head with a stick and dragged him outside his tent while his wife and young children screamed. He temporarily lost consciousness and was hospitalized for four days. His brother also was injured and hospitalized when he tried to intervene. After about fifteen minutes of mayhem, the settlers walked across the valley to the Susya settlement. Although there is an Israeli military base only a few minutes away, it took one and a half hours before soldiers came to the village. Settlers cut around two hundred olive trees and grape vines in Susiya during the night of April 27. On September 18, seven Israeli settlers attacked an elderly man with sticks and pipes. Soldiers accompanied the settlers and did nothing to stop them. The settlers' faces were covered. The injured man was taken to the hospital in an ambulance. Team members at various times spent nights in Susiya.

I talked with Amos Gvirtz, a longtime Israeli pacifist friend.

He also planned to go today to a Bedouin village in Israel, near Be'er Sheva, where in the past few weeks the Israeli military has demolished over thirty Bedouin homes. Earlier, the Israeli military had removed these Bedouins from their lands, and now wants to remove them again. The ethnic cleansing never stops. We talked about getting Israelis to live in the Bedouin village as we do in At-Tuwani.

Amos said the present Israeli government is too weak to do much of anything, and the Israeli people do not believe they can change anything. We talked about how that could be changed. How can we give people hope? He said Amir Peretz, the current defense minister, a leftist who promised reform and social justice, now appears to have sold out, a source of disillusionment for many.

One of the Palestinian speakers gave a warm welcome to the Israelis and said, "You understand the conflict here better than do the leaders of the Israeli government." I thought about how the oppressed understand their oppressors very well, while the oppressors tend not to understand the people they oppress. This definitely holds true here as the Palestinians understand the Israelis very well, but the Israeli soldiers here have almost no understanding of the Palestinians. The same holds true in Iraq where the Iraqi people understand the Americans, but neither American soldiers nor U.S. government leaders understand the Iraqi people. This is one reason why oppressors are so afraid of the people they oppress, and occupation is a very unstable way of organizing society.

Most of the people were gone by three o'clock. I had agreed to spend the night in Susiya. The few Palestinians and Israelis that were left were served a simple meal. Then everyone left, except for Ezra and four young Israeli refuseniks. We then feasted on machlube that the Nowajah family prepared for us.

I spent some of the time talking with Itimar, a former soldier who now is a refusenik. He spent part of the time last summer in prison during Israel's war on Lebanon. The Israelis had many questions about CPT, especially the basis of our willingness to take risks. I talked about my support for Peggy's work in Iraq. We talked about the freedom that results from trusting in God and being ready to die. I sensed a deep searching spirit among them.

After they left, I had a delightful time with the Nowajah family. It felt so peaceful with them in their tent. But as I looked out the opening in the tent I saw the lights of the Susya settlement across the valley, and I thought of the possibility that in a few weeks this tent may be bulldozed into a pile of rubble. I also wondered if there could be settler attacks tonight in response to our action today. This family, however, did not appear to be worried; they have found peace in the middle of horrible oppression and threats.

January 14, 2007, Sunday

We got up early, fed the sheep, had breakfast, and when we were ready to leave to take the children to school in At-Tuwani, the car would not start. The battery was dead. I thought about all the problems this family has, including driving a car that is literally falling apart, and now they have one more problem. We did get the car started and soon we were back in At-Tuwani.

At around half past ten, we were told there were settlers in Mufakara. John and I headed up there, walking up the road that goes toward the Avi Gail outpost. We decided to walk toward Mufakara from the direction of the outpost to possibly meet the settlers as they left Mufakara. That felt a bit crazy, but right. We saw no settlers. The people in Mufakara told us that two young settlers came to the edge of the village, frightened some young children, and then left. Recently, almost daily, the people of Mufakara are receiving minor harassment from settlers.

January 17, 2007, Wednesday

I went down to the road early this morning to meet a Spanish Television film crew that wanted to film the children on their way to school. The crew was a little late, so I had them drive up the road toward Ma'on. The children also were a little late, which gave the crew some time to get organized and then interview me about the need for soldiers to accompany the children.

It wasn't long before Gdalia drove up in his white pickup truck. We must have looked suspicious to him with four extra people. I greeted him in Hebrew and explained the crew was from Spanish Television. I then actually had a conversation with him, my first. He seemed to be in a fairly good mood. I told him I really would like to come to Ma'on and listen to him and his friends in order to understand their perspective. Gdalia said, "No, that is impossible. You people from CPT support the Arabs, so we cannot talk with you. Look at your website. It is totally pro-Arab, full of lies and small incidents blown way out of proportion. There were no problems here before your team came here." I asked him if he saw any answer to the conflict. He said, "No, because you can never trust the Arabs. They violate every agreement they have ever made. Their only goal is to destroy Israel and drive all the Jews into the sea. Hamas is worse than Iran. How can you talk to or make agreements with people like that?" "So what is the answer?" I asked. He said the only answer he could see was the status quo, trying to maintain the current situation.

I listened. I could have replied to everything he said, but I do not think arguments or facts would have been helpful. I have no idea whether my reaching out to settlers will do any good, but I must try. I keep asking how to respond to the myth of Israeli innocence. Does Gdalia really believe the Ma'on settlers are not part of the problem? Maybe he does believe that. I felt a lot of compassion for Gdalia as I listened to him. There is something good about him. He can probably not see any way out of the box he is in. Gdalia probably sees the conflict as a win/lose situation. For there to be peace, the settlers would have to lose something, so his vision is of domination, of victory over the Arabs. I wish he could see that peace could be a win/win situation for everyone. For many people, everything has to be either/or. Either you are for me or against me, either for the Palestinians or the settlers. A more helpful way of thinking is to think in terms of both/and. I can be open to and love both Palestinians and settlers.

I told him again I want to sit and listen to him and the Ma'on people. He seemed to hesitate, almost as if there was a glimmer of hope in him for the possibility of dialogue. Or maybe this is wishful thinking. I choose to take the risk that there is hope.

The children arrived and the film crew should have gotten some good footage by the gate of the soldiers and of the children walking to school. They interviewed the principal and did some filming in the classrooms.

On the way up to Khoruba this afternoon we met a tractor with a wagonload of people from Mirkez and Jinba. Issa and Mussa were on the trailer. It was good to see them again. I am afraid I will not get down there to see them this year. They asked about Peggy.

The two Doves went to Karmil to document damage done by soldiers last night. At two o'clock this morning, fifteen soldiers in three jeeps came to a house, threw stones at the house, and woke up the family. They broke three doors and forced their way into the house, which they occupied for about two hours. The soldiers ordered the family to leave the house, after which the soldiers did a search of the house, scattering clothes. We are sending a report of this, along with pictures, to human rights groups.

January 18, 2007, Thursday

Ta'ayush people brought four clowns here this morning to give a performance at the school. Before the performance began, we were told there were soldiers in the village. We headed toward the store and saw three soldiers looking suspiciously at a white van with Israeli license plates parked between the school and the store. The soldiers seemed angry. This was the same group of soldiers who have accompanied the school children the past few days. When I realized they were concerned about the van, I mistakenly told them that the Israelis who came in the van were at the school. I soon learned the Israelis came in another van. The soldiers angrily told me there was a problem and headed toward the school where I put them in touch with Liat, an Israeli woman.

The soldiers headed back to the van, arrested the driver, and tied his wrists behind his back. The soldiers were horribly rude, arrogant, and aggressive, but not physically abusive. They told a team member she could not film them. She continued filming them. Soon a dozen village women, including Hajji Fatima, who was lecturing them in Arabic, surrounded the soldiers. I felt sorry for the poor soldiers. They seemed frightened. They ordered everyone to move away, but the villagers only moved closer. Not one person obeyed any of the soldiers' commands. They were practically powerless. What can one do, even if armed with an M-16, when one's orders are ignored and everything is being filmed? They moved the handcuffed young man to the other side of the jeep, but the women also moved to the other side of the jeep. The village women were calm but strong. They provided the handcuffed man a lot of emotional support.

After about ten minutes the soldiers put the man into the back of their jeep and drove away. I was worried. What would they do to him? They drove to below the village, stopped, and let the man out of the jeep. Soon Palestinians in a pickup truck stopped beside the soldiers and, after a few minutes, brought back the man the soldiers had taken. I said to some men, "I do not understand." They told me, "It is better to not understand." I was upset with the whole scene but realized the Palestinians were calm. They consider the soldiers to be ignorant and crude and were not surprised by how the soldiers act. The villagers are not as naïve as I am.

As I now understand the story, the soldiers knew that many Palestinians would be coming back today from work in Israel and that the van parked in At-Tuwani was waiting to pick up returning workers. When the soldiers entered the village, about six men ran and hid until the soldiers left. They were then picked up by another vehicle. I learned that the white van is used to transport workers at a very high price, similar to "Coyotes" on the USA/Mexican border. If one tries to get into Israel without using these transports, one is more likely to be arrested. The whole thing is a racket. The transporters are collaborators. A villager explained that the soldiers took the man to get information or money and released him when they got what they wanted.

I headed toward the school to watch the four clowns entertain the children who loved every minute of it. These clowns came to the village with a different attitude than did the soldiers. They came in friendship, without guns, and received a positive response. I wondered, "Are the people who sent the young soldiers here really that ignorant and naïve, that clueless about what makes for peace?" The clowns arrived at the school quite late because Israeli soldiers held them up for a long time. Do the soldiers also feel threatened by clowns?

John and I went with the children at one o'clock. The soldiers were waiting. I went up to the soldiers in the jeep and apologized to them for telling them that the white van was Israeli, which was not true. I wanted to say something to break the tension between us from this morning. They accepted what I said and told me there is no problem.

Some boys told us at six o'clock this evening that there were soldiers down on the settler road. John and I headed down there and saw the soldiers maintaining a flying checkpoint on the road. The soldiers were stopping most every vehicle but didn't seem to be causing any problems. They held one car for maybe fifteen minutes. After an hour they dismantled the checkpoint, just as two villagers were returning from work in Israel, so we walked up the road with them. That was neat.

We got a call at quarter of nine saying soldiers were down on the road again and had stopped people who wanted to come to

Flying checkpoint.

the village. We could see soldiers in the darkness when we got near the road. Soon there were lights being pointed at us. I knew these lights were mounted on their guns so they could see us in the dark I didn't like having those guns pointed at us, but this time I didn't yell at them to not point their guns at me. I wanted to de-escalate the tension. I called out, "Shalom, shalom." They said "Halt," but I said "Shalom, shalom," and we kept walking toward them.

When we got close to them we saw there were six soldiers with no vehicle. A Palestinian car was stopped across the road. The soldiers were fairly hostile, told us they don't speak English, and acted like they didn't want to talk with us. But almost immediately we were talking. They asked us all kinds of questions, anything from where we came from to what we were doing there. They seemed to know quite a bit about us. We told them we came from the village because we heard they were preventing people from coming into At-Tuwani. They denied that and said that they had only arrested one person who was driving a stolen car. We didn't know if that was true.

They began a critique of CPT, saying we side only with the

Arabs and are anti-Jewish. I told them we want to talk with the
Ma'on people, but they refuse. I said we want to work with both
sides, but that is impossible. When I told them many Israelis
come here to At-Tuwani, including today, they dismissed that,
saying only people from the extreme left come here. They
described their accompanying school children past the settlement as unnecessary, saying the children just need to learn to live
in the real world, that no soldiers protected them when they
went to school, even though they sometimes were beaten on the
way to school. It may be true that some of them were beaten on
the way to school (I was too), but I doubt that the people who
attacked them were adults, or that their attackers had the power
of the Israeli establishment behind them.

They questioned why we are here. "Why don't you deal
with your problems in America?" I told them that we work in
the United States and Canada also. "Why don't you go to Iraq?"
I said my wife is there and I intend to go there in two weeks.
They wondered if we relate to American soldiers in Iraq. The
more we talked the more they warmed up to us.

I wondered, how could we do things differently so as not
to appear totally pro-Palestinian? The problem is that the injustice and violence here comes mainly from one side and that it is
impossible to stand with the settlers. Have I been one-sided
recently? I related to both Israelis and Palestinians in positive
ways today. How did I take sides today? I was ready to protect
Jews if they were being attacked.

I walked across the road to talk to the Palestinians in the
stopped car. They said they thought there was no problem.
They were just waiting to get back their ID's. After a half hour,
a big military troupe carrier arrived, the Palestinians got back
their ID's, and the soldiers left.

January 20, 2007, Saturday

About twelve Israelis came this morning to accompany
farmers as they plowed their fields near settlements. John, Bob,

Israelis and team members accompany a plowing.

and the two Doves went first to Mufakara, and then to Khoruba where villagers plowed with four donkeys while soldiers were up by the Ma'on outpost. They saw a few settlers, but there were no problems. Ezra and others went to a small village near Beit Yatir where a settler gave them trouble. Soldiers came and threatened the Israeli activists, pointing their guns at the Israelis and shooting in the air. Police came and took Ezra's ID, claiming he had assaulted a soldier. Ezra then went to the Kiryat Arba police station to make a complaint against the soldiers. The Ta'ayush people had it all on video.

January 22, 2007, Monday

I greeted the Tuba children as they came to school. They said two settlers yelled curses at them as they walked past the settlement this morning.

The children got out of school at 10:30 this morning. We waited until about 12:50 when the soldiers came. I had a good time with the children, talking about religion, my children, America, etc. I helped one boy read his English book. Some of the children gathered herbs.

At about 12:40, Gdalia drove up in his white pickup truck. I walked toward his truck, greeted him in Hebrew, and explained to him that we were waiting since 10:30. He immediately called the military and also informed them that they should come every day this week at 11:00, because there are exams this week. I thanked him.

I then told him I will be leaving for Iraq in a week and that I really want to sit and listen to people in Ma'on. He said, "I think you are a lost cause." I said, "I probably am a lost cause, but I really do want to listen and understand." Then I told him that every week back home I go to the synagogue on Friday evenings for Shabbat prayers. He seemed impressed with that. I then asked him to take my telephone number, so he could call me. He agreed and put my number into his cell phone. He didn't commit himself to anything, but I suspect he will talk with others in Ma'on about me.

We then had a short conversation about the horrible situation in Iraq. He said it is worse there than for the Palestinians here. I agreed and said a bit about how the Palestinians are suffering in Iraq, and how our team has accompanied Palestinians to the Jordanian and Syrian borders. He actually used the word "Palestinian." He wished me well and drove away.

Within a few minutes the soldiers arrived. Soldiers do what Gdalia tells them to do. I greeted the soldiers, the same ones who were at the checkpoint Thursday evening. They seemed just a bit hostile. I explained that they should come every day this week at 11:00. I them told them it is important that they walk with the children because they need the exercise to be strong. They said they get enough exercise.

Instead of driving through the mud at the gate, two soldiers walked with the children, and the other two drove around to the other side. One of them asked us to walk with them, so we walked with them to the gate. They wanted us to walk with them the whole way past Ma'on, but I told them we were not allowed to accompany the children past the gate. They didn't seem to know that. They asked me if I know Ezra. I said, "Yes." They claimed that Ezra assaulted and pushed a military officer on Saturday. The Israelis on Saturday said this was not true and could prove it with their videotapes. I said I wasn't there, did not know what happened, and do not approve of anyone assaulting anyone, no matter who it is. I agreed to talk with Ezra. I think my conversation with the soldiers may have broken some ice between us.

This evening during our worship time we read the story of Jesus and the woman caught in adultery. Her hypocrite accusers (Where was the man?) had judged and condemned the woman, and had decided to exclude her, as they considered themselves better than she. They would decide her fate for her. But Jesus' response opened new possibilities, new beginnings, for everyone involved. That is our task. Instead of building walls and barriers to exclude people, instead of cutting off possibilities, we can offer hope and new beginnings to everyone. That is the meaning of grace. It would be a horrible sin to put Gdalia and the Ma'on settlers into a box, to label them and not be open to them. If we harden our hearts to them, we have become like them. Before God, each day we are offered new beginnings and the possibility to start anew. Why not extend the same grace to others?

This evening the sky became dark from a huge cloud of smoke coming from the Hebron garbage dump between here and Hebron. I thought, "There in the sky is the trash the Hebron team produces each day." Burning trash is standard procedure here. One way to get rid of garbage is to dump it into the atmosphere, into the air we breathe. I shared my disgust with some of the village men. It seemed to be a new idea for them, but they saw the insanity of poisoning the air we breathe. The injustice of the Occupation is so small compared to our trashing the future of all life on this planet. There is a simple way to stop putting all that pollution into the air: stop producing trash.

January 23, 2007, Tuesday

This afternoon I saw a short video of an interview with a young couple from Pittsburgh who lives in Havot Ma'on. They said CPT bought a car for a terrorist in Hebron, gave money to Arabs, were leftists, and made up the stories about settler violence. One example they gave was how we made a big deal about settlers yelling at the school children. There was no hint that the Ma'on settlers ever do anything wrong. But we all try to justify ourselves, don't we? It is difficult to accept that we are justified by God's love and grace. How different things would be if we could accept grace.

Seeing the video made me even more want to talk with those settlers. But why would the settlers want to talk with us? The settlers here believe that Jews are a superior race, better and different than all other people, the only people loved by God. Add to this their belief that since Jews are hated by all other people, Jews must stand together in solidarity against everyone else. They believe there is no other country or people on whom they can depend. So why would they in any way cooperate with us?

This minimalist view is an extremely dangerous view, and is not supported by history. It is significant that during the Holocaust, over half of the Jews survived in eight of the twenty-one countries allied with or occupied by Germany. Non-Jewish support was essential to the survival of those Jews. It is not true that Jews stood alone. It is true that non-Jews should have done much more (See Murray Polner and Naomi Goodman, *The Challenge of Shalom*, Philadelphia, New Society Publishers. 1994, pp. 59-81). Any group that argues that they must stand alone is pointing to disaster. We all need each other. To cut ourselves off from others is to cut ourselves off from God.

Not all settlers are closed to others. About a month ago some of us decided to walk up Shuhada Street in Hebron, since it is now a Jewish-only street, even though the Israelis promised to open it after the United States spent millions repairing that street. It felt a bit scary walking up the street. When we got up to the Beit

Hadassah settlement, I saw Arnold Feurerstein standing in front of Beit Hadassah, a settler I first met twelve years ago. We enthusiastically greeted and hugged each other to the amazement of the other settlers there. He obviously was happy to see me. We then engaged in an animated conversation. Other settlers watched us, looking very unhappy with us talking together in front of their settlement, but they did not interrupt us. I considered this a victory: a friendly conversation with a settler in front of Beit Hadassah and the settlers not feeling free to interrupt us.

Then another settler drove up, a hostile man from Florida with whom I once had a conversation but who has since ignored me. Arnold introduced me to him, and he seemingly had no choice but to be civil with me. I asked him how he saw the situation here. He said he sees no hope, that you can't make peace with the Arabs. "As long as there are Arabs here, there will never be peace."

January 24, 2007, Wednesday

A man came by this morning and said that they were again having problems from the soldiers and wanted us to come to his home in Karmil where team members visited January 17. Some of us visited the family. We listened to their story. A week ago soldiers came to their house at 2:00 in the morning and stayed until 4:00. They were looking for three sons who were not there. Instead, the soldiers ended up kicking and beating three other sons. Again this past Monday, soldiers returned to the house at 2:00 in the morning and searched the place. The soldiers handcuffed and blindfolded the father and three sons, took them about ten miles to Al-Farrar, and left them there along the road at 3:30 a.m. They walked home from there.

This morning Captain Zohar, who participated in both raids and claims to be the commander of intelligence for Shabbak in the Hebron District, called and told the family that unless twelve family members went to the DCO in Hebron within a half hour, "I will come with my soldiers and it will be very violent."

Rich Meyer called lawyers, human rights groups, and Israeli journalists. Because Captain Zohar had called the family on the telephone, the family had his number in their phone. Rich gave Zohar's number to the people he called. We know some people phoned Zohar. The family told their story to journalists. We expect their story to be in the Israeli media. The family got a call this evening from the International Committee for the Red Cross, so we know they are involved.

After conversations with family members, the question arose as to whether we should spend the night with the family. If soldiers come in the night, would it be better or worse for the family if we were there? We told the family that this was not a matter of politeness or hospitality, but that they should decide on the basis of what they think is best for them and that we would not be offended if they asked us to leave. The family seriously wrestled with this question away from our presence and concluded that they wanted us to stay for the night. Our team has often wrestled with this question. We think that sometimes our presence has made things worse for Palestinians, but over all, we believe our presence usually has reduced the violence and harassment.

Rich and I spent the night with the family. I took some time to orient myself as to where Rich and I would sleep, the location of the door soldiers most likely would come to, and where the various family members would be sleeping, and to plan for what we would do if soldiers came in the middle of the night. We agreed that Rich would have the video camera, and I would be the person to cheerfully greet the soldiers. I felt comfortable with that.

I thought of stories from other CPTers who experienced midnight raids. I thought back on the night of February 2, 2003, when I slept in a home in the Beqa'a Valley, two days after two Palestinians killed Dov's friend, Nati, and settlers rioted, destroying much Palestinian property. Settlers had broken most of the windows in the house in which I was sleeping. At about midnight, I was awakened by yelling, screaming, and pounding on the doors. My heart raced. I was sure it was settlers attacking the house again. I quickly jumped out of bed, got dressed, and prepared to face the settlers and to try out some of my non-violent tools. To my great relief, when I entered the living room, there stood four Israeli soldiers, yelling and screaming at the family, treating them like animals. Within ten seconds, the soldiers realized I was an American and instantly calmed down and began to treat the family with some degree of respect. They said they were looking for weapons. They still did a house search but didn't steal anything, destroy anything, or urinate or defecate on the beds and clothes as they often do. I believe my presence made a difference that night.

I thought of the nightly raids on Iraqi homes by American soldiers. They are trained to start with thirty to forty seconds of absolute furry in order to totally subdue the family and "ensure the safety of the soldiers." They do not seem to understand that treating Iraqis in this way builds up resentment and in the long run makes American soldiers less safe. I thought about Israeli soldiers training American soldiers how to do midnight raids. I knew something of what to expect if the soldiers came tonight.

We sat around the fire outside their house, ate, chatted, and enjoyed the beautiful night sky with all the stars and constellations. I experienced a deep peace as I sat with the family, not knowing what the night would bring. They seemed at peace.

January 25, 2007, Thursday

There were no problems last night. Was that because we were there? When we got up at six o'clock this morning, Mohammad was there with warm water and a towel for us. We were served a breakfast of taboon bread, olive oil, and hard-boiled eggs. We then left in time to walk to At-Tuwani and meet the children as they came to the gate.

On our way to meet the children, we walked past the olive grove that was demolished during the night of January 5, 2006, last year, where Israelis had trimmed the stumps and helped clean up the branches. It was encouraging to see green shoots growing out of the mangled stumps and limbs. What a sign of hope. Life springs anew. Death and destruction do not have the last word. Last year, Shaul Mofaz, then head of the Israeli military, said the farmers who lost trees would be compensated. I checked on that and was told there has been no compensation.

As we waited for the children, I realized that this was my last day with the children this winter. I again said my goodbyes to them.

At about half past ten, someone told us there were settlers up near the trees above the village. Rich and I rushed up there and saw some of them in the trees. We learned some settlers had come out of the woods and thrown stones at a shepherd and his flock while they were grazing up the Humra valley above the village. Rich tried to get some video footage of them. I didn't see any faces, but I did see a hand swinging a slingshot. A few stones landed around us.

I really wanted to just be vulnerable and walk up into the woods and face the settlers. That is what I wanted to do, but I was not clear that that was the right thing to do.

Then Gdalia drove up in his white pickup truck. I walked toward him, greeted him, and asked him how he was doing. "On such a beautiful day, I am doing fine." He then asked me when I am leaving to go to Iraq. I felt encouraged by that and said, "I really want to talk with some of you before I leave." "Maybe," he said. I told him, "I have two requests. I would like to meet with a group from Ma'on. If that is not possible, I want to talk with you." "I will see what I can do," he said. I was elated.

I then told him that there were people in the trees who were throwing stones at us and at the shepherds. He immediately called someone on his radio and then his cell phone. He had called the army, he explained. He then got out of the truck and looked into the trees with his binoculars. We could see the feet of settlers. After a bit he suggested we call the police and drove away. Rich then called the police at eleven o'clock, and described the situation. The police said they would call Gdalia. After ten minutes we saw Gdalia's truck up on the ridge to the west, above Mufakara.

I keep thinking about Gdalia. Why did he seem so concerned about the rock throwing? Is settler concern about being evicted part of the equation? The Israeli government has been saying that they will dismantle the "illegal" outposts. Last summer, the defense minister promised to remove the Havot Ma'on settlers, and the Israeli military was beginning to make preparations for the evacuation, including preparing a staging area across the road for the many soldiers and police that would be involved. After the war against Lebanon started, those plans were put on hold. This past fall, the defense minister again promised to remove the Havot Ma'on settlers. The people of Havot Ma'on have created many problems for the Israeli military and police, and there is strong pressure to remove them.

January 26, 2007, Friday

At 9:30 this morning we were told there were soldiers down on the road. Two Doves and I went down to the road. They had a regular flying checkpoint with signs and spikes on the road to ensure that people stop. It didn't appear that they were causing any trouble, but it still irked me that they were there. I decided to walk up to them and greet them. I had a bit of anger in my heart as I approached them, but greeted them in a friendly, welcoming way. I need to remember that I do not have enemies. It is the principalities and powers that we struggle against, not people. To act in love is a decision we can make. I wanted to go to them and vent my anger on them but that would not have been helpful. I greeted them with "Shabbat shalom." I recognized them from school patrol the past few days. I suggested that since there would be no school for two weeks, they could go home to be with their friends.

I talked mostly with a guy from Brazil. He asked what we

are doing here. I told him we are human rights observers and are concerned with settler attacks on Palestinians. He responded by saying that settlers never attack Palestinians. All the attacks here have come from Palestinians against settlers. I think he believed what he said. I assume settlers had told him these things.

How do we deal with perceptions that are based on lies? The last Palestinian attack on Israelis in this area that I know of was when Palestinians killed Dov in May 1999, about eight years ago, and that confrontation was initiated by Dov. Israeli activists just gave us a poster with a picture of a Palestinian girl killed by Israeli soldiers around a week ago. The poster points out that over eight hundred Palestinian children have been killed by Israeli soldiers since 2000. Apparently these soldiers do not know that. Apparently they do not know why they escort children past the Ma'on settlement. The other soldiers started dismantling the checkpoint as we talked.

We got a call this afternoon saying that the family in Karmil got another threatening phone call this afternoon from Zohar saying that the Red Cross, journalists, and foreigners will be of no help to them. Furthermore, the entire family must immediately report to the DCO or there will be big problems. Bob Holmes and I walked up to Karmil and visited the family. We were prepared to spend the night, but it became clear that they just wanted us to check in with them, not spend the night.

January 27, 2007 Saturday

I talked with a villager about my leaving on Monday to go to Iraq. I told him that it is difficult for me to leave, that my heart is here in At-Tuwani. The only thing that makes it less difficult for me to leave is my belief that the work I do at home for the cause of peace and justice in Israel/Palestine is much more important than the work I do in At-Tuwani, since the problems in At-Tuwani are rooted in America. His face lit up, he became animated, and he said, "Yes, yes. You understand." He gave me his blessing for the work I must do in sharing a vision of hope and peace for the Israeli and Palestinian peoples. As I go home, I want to work together with others to oppose injustice and work for that day when "Justice will flow like waters, and righteousness like a mighty stream." Inshallah.

November 29, 2007-February 29, 2008

November 29, 2007, Thursday

Danny Yahini and Patty Mercer, friends from Ohio, met me at the airport in Tel Aviv and drove me to Jerusalem where we had lunch in the Jewish market, a place of suicide bombings in the past. We then drove south from Jerusalem, past Bethlehem, toward Hebron and At-Tuwani. I told stories of places we passed along the way. We stopped at the Jabers in the Beqa'a Valley and had a delightful visit with them. They are doing well, but there have been home demolitions and problems from settlers. I continue to feel part of the Jaber family.

We then drove into At-Tuwani. I was thrilled to see that the wall along the settler road was gone. The Israeli military had been refusing to remove the wall, but this summer finally agreed to remove the wall that the high court had declared illegal last December. Peggy was here in July when the military removed it. All the work people put into opposing that wall did pay off.

I also was pleasantly surprised to see how much the damaged olive trees below the village had grown in the last year. Those trees are not giving up.

I spent time with the team and learned there are no Doves here right now. Jan Benvie from Scotland was here last year. Jonathan Stucky is from Colombia, in South America. His father is a Mennonite pastor who I remember meeting some years ago. Josh Hough is from Oregon. He said an important part of his motivation for working here was the impact of Rachel Corrie's death on him. Josh told me that Rachel's death "set a fire in me that would not die. A movement against such injustice demanded my involvement." Since I knew Rachael and have seen two versions of the play "My Name Is Rachel Corrie," it means a lot to me to meet a person so influenced by her death.

I saw and greeted people at the beautiful, newly completed mosque. This past Monday, at the very same time as Palestinians and Israelis, along with representatives from forty-four other countries, were meeting in Annapolis, Maryland, with George Bush for the first peace initiative in years, Israeli soldiers came to At-Tuwani and delivered a demolition order on the new mosque. I have been quite cynical about the lofty, empty rhetoric coming from Bush, the Israelis, and the Palestinians at that meeting. I did not hear one thing specific that gave me any sense of hope. Issuing this demolition order for the mosque on that day makes me even more cynical. I would like to see just one thing that indicates that the Israeli government has decided to give up its policy of taking more and more from the Palestinians and instead now will seek peace. I will be looking for signs of change during my three months here in At-Tuwani this winter.

The villagers have decided to ignore the demolition order. I have been thinking about doing civil disobedience if the soldiers come to demolish the mosque. I am ready to do that, but I am also asking if I am willing to face the possibility of getting arrested and not being allowed to come back here again. That would be horrible. But if I am to be faithful, I also have to be willing to give up that.

Merefat, Juma and Sarriya's twelve-year-old daughter, died suddenly a few weeks ago. I remember her well. I gave my condolences to the family. They said, "Allah karim."

November 30, 2007, Friday

This morning Jonathan and I sat at the top of the hill south of At-Tuwani, right below the Ma'on outpost, accompanying a villager as he plowed his land and planted barley. This is the fall planting season. We heard music and voices coming from settlers in the trees just above us, which made me feel somewhat nervous. I asked myself if I was ready to be beat up today by settlers.

December 1, 2007, Saturday

This morning, between 150 and 200 activists, mostly Israelis from Ta'ayush and Combatants for Peace, came into the village for a big demonstration. People from other villages also joined us and Palestinians from as far as Ramallah. The plan was for us to march to Tuba to accompany plowing there, protest the closing of the road to Tuba, and call for removal of the settlements. We marched up beyond the village where soldiers and police stopped everyone. I had worried that they might not even allow the buses to come here as they sometimes have done in the past. Now I wondered if they had declared the area a closed military zone and would prevent anyone from going anywhere.

Within thirty seconds I noticed that the Israelis were gently pushing through the soldiers' line. Ta'ayush has a lot of experience pushing through lines of soldiers. The soldiers pushed back a few Israelis, but it was too much for the soldiers, and soon they were trying to keep up with the mass of people who were surging ahead.

I felt sorry for the poor soldiers. Their guns were useless. They were powerless. They were not going to shoot a group of fellow Israelis. If it had been Palestinians it may have been different.

I was clear that I did not want to get arrested. In fact, I had some misgivings about participating in the demonstration since the Israelis were calling for the removal of the settlers. It is not for CPT to say whether or not the settlers should be removed. That is between Israelis and Palestinians. If there were a one-state solution, many of the settlers would remain. Our work is to support Palestinian nonviolent resistance and help balance the power equation between Israelis and Palestinians as they face questions like that. We do stand for justice, but it is not for outsiders to tell the people here what they should think or decide. I did feel comfortable being an observer for the demonstration, prepared to intervene in problems.

It quickly became clear to me that I should walk with the Palestinians at the end of the march and be prepared to protect them in case they were attacked. It was not clear to me how to intervene in possible fights between right-wing and left-wing Israelis.

When we got to the top of the hill, Ezra told me to stay there to accompany an At-Tuwani family plowing there. I didn't want to hear that, since I really wanted to march in the protest to Tuba and be part of the action there. I knew, however, that Ezra was probably right about my needing to stay there. I also remembered that when I am submitted to doing God's will, things go much better than when I seek to do my own thing. To make sure, I checked with other At-Tuwani people there and they agreed that I should stay with them in case settlers attacked, something that seemed like a real possibility. I resigned myself to staying there.

I spent much of my time listening to conversations between villagers. Occasionally we would see settlers up the hill at the edge of the trees. At about quarter past twelve we saw a few settlers coming toward us. Two Israeli men walked toward the settlers. I was not sure what would happen, but they soon got into an animated conversation. About six local Palestinians walked up and joined the conversation. I also went to listen. Soon there were about twelve people on both sides.

I could hardly call it a conversation. About five people on each side were yelling at the people on the other side. Actually, it is possible to be yelling and at the same time hearing what the other side is saying, but I would rather people spend more time listening than talking. If we are serious about reconciliation we must stop considering others as evil and as enemies to be defeated, stop labeling them, treat them with love and respect, and actually listen to their concerns. We need to build bridges.

The settlers seemed hostile and the others condemning. Afterward one of the Israelis was quite upset and said the settlers sounded like Hitler. He refused to translate for me what the settlers had said "because it was too bad to repeat." I know they accused the activists of sleeping with Arabs. I stayed off to the sidelines, but a few times I repeated the Shema in Hebrew to everyone. I am not sure if they understood the point or not.

A little later, Combatants for Peace people walked up close to the trees where about twelve settlers had gathered, and there was another big confrontation with Israelis yelling at each other. There was a lot of animated dialogue between a young settler woman and a woman Combatant for Peace.

I stayed on the sidelines. I got to talk a bit with one of the settlers and told him I wanted to come to Ma'on to listen to and try to understand them. He said that was impossible because we stand with the Arabs. I persisted in saying I want to understand, that one reason we are always with the Palestinians is that we are prevented from relating to the settlers. He seemed to hear that. I told him I worship in the synagogue back home each Friday evening.

At the end of our conversation, he seemed somewhat open to us talking. I suggested he talk to Gdalia about me and my request to meet with settlers. I was overjoyed that we even had this conversation. I refuse to give up on anyone or consider anyone my enemy. I missed talking to Gdalia, but I saw him driving around in his white truck.

I then talked with the woman from Combatants for Peace who had been in the army in Gaza, experienced horrendous things, and left the army full of anger at the military and her father who had forced her into the army. She has worked through that anger and is now working for peace. She told me two hundred former Israeli soldiers and two hundred former Palestinian militants came together to form Combatants for Peace. I was quite impressed with their nonviolent vision for ending the Occupation, their vision for Israelis and Palestinians to come together, and their personal radical commitment to work for change. She said our conversation gave her a new sense of hope.

When the villager finished his plowing and was ready to head back to At-Tuwani, soldiers stopped him and made him wait, after which two older At-Tuwani women started screaming at the soldiers. One soldier became very aggressive, yelled at the women to shut up, pointed his gun right up close at the women, and became very hostile. I was worried. Apparently so was the squad leader, who tried to calm him down. The soldier became hostile to his leader who then ordered the soldier to go up to the jeep, and stand there for a while, the way one would make a child stand in a corner for a time out.

Soon we saw the large group heading back from Tuba. It was an impressive sight to see all those hundreds of Israelis and Palestinians coming over the ridge, walking around the outpost and chanting as they marched. Police were at the head of the procession, with lots of soldiers walking among the trees above the marchers, with more soldiers at the rear. This time the soldiers were prepared to protect the demonstrators.

Things went well over around Tuba. Various villagers were out plowing with their tractors or donkeys as the Israelis milled around, watched, and engaged in conversation. There were two problems. Three soldiers confiscated the tractor keys of a farmer who was plowing. The farmer got the tractor restarted and continued plowing. A settler also beat up a Tuba boy and stole his donkey. Note: As of February 28, 2008, the settlers still have the donkey.

Jan and Jonathan and two people (David and Martha) from Michigan Peace Team stayed on in Tuba as protection in case settlers attacked during the night in retaliation for today. It is important that people stay behind after an action in case there are problems after others have left. Maybe some Israelis need to stay behind after they do actions here.

I deeply appreciate the Israelis coming here, but there are also things I do not appreciate. Israelis are so assertive and in need of being in control. It was interesting that during the speeches, all Arabic was translated into Hebrew, but no Hebrew was translated into Arabic. Things look different from a position of power than from the bottom.

December 2, 2007, Sunday

It started raining during the night and continued through the morning. What a blessing right after all the recent planting. This was the first good rain of the season. We got between a half and three quarters of an inch.

It was a joy to meet the ten children again this morning on this first day of school since my return. There now is school only five days a week, with Fridays and Saturdays off. They did ask if I had prayed. I was sorry I did not see them yesterday in Tuba. We walked together to At-Tuwani in the rain and mud.

This afternoon Jan and I went to Khoruba to watch for the children. The soldiers came two hours late, so we got cold sitting in the wind. Was the soldiers coming late a way to punish the people here for the action yesterday, lest we forget who is in control? It ends up with the children suffering. What does it do to the children to have to stand in the cold for two hours? Yet this is the one place in the occupied territories where children run toward the soldiers when they see them coming.

I spent the evening with Nasser, Kiefah, and children. That was a delightful time. Adam was afraid of me at first but then warmed up. We ended up playing ball together.

December 3, 2007, Monday

I spent some time this morning with shepherds over north of Ma'on where we had confrontations with soldiers three years ago. We saw no soldiers or settlers. There was little grass, but the sheep did nibble on the brush. I thought of how unsustainable this grazing is. Before the little blades of grass are eaten, they need to do some photosynthesis to restore strength to the roots. I saw sheep nibbling the crown of the plants just above the roots, destroying the little grass that is there.

December 4, 2007, Tuesday

There was no school because of a teachers' strike to protest not having been paid from last year.

Jan and I rushed down to the road at 2:20 and saw maybe twenty soldiers who informed us that settlers were having a race on the road this afternoon and that the road was closed. The soldiers had put rocks across our road near the settler road. Two years ago a bulldozer dug a ditch across the road to close the road for a similar race. Since there was Israeli traffic on the road, I told the soldiers that the road did not look closed to me. "It's closed for Arabs," a soldier told me. I asked why Jews could use the road but not Palestinians. "We do what we do because we can." I asked him if he thought this would bring peace. "There can never be peace with Arabs," he said. "They do all the bad things here."

Soon we saw runners on the road while Israeli cars kept whizzing by in both directions. An Israeli woman on a horse went through a group of runners and struck one of them. One of the runners had a rifle slung over his shoulder.

The Israeli soldiers were acting in a horribly racist manner, humiliating the Palestinians. The Palestinians engaged the soldiers in conversation and seemed to be doing a good job of breaking through the walls in the soldiers' minds. I hope that helped break down some of the stereotypes these soldiers have of Palestinians. Probably some of them had never before spoken with Palestinians. At one point in the conversation they were talking about peace. A Palestinian said, "Shalom is from Allah." I chimed in, "Shalom is from Allah, not from the military or from guns."

By quarter past three, the race was over, but the soldiers said the road would be closed until five o'clock. An At-Tuwani woman tried to cross the road at 3:40 with her donkey and two children, one of whom was sick. Jan intervened to get the soldiers to allow the woman to go home. The soldiers refused even though the race was over. They did open the road at 4:10.

Could the soldiers have not known that what they were doing was racist, humiliating, and wrong? Our continual presence there kept reminding them of that. Forcing people to do things they know are wrong creates horrible psychological problems for those soldiers in the future, something common among soldiers. I doubt people can ever be adequately trained to enforce occupation, a task more difficult than fighting a war. Oppressing people is so contrary to how God has created us.

Why did the military act as they did today? Certainly there is nothing wrong with closing a road for a race. But they didn't close the road for a race. The traffic kept whizzing by. Part of the reason probably was to prove again to the Palestinians who has the power. Part of it is simple racism. But part of it also is paranoia. The Israelis live in deathly fear of the people they oppress. If they want to have a race, they want security for that race. The simple answer was to remove all the Palestinians from the area. But their simplistic answers only make Israelis less secure. Actions like this only store up trouble for the future. How sad. Better would be to invite Palestinians to join the race.

December 6, 2007, Thursday

The children got out at 11:00 today. We called the army at 10:25 to remind them. I waited until 11:20 and called the soldiers again. They said they were on their way, but it took twenty more minutes for them to arrive. It was cold waiting. When the soldiers arrived at 11:40 I went up to the jeep to greet them. They opened the door a crack, and I said, "Shalom, shalom, Happy Hanukah." They closed the door and were on their way. These soldiers are not friendly. I will take it as a challenge to break through some of the walls these soldiers have built up.

I had a good time with the children as we waited. They started asking me what kinds of food I like. They listed many foods, half of which I recognized. That was fun.

We want to do something about the soldiers continually being late for school escorts. We are going to make a list of all the times in the last three months that the soldiers were late. We will then give this list to the Israelis who have been working on this issue.

December 8, 2007, Saturday

This afternoon three of us walked over to Mufakara to visit a family. I met a daughter and two grandchildren of Maher, a Mufakara nonviolent leader who was killed in an auto accident about a month ago. I expressed my condolences to the family.

Shortly after we got back, we learned there was a problem with soldiers down on the road. The soldiers had made villagers on a tractor wait for a half hour before allowing them to go home. Jan and I walked in the dark toward the road. I thought of our times there on the road after dark last year. Soon we saw the lights of an army jeep across the road. Four soldiers had made about ten people get out of a van and stand in the cold along the road. After a few minutes the people got back in the van and went on their way.

Soon other vehicles came and were stopped. As each vehicle approached, the soldiers walked toward the car with their guns drawn, ready to shoot. After we got there, only the drivers had to get out of their vehicles. By the end of our time there, no one needed to get out of their vehicles. The last car did not even need to stop.

In between stopping vehicles, soldiers surveyed the whole area with their night vision goggles. They probably were afraid. I would have been afraid if I had been one of them. We tried to engage them in conversation, but they didn't seem to want to talk.

At first, Jan and I stood maybe twenty-five feet apart, but it was cold and soon we were standing downwind near the jeep with its engine running. That kept us warm. Gradually the soldiers showed interest in talking. They asked who we were and what we were doing. They told us the problem here is the Arabs who cause all the problems. They said the answer is to arrest all Hamas people.

We told them we want shalom. They said there can never be shalom with the Arabs. "The Arabs are animals." I challenged that and said, "God is one and created us all." I repeated the Shema in Hebrew. One soldier said he didn't believe in God. I didn't respond to the subject of God but said, "There is no hope for peace if we accept racist attitudes toward people. It is important that we affirm our common humanity."

I asked them why they needed to escort children every day. "Oh, the people in Ma'on are stupid," they replied. I said, "So there are problems on both sides?" They didn't reply.

I told them my generation messed up things and I hoped their generation will do better. "We need to think creatively and find better answers," I told them. One soldier said, "Oh, like John Lennon said in his song 'Imagine …'

You may say I'm a dreamer,
But I'm not the only one."

Everyone wants peace, but the leaders of the domination system have convinced many people that peace is a pipe dream. I referred to the fact that last Saturday about two hundred Israelis came here to stand with the Palestinians here. "I know peace is possible. I saw it again last Saturday." I would guess they were among the fifty or more soldiers there.

At this point one of the soldiers started cursing, and I knew that the conversation had gone as far as possible. When people get agitated, it is a sign that something deep was touched within them. At this point, everything must be left to God. Our task is to plant seeds.

Soon the soldiers gathered their stop signs and strips of spikes they put across the road, and were on their way. We wished them goodnight in Hebrew. It was half past seven. We had stood there for two hours. It seemed to us that the soldiers became less aggressive the longer we were there.

December 9, 2007, Sunday

We had some unexpected "guests" today. Settlers organized an "educational" hike today for Israelis to become acquainted with the settlements and all the land that they think will be theirs. They hiked from Susya to Ma'on. We first saw the group of over fifty Israelis sitting and milling around in an olive grove below the village. It was not clear what was happening. Soon they all started hiking toward At-Tuwani. They were all wearing backpacks and looked like middle class Israelis out on a hiking trip. They casually walked through the village, taking pictures of buildings and caves, acting like the village belonged to them.

I asked a woman, maybe fifty-five, where she was from. In a condescending tone of voice, she said, "Israel." She asked me where I was from and what I was doing here. I said we are here to try to lower the violence against the people here. She became defensive and said, "But what do you think about these villagers attacking the people in Ma'on?" At that point her phone rang and that was the end of our conversation. I could have told her that according to the Israeli military, seventeen Israelis were killed by Palestinians in 2006 and 652 Palestinians were killed by Israelis. That is a ratio of 38 to 1. I suspect that before the hike, they had been told that these villagers were very violent. I was impressed, however, with how they walked around the village seemingly without any fear. Actually, they were quite safe. No one from this village was going to attack them. Jan did tell the hikers that coming into the village like that was frightening for the villagers, and they should not do it again.

Josh and Jan walked with the hikers up to the cistern on the right in the Humra valley. It looked to them like a hiker poured something into the cistern. We wondered if it was poison so we alerted the villagers, and the water will be tested. Note: The water was tested and had a ph of 2.4 (7-9 is normal, meaning the water was very alkaline). It also had a high concentration of solubles. Action Against Hunger, a Spanish aid group, came to look at the cistern, and has paid for cleaning and repairing the cistern.

I went to the gate with the children this afternoon. I called the army twice and then called Iudit, our lawyer at Yesh Din. I told her the army has been consistently late. She said she would work on it. The jeep finally came at 2:00, an hour and a half late.

December 10, 2007, Monday

The soldiers were late again this morning. They arrived at the gate at 8:22, almost an hour late. The soldiers stopped before the gate so I did not get their jeep number.

The school closed at 10:15 this morning because the teachers went on strike again. We immediately called the army to let them know, but they didn't come until 12:07. Jan and I were at Khoruba, so we had another long wait up there.

December 15, 2007, Saturday

Jan, John Funk, and I went up to Sarura to accompany an eighty-six-year-old man and his grandson plowing with two donkeys. I met the man yesterday, the father of a woman here in the village, and learned that he used to live in the abandoned village of Sarura. He left in 1999 because of settler harassment. Our neighbor grew up in the cave up the hill west of Sarura. Her husband lived in Sarura when he was a child. It is good to make this connection since we have so much interaction with their children. It felt good to have that contact with the abandoned village that we pass every day on our way to Khoruba and be able to connect that land with specific people.

December 16, 2007, Sunday

I left At-Tuwani early this morning, walked to Karmil, and got a car to Yatta, then to Hebron, and on to Bethlehem. I was surprised by the vast amount of settlement expansion in the last year. I am still waiting to see evidence of any movement toward peace.

I was dismayed to see quite a few Palestinian police on the streets with rifles. In my twelve years of visiting the West Bank, I have rarely seen Palestinian police with guns. It is discouraging to see this new development. I have been aware that the CIA is spending huge amounts of money to train and arm the Fatah Palestinian faction. Does America want to militarize everyone around the world? I wish the United States would teach nonviolence instead of violence to the world. The last thing the Middle East needs is more guns, more training in violence, and more encouragement to use violence to solve problems.

The trip to Bethlehem took three hours. Using Israeli roads, I could have made that trip in a half hour. Seeing Israeli settlers waiting at Israeli bus stops near the settlements reminded me of the apartheid system the Israelis are creating, the separate transportation systems being only one example. Having separate vehicles and separate roads for Israelis and Palestinians is a serious rejection of the oneness of God. I thought of the exciting possibilities that could come out of Jews, Muslims, and Christians joining together to rediscover their common religious roots, and witnessing our common belief in the oneness of God, in order to oppose this apartheid system.

After worship in Bethlehem I went to the Beqa'a Valley and spent the afternoon and night with the Sultan family, and renewed my relationship with them. They are doing well.

John and a Dove went to Sh'eb Botom to accompany Abu Khalil as he plowed below the illegal outpost of Mitzpe Yair. Soldiers told Abu Khalil that he could plow the land, but it was foolish because the settlers will destroy the crop. They plowed the land to keep ownership of the land for the future. Peggy spent three days there this past summer accompanying shepherds grazing their flocks near a settlement.

December 19, 2007, Wednesday

I went up to the mosque at 5:00 this morning for Eid prayers. We chanted until 7:00. We did the chanting as two groups, each group trying to be louder than the other. The children really got into that. It was an inspiring time for me.

I was invited to go up and join the Adara family in sacrificing a sheep. I helped just a bit. There were more workers than work needing to be done. I met a lot of extended family who stopped by for short visits. After lunch I came home.

December 23, 2007, Sunday

Sean O'Neill came back yesterday from a break back home in Springfield, Ohio. He was here with Peggy last summer. We now have two Doves with us again, after having no Doves here for several months.

School started again today. Sean and I went to the gate this afternoon. The soldiers were waiting at one o'clock, but only two children were there. We waited until after half past one before the rest of the children came. The soldiers seemed patient and asked what we do here. I told them the history of the school patrol, about which they seemed to know nothing. They didn't know that we are not allowed to walk with the children past Ma'on and seemed surprised that we write reports on what happens each day, like if they are late, walk with the children, etc. The driver said he didn't know they were to walk with the children. The commander said he did know that and then walked with the children without a gun. That surprised me. In response to my saying that there have been many attacks from settlers on the people here, the commander said there are many stories told that are not true.

December 24, 2007, Monday

Villagers burned the trash in the dumpster this afternoon. There was a huge plume of black smoke. One family was sitting out in the smoke. Much of what they burned was plastic. I worry about the health effects ten or twenty years from now. What can I do? The answer is written on the wall of our house here: Refuse, reduce, reuse, repair, and then recycle. We need to do that, in that order. Stop producing trash. Refusing and reducing are the most important.

I have been thinking about the soldiers saying to us "Because we can" as to why they do what they do. I am always horrified by that because it is an explicit rejection of any ethical guidelines in relationship to one's behavior. The soldiers can do anything they want "because they can."

How different are we from those soldiers? Why do we use our privilege, be it Western, educational, class, race, gender or what ever, to justify our oppressive, wasteful behaviors? Why do we consume more than our share of the world's resources? Why do we turn on lights when we do not need to? Why do we dump huge amounts of carbon and toxins into the atmosphere every day for frivolous reasons? "Because we can."

Why do we buy the products of corporations who steal, oppress, and ravage the earth, even when there are other products available or the products are not even necessary for living a good life? "Because we can."

I have no moral standing to look in judgment on those soldiers. I am no better than they are. I also am in need of grace.

December 25, 2007, Tuesday

There was no school today because of Christmas. It was a beautiful, warm, sunny day in the mountains of Palestine. Jan and I spent the morning accompanying a villager and his children plowing and sowing wheat with two donkeys. We were working in a narrow valley just below the village of Sarura, which the villagers abandoned in 1999 because of repeated attacks on the village from Israeli settlers. The family we were accompanying lived in that village before settlers forced them to leave. The father showed us the cave he used to live in. Since Sarura had been a Roman village, I thought of the Roman occupiers at the time of Jesus. The Roman caves are still there, as are the ruins of Roman houses.

The Romans are long gone, but, like two thousand years ago, this is occupied land, controlled by people who wield worldly power. We were standing with the shepherds, with the dispossessed, people like those to whom the angels announced good news two thousand years ago. There were flocks of sheep on the hills around us, an ideal setting for thinking about the birth of Jesus.

In spite of God's revelation in Jesus, people still rely on violence and oppression, still reject the promise of peace on earth as a gift from God. We, however, experienced God's peace as we broke bread and drank tea together as the donkeys rested and snacked on the wheat they were helping plant. We then ate lunch with the family when we came back to At-Tuwani.

The larger Adara family came to have a Christmas party with us. We made mtabug, a pastry something between cinnamon rolls and baklavah, which we enjoyed together.

December 27, 2007, Thursday

We had a team meeting today. What a relief to actually have a team meeting and talk to each other, instead of making decisions informally. Informal decision making leaves too many opportunities for control and power manipulation. Informal decision making is a use of power that is unaccountable and undemocratic. It does not encourage all voices to be heard. For example, I was informally asked to approve an important decision others made. It would have been very difficult for me to oppose the decision. I said I thought we needed to talk about it in an open way, which we did, and all of us agreed with the original suggestion. That felt a lot better to me.

December 29, 2007, Saturday

Yesterday afternoon two Israelis and two Palestinians died in a firefight west of Hebron. I was feeling very heavy and feared there would again be retaliation, and collective punishment, and the cycle of violence and repression would continue. We got the batteries charged up in the cameras last evening just in case there is trouble. We want to monitor the road more closely in the next few days. Soldiers down on the road did make people wait an hour and a half yesterday. It now appears that there will be no collective punishment. We heard that the Palestinian police have promised to take care of this, so maybe the Israelis will give the PA police a chance to prove they can do what Israel wants. Neither side is making a big issue of the killings.

December 30, 2007, Sunday

We got a call around half past eleven at night that there were settlers up at Juma's house. Since the others were going up I decided to stay here. By the time they got there the settlers were gone. The family heard noise on the roof, and then whoever it was ran away, scaring their sheep. Sean and a Dove ended up spending the night there. Everything was quiet the rest of the night. This morning we had a time for debriefing, talking about what we could have done better. Everyone felt they had handled it well. Much of the conversation was about who and when to call when there is real trouble. That conversation felt good to me.

December 31, 2007, Monday

Nasser asked for me to go with him to Susiya. Everyone agreed that today was a good time to go. It was a joy to be back in Susiya and greet people. They made me feel right at home.

I accompanied three Susiya villagers as we led a flock of sheep to Yatta. I think they sold them because of lack of food for the sheep. We walked west toward the archaeological ruins of a second century synagogue and church building, and the remains of Susiya village that was demolished, all of which is surrounded by a high fence and is closed to Palestinians. On our left was the military base from where the soldiers protect the settlers and enforce the Occupation. Much of the way was a forbidden area for Palestinians. It felt like they wanted me to accompany them for their protection.

We walked part of the way on the road that used to be the road from Jinba to Yatta, which now is supposed to be for Israelis only. Part of the way we walked along a narrow strip of land between the fence and the road. It was a great boost to my ego as the sheep followed me part of the way. We saw a few soldier jeeps drive by, including one that soldiers regularly use for the school escort. We had no problems from soldiers. Nasser told me sometimes they enforce the rule of no Palestinians and sometimes not.

After walking over a mile (Susiya is not far from Yatta if they could go straight there), we were close to Yatta, where about six Palestinians met us and took the sheep the rest of the way to Yatta. We headed back toward Susiya. They insisted that I ride the donkey on the way back. I denied that I am an old man and insisted that I am a shabaab (youth), but I had to ride the donkey. I also felt bad making that poor donkey carry me. This was my first time to ride a donkey, and I soon realized how inexperienced I was in keeping my balance. It was different from riding a horse with a saddle. I had to hold on tight. I also began to feel pain in my leg muscles, muscles that not much earlier I was not aware of having. After going a half mile, I had to stop. I ended up falling off the donkey as I tried to get off. So much for my youth. I did develop a friendship with the donkey as I gave it some love. The donkey snuggled its head in my arms as I rubbed its head. Donkeys do not get much love around here.

It was a lazy time the rest of the afternoon as I sat in the sun with various villagers. I then helped feed the sheep, helped take care of three small children as their parents did chores. This evening was a pleasant time with the family, but the whole time we sat in the tent I could see the light of the Susya settlement on the next hill. I wondered if settlers would attack us tonight. I wondered if the Israeli military will come and demolish all these primitive tents tomorrow morning and steal this land for the Susya settlement. Nothing has happened in the courts since last winter, which means that the Israeli military can demolish all the tents and remove everyone anytime they please. Only their fear of world opinion or an act of God can stop them now.

I thought of how fortunate I am. I have been given the gift

of intimacy with these simple Arabs living in tents, in danger of having their homes demolished any day, any hour, any minute, yet so full of love and joy. I thought of the settlers in the brilliantly lighted settlement on the next hill. They look down their noses at these poor Arabs, despise their very existence, and want the land cleansed and purified of these non-Jews. I wish they could see what I see.

January 1, 2008, Tuesday

Happy New Year! There was no school today. Mohammad came to the tent at five o'clock this morning, turned on the light (the electricity comes from a solar panel and a small wind turbine) and made tea for us.

I walked out this morning and saw the thirty-two olive trees that settlers cut down the night of December 6 in the valley between us and the settlement. One of our team members came here to Susiya the next day to take pictures to document the loss.

I helped feed the sheep, fed a lamb with a bottle, and again spent most of my time playing with and taking care of the three little children. I held the little girl most of the time, as I did yesterday evening. I came back to At-Tuwani this morning.

January 2, 2008, Wednesday

This evening about five boys, ages ten to thirteen, came with their wagon and wanted to haul some of the firewood from Hafez's house to our house. We are dividing a truckload of wood with Hafez and his family. Apparently they saw this old man carrying armfuls of wood and felt sorry for him. Later I saw them struggling with a load that kept turning over. I helped them get that wagonload down a steep hill and up another hill to our house. I thanked them profusely, and they replied, "But we love you, Jaber." I am deeply moved by that expression of love from those boys. I also feel a deep love for them, for everyone in this village. Every day, both here and at home, I pray for the people here.

January 3, 2008, Thursday

I went over to the gate at half past ten, and the seventeen children were already there. There are now seventeen children because families have moved back to Maghair al Abeed after spending the fall in Yatta. We waited for over an hour for the soldiers to come. I called twice. It was a rowdy time, with both boys and girls wrestling (separately). They made me recite the first chapter of the Qur'an, count in English and Arabic, etc. They were really sweet.

We then saw about fifteen settler teenagers up near the outpost. It looked like they were learning to ride horses. The children expressed fear as they started walking. We could hear the teenagers yelling curses at the children. A few settler teenagers threw a few stones at the children, but an adult settler stopped them. The children huddled around one side of the jeep. No soldiers walked with them.

January 6, 2008, Sunday

I went to the East Jerusalem Baptist Church today. It was good to see people there again. Jan Benvie and Eileen Hanson got on the same bus back to Hebron. Police stopped our bus, the same police women as stopped our bus this morning and checked documents to enforce the ban on Palestinians entering Jerusalem. I found it disgusting. I said to Eileen, so that the police women could hear, "This is done to enforce the Apartheid system." They must have heard me. The whole trip today was difficult for me. I don't think I have ever been so aware of the apartheid system as I am this year. I am totally appalled. The walls, the separation, the inequality, the oppression, the racism, the fact that Palestinians have to drive so much farther and longer to get anywhere, all are part of the Apartheid system. The Israelis are getting much stricter about keeping Palestinians out of Jerusalem. That is illegal, immoral, and disgusting.

January 7, 2008, Monday

I brought Steve's backpack from Hebron for him. It was huge and heavy. I was amazed at what happened to me as I carried that burden. I was a different person. I was uninterested in meeting or talking with anyone on the street. I didn't do all the shopping I intended to do. I lost my freedom. I became almost totally concentrated on my burden. I realized that is what happens to us when we carry burdens, when we carry extra baggage. I want to be free. I want to look out beyond myself. I want to reach out to others.

Steve, a Mennonite pastor from British Columbia, and I went to evening prayer at the mosque. They made it clear that he was welcome. It was a special time of prayer. Someone from Yatta led the prayers, and there was quite a bit of silence. After the prayers we continued kneeling in silence for maybe five minutes. I had a special sense of the presence of God's Spirit with us. Steve sensed that also. It was a good introduction to Muslim prayer for him.

January 10, 2008, Thursday

We had a team meeting this morning. That seemed like a real breakthrough. We actually talked to each other and wrestled with issues, and then had a check-in at the end. A lot of good sharing of feelings came out which did a lot to clear the air. We have been getting along pretty well but have not been close. I hope that will change now.

We agreed to have regular worship. Steve will be responsible. I feel grateful for that because I believe worship is essential for team life and we have seldom had worship this winter. That is sad. Team life suffers when the team is not worshipping together. Worship is at the heart of who we are. When that is missing we lose our center. I think a lot of team problems in the past were related to our lack of worship in the At-Tuwani team. Or, was our lack of worship a sign of other problems?

Worship is important for the quality of our team life. Even

if we are getting along fine, our relationships can be shallow or hollow. Worshipping together does not guarantee deep or even peaceful relationships, but it can help. Relationships need continual attention and commitment. Coming together in prayer can deepen and create new openings for our relationships. The point is not that we are required to worship, but that we are missing something essential if we do not worship together. If we do not pray together, if we do not listen together to God's Spirit, if we do not share in deeper ways, the quality of our team life will suffer, even if we all are working well together.

Worship is important for each of us personally. We need to personally find a sustaining source of power to continue the struggle, a source of strength that can keep us going for fifty years. I have seen too many activists burn out after a short time of struggle. Too many team members run on spiritual empty. I have watched team members burn out, all the while claiming they were doing fine, even though it was obvious that they were spiritually empty. These same individuals claimed they had no need for worship.

There is not only one way to find that source of strength in our lives. I know people who call themselves atheists who apparently have that spiritual connection. People of faith find that in their own personal devotional lives and in communal worship with others. Both are of utmost importance.

There is an understanding in CPT that we are engaged in spiritual warfare against the principalities and powers, that we are struggling not merely against individual people. In fact, I would argue that this understanding of spiritual struggle is at the heart and soul of what CPT is about. Our actions come out of a spiritual center rooted in prayer. If we lose that center, we will become something different. To not see worship as essential is to not understand the essential core of what CPT is about.

The spiritual center of CPT helps define who we are, what we do, and how we do it. When our actions are rooted in prayer and led by God's Spirit, they have greater power. Why would we not want our actions rooted in prayer? The work we do is too important to choose second best approaches.

January 11, 2008, Friday

Sean and I went up to Khoruba this morning to accompany a Tuba shepherd with his flock of goats below the Havot Ma'on outpost. After maybe a half hour, two settlers drove in a car and stopped maybe two hundred yards above us. I sensed some fear. Will the settlers attack us? We saw one of the settlers talking on the telephone. Was that to call other settlers or to call the soldiers? I was relieved when Gdalia drove above us and watched us, because I think other settlers may be less likely to attack if he is there watching. I followed the shepherd a little way down the hill while Sean stayed where we were in order to continue video-taping the settlers.

The shepherd started a little fire to make tea as we waited. If there was a problem, he was prepared to leave with his flock, which was munching on the thorny shrubbery. There still is no grass. I became friends with a large ram who appreciated having his head scratched.

Soon four soldiers arrived and walked toward Sean. The soldiers asked what we were doing there. Sean said we were accompanying the shepherds. "They are not allowed to be here. This is not their land." "They can be here because this is their land." "Do they have papers?" "Yes, they have papers." Then Sean told them, "You need to check with the DCO instead of just doing what Gdalia tells you." The soldiers told Sean we are just causing trouble. "No, it is the settlers here who cause the trouble and attack the shepherds. Why don't you enforce the law on these illegal outposts and carry out the order to disband this outpost?" "We can't do that." Sean said, "You mean to say that these settlers here have more authority than the Israeli military?" The soldiers agreed that was true.

Then, as the soldiers walked away, they pulled down their pants, bent down, and exposed their rear ends to Sean. Sean got it all on videotape. Note: The media picked this up, and it became a big media story in Israel. The military was quite concerned about the negative publicity concerning the lack of discipline in the military. The three soldiers were given twenty-one days in jail and removed from combat operations. Obviously they are not moral enough to be killing people or driving shepherds off their land. I have some misgivings about this incident. Why is there a public outcry about Israeli soldiers taking down their pants but no public outcry about soldiers not allowing Palestinian shepherds to be on their own land? At least some of the media is mentioning the fact that the soldiers are taking orders from the settlers. One Knesset member said that serving in the Occupation is inherently immoral. The video clip "Israeli Soldiers Bare All" is publicly available.

January 12, 2008, Saturday

I met the CPT delegation down by the road and started an hour and a half tour by talking about issues related to the road before giving them a tour of the village. Village women prepared a great lunch. After lunch, I headed for Hebron where I plan to spend a week.

January 13, 2008, Sunday

I spent most of the day with a group from the Evangelical Covenant Church in Rockford, Illinois. It was a wonderful, inspiring day. They were very open and God's Spirit seemed to be moving among us. After showing them around Hebron and telling them about problems with settlers, I saw Arnold Feuerstein, who lives in Kiryat Arba. When he saw me, he seemed overjoyed. We enthusiastically greeted each other and had a conversation about the situation here. The tour people were surprised after all the negative things I said about the settlers, but it made a good point that peace is possible between opposing groups. Arnold gave them a moderate Israeli perspective, but still maintained that the Palestinians are the problem.

January 14, 2008, Monday

I went with Jan this morning to take Mohammad abu Sneineh to school. Mohammad is eight years old and in a wheel chair. He lives less than a block from the Ibrahimi school, but soldiers blocked the street between his home and the school. To get to the school, he must go about half a mile up a long, very steep hill and then down a long, steep hill to the school. It was hard pushing that wheelchair up the hill and holding it back coming down the steep hill. Then we had to go through the Yatta Road checkpoint.

He is a sweet, shy boy who has to suffer because the Israeli military closes streets and restricts the movement of Palestinians. The Red Cross is supposed to be working on getting him easier access to the school. This is not normal CPT work, but it is a witness to the soldiers and the neighborhood. What we need to do is get the street opened.

January 15, 2008, Tuesday

Soldiers detained Tarek at about half past three this afternoon at the mosque. Tarek Abuata, a Palestinian Christian, is the new support person for CPT in Palestine, replacing Rich Meyer. Even though he is a U.S. citizen and has a U.S. passport, he is not allowed to enter Jerusalem or anywhere else in Israel because he is Palestinian. Tarek is spending six weeks with our teams in Hebron and At-Tuwani.

Tarek was talking with some Palestinians who were being detained. A soldier started giving him a hard time and, before long, detained him. They told him to sign a paper in Hebrew and they would release him. He refused to sign anything he could not read. Police then took him to Kiryat Arba police station. We didn't know what to think. We heard the police were concerned about his having no visa stamp in his American passport. We sprang into action, calling Christoph at the Red Cross, the U.S. consulate, Jonathan Kutab, Israelis, Rich Meyer, Doug, and various other people. We prayed for him during supper.

Then after half past eight, someone rang the doorbell. We wondered if it was soldiers. It was Tarek. I thought of the story in the Book of Acts when Peter got out of jail. Everyone was overjoyed and excited to have Tarek back and to hear his story. The soldier claimed Tarek refused to show his passport, which was not true. He had done nothing wrong and the police knew it.

January 17, 2008, Thursday

There is turmoil in Hebron in response to Israel killing twenty Palestinians in Gaza two days ago. Yesterday Palestinian youths burned tires on the streets and threw stones at Israeli soldiers. The Israeli soldiers responded with volleys of tear gas, percussion grenades, and "rubber" bullets. The youth ran away when the soldiers shot at them, only to quickly return and throw more stones. The soldiers announced curfew and the streets emptied.

Tarek and I went out on patrol this morning. The whole Old City was under curfew, which meant all shops closed, yet there were some people on the streets. We saw soldiers blocking the street one block below BabiZawia. They were in a crouched position, guns raised, ready to fire. That didn't look good. Were they just training, or were they ready to start shooting? There were journalists there, which made me feel a little better.

After our team meeting, Dianne and I went on patrol. Since the soldiers would not let anyone through, we walked a short distance to the right, and then on to BabiZawia where the soldiers were shooting tear gas and rubber bullets at the shabaab up the street. The youths were throwing stones at the soldiers. We stood on the sidewalk as the soldiers right in front of us on the street fired their guns with the media and ISMers right in the middle. There was a strong breeze from the south that effectively blew away all the tear gas. Rocks, "rubber" bullets, and tear gas canisters littered the streets. We were in the middle of a war zone, but I felt safe.

The whole scene seemed absurd. Both sides were stimulating the violent response of the other side. It was a game of teenagers on both sides attacking each other. I thought how stupid both sides were acting. Throwing stones at soldiers is not a very creative response to oppression and does not accomplish much positive results. The soldiers were acting even more irresponsibly and irrationally. The response of the soldiers only encouraged and emboldened the youth. The simple way to get the youths to stop throwing stones would have been for the soldiers to leave the area. Shooting at the stone throwers is hardly a way to peace.

While some soldiers were shooting, other soldiers tried to keep Palestinians out of the area. A middle-aged Palestinian woman started walking to the other side of the area, beyond the trouble spot. A soldier told her she could not cross the area and ordered her to turn back. Not only did the conservatively dressed Muslim woman not go back, she continued walking toward the other side of the intersection. The soldier tried to stop her and got in front of her, but the woman just walked around the soldier. The soldier gave up, and the woman walked on her way. The actions of the woman left the soldier with his M-16 powerless. With internationals watching, he was not going to shoot the woman. The simple act of resistance by the woman was more powerful than the actions of either the soldiers or the stone-throwing youth. Suppose more people simply refused to cooperate with evil and simply did the right thing. The idea that people should obey unjust laws is superstition.

January 18, 2008, Friday

Paulette, Jean, and I went to al Khader for a demonstration against the Wall that will cut Bethlehem off from Route 60, and from five thousand acres of land across from Route 60, a major theft of land. I doubt that Israel wants peace before they take more of that important agricultural area. We met at the gas station at the south end of Bethlehem. I greeted quite a few people I knew. The event began with Friday Prayers on the road. That was impressive. We then marched up the road a short way to where a line of soldiers three deep stopped us. There was a short speech and it was over. They plan to have this every Friday. A local Popular Committee planned the action, one small part of a much larger, growing nonviolent movement.

January 20, 2008, Sunday

Tarek and I attended worship with the Immanuel congregation in Bethlehem. I appreciated the special prayer time for Gaza. Israel has recently killed forty people there, and Israel is even cutting off food supplies. The electricity goes off this evening. How much more of this oppression will the world allow?

I planned to meet a friend in Jerusalem, so I started walking toward the checkpoint between Bethlehem and Jerusalem. I was horrified as I walked by the Apartheid Wall. It is incredibly ugly, both in appearance and purpose (separating and removing people and stealing land). That Wall is about the most despicable thing I have ever seen. I shuddered with horror. I thought of the shattered lives, broken relationships, stolen land, shattered economy, and divided families. The Israelis are building a wall around Bethlehem, turning Bethlehem into a prison. I had to do extra walking in order to get to the checkpoint because of the Wall snaking through Bethlehem.

I started walking through the checkpoint. I was shocked at the massive nature of that place. It feels like a major international border crossing, consisting of long cattle ramps, horribly oppressive, unwelcoming, and foreboding. The place feels cold and harsh, almost threatening. It is sick. The cattle ramps go unnecessarily up hill and then back down. Inside the building there were soldiers on walkways above us. The mural in the distance, depicting peace between Israelis and Palestinians, seemed totally out of place and inconsistent with the reality of the place. I have never been in a place that felt so oppressive. The place tells volumes about the nature of Israel's soul.

I got through the first checkpoint, walked along another long cattle ramp, and came to the actual crossing. There were hundreds of people waiting to get through. People said the checkpoint would be closed for a few hours.

My friend called and said he was busy and we should cancel our plans to get together today. I turned around, walked back through all those cattle ramps, and was back in Bethlehem.

I got a Yatta taxi to the Beqa'a. The Jabers were harvesting turnips, so I worked until dark helping them. That brought back memories from when I lived with the Jabers. I got to talk with many of the family members as I cut off the tops and roots of the turnips. When we finished, I spent the night with Atta and Rodeina. They are doing well.

January 21, 2008, Monday

I got up early and walked into Hebron. As I left the house I saw the rubble of two nearby recently demolished houses. Horrible! The Israeli military has recently issued twenty-five demolition orders or stop work orders on homes and the new medical clinic in the Beqa'a. The Israeli military demolished two or three more homes here in the Beqa'a in the last year.

This afternoon at about half past one, Kathie and I went down into the market where soldiers were forcing all the shopkeepers to close their shops so that a group of about forty young Israeli men could pray at a Hebrew plaque in the market. I was incensed as I watched those young Jews praying while the soldiers used their guns to force all the Palestinians away. What kind of prayer, what kind of religion is it that uses guns to close stores and remove the people who live here so that outsiders can pray here? What has happened to Judaism? There is no morality in what happened here. The power of the gun has replaced morality and decency.

I confronted the soldiers about what they were doing. I repeated the Shema. Tarek came and started preaching that what they were doing was a violation of Judaism. More soldiers came. That attracted the "worshippers" who came to confront us. They cursed us, mocked us, and told us to go home. One came up to me with his face practically touching my face and tried to stare me down. I stared at him. I repeated the Shema to him. I repeated, "Baruch Hashem Adonai." The soldiers soon removed the "worshippers."

One elderly Palestinian man sat down near the soldiers who ordered him to leave. He ignored the soldiers. The soldiers backed down and let him stay there.

January 23, 2008, Wednesday

Our worship this morning focused on Gaza. I am deeply excited by the recent actions in Gaza. Hamas tore down maybe seven miles of the fence between Gaza and Egypt and hundreds of thousands of people from Gaza are streaming into Egypt to get provisions before returning home. This must be the biggest prison break and one of the great civil disobedience actions in history. My hope is that this incredible event will plant the seeds for others to take similar actions and tear down walls, will give people courage to resist the Occupation, and will start a new nonviolent intifada. This must be a real dilemma for the Israeli government. What can they do? They already have taken a severe blow in international opinion for cutting off all supplies to Gaza. How can they stop people from getting food?

Two men came this morning and talked about their nonviolent activities with PalestineSolidarityProject.org. They work closely with other nonviolent groups, go to At-Tuwani and Susiya, organize demonstrations, and work closely with Israelis and internationals. That was exciting to hear. Last evening seven young Palestinians who recently went through nonviolence training came for supper. The most exciting thing I see here is the development of a nonviolent movement, starting with grassroots training in order to create the infrastructure for such a movement.

January 24, 2008, Thursday

This morning the whole team came to At-Tuwani for a joint team meeting. I was eager to get back to At-Tuwani, but also reluctant to leave Hebron, both because I am excited about the work the Hebron team is doing and because I have felt so spiritually fed by the Hebron team.

We had a very good meeting. Kathie led worship. Joy Ellison did a superb job of facilitating the meeting. She kept us on track and we wasted no time. We did planning for an upcoming strategic planning retreat to rethink our work here and shared details of what has been happening with both teams. It is exciting to be back in At-Tuwani.

January 25, 2008, Friday

A Dove and I went down to the road to watch soldiers. The soldiers had stopped a medium-sized car with two camels in the backseat, with their heads and necks stretched out the window. I couldn't believe it. The camels seemed very angry. I would guess their legs were really hurting from being crammed into the car. I asked the driver if there was a problem. He said there are always problems with the soldiers. Soon they let him go. We watched as the car with the camels traveled up the road.

January 27, 2008, Sunday

A major task for the team in the past two weeks has been accompanying Tuba and Maghair al Abeed shepherds in the Meshaha Valley, the next valley just southeast of Khoruba, near where settlers attacked Johannes three years ago. Settlers have been coming out, calling the soldiers, and threatening the shepherds. Sometimes the settlers carry clubs. On January 12, the day I went to Hebron, the settlers fired six shots in order to frighten the shepherds, and then ran into the trees as if they had been shot at. Gdalia has been ever-present. The actions of the soldiers have been inconsistent. Sometimes they drive the shepherds away, sometimes do nothing, and at least once they said the shepherds could be there.

Tarek and I went up to accompany the shepherds this morning. It wasn't long before soldiers arrived with twenty-three-year-old "Ehud" in charge. Ehud announced that the shepherds may not be anywhere in the area. He said the reason was that it is not safe for the settlers if Palestinians are anywhere where they can see the settler outpost. That would mean a huge area of land is off limits for the shepherds. We pointed out to the soldiers that the Israeli High Court has ruled that the shepherds may graze their sheep in most areas. We suggested they follow the laws of Israel instead of taking orders from Gdalia and the settlers.

We reminded the soldiers that this is Palestinian land. A soldier quickly told us, "This is Israel." I told the soldier, "This is not Israel. This is Palestinian territory. Even President George Bush recognizes that this is Palestinian territory, not Israel." We did a little preaching to the soldiers, telling them "There will never be peace here as long as you claim everything to be Israel, as long as you intend to steal all this land from the Palestinians. The real reason for not allowing these shepherds to be on their own land is that you are helping the settlers to steal this land."

I reminded the soldiers, "You do not need to protect the settlers. It is those settlers who continually are attacking these shepherds, and even attacking little school children. Repeatedly soldiers have stood by and watched as settlers have attacked Palestinians. The question is, do you want peace, or do you want to take the land?"

Gdalia stood up on the mountain above us. I wanted to talk to him, but I was busy.

Ehud ordered us to leave. Instead of leaving, we argued with him, telling him he was not following the law of his own government. We said we wanted to talk with his commander and that he should call the DCO. Even though the soldiers ordered us to leave, they didn't seem to have the will to enforce the order. I think we touched something in them that countered their training as soldiers. Ehud became almost passive. We undermined the authority of the soldiers, which made it easier for the shepherds to ignore the soldiers' orders. We were a real bother for the soldiers. I felt sorry for Ehud.

At 11:50 a higher-ranking officer came and immediately took charge. He started yelling at the shepherds. I told him to treat people with respect. He then walked down and started to talk with one of the shepherds. The whole time he kept his hand on the shepherd's shoulder, an obvious non-verbal power move, while telling him he had better be careful or he would kill the sheep if he sees him there again. Someone told us that this is a new commander who does what the settlers want. A villager told us that when confronted with a fact of Israeli law, the new commander said, "I am the law."

We waited there until the soldiers drove away, and then walked down into the valley and up a short distance where the shepherds were making tea over a small fire. We shared tea and bread and had a pleasant conversation for over an hour. Tarek and I wonder if we took too much initiative, instead of staying more on the sidelines.

January 28, 2008, Monday

There was no school today because of a teachers' strike. Yesterday morning Samaia told me there would be no school today. Throughout the day we heard from various people that there would be a strike, there would be no strike, it would be one day, a whole week, etc. Four-year-old Samaia was right after all. I am always going to believe her. Today she told me it will snow tonight.

January 31, 2008, Thursday

I woke up and saw six inches of beautiful snow on the ground, the first snow to accumulate here in ten years. I ate breakfast and got ready for action. At a little before half past seven, I saw the neighbor boys, and a snowball fight erupted just as I had been warning everyone for the past few days since

snow had been predicted. It was a wonderful time. That snowball fight continued for four hours, involving most of the villagers. I threw a snowball at a seventy-five-year-old man who
returned the fire. I made sure to bombard all the small children
a number of times and let them bombard me. Hafez and Aisha
had an intense battle.

I went to about every home in the village to instigate a
snowball battle. I didn't want to leave anyone out. I didn't see
anyone when I went to Juma's house. I waited a bit and when
I saw one person, I threw a snowball at him. Almost immediately, like hitting a hornets' nest, at least fifteen people came out
of the house, all of them attacking me. It was great. Later in the
morning much of the battle centered around the Hereni homes.
Snowballs were whizzing from every direction, and you never
knew who was an ally or an enemy.

What an amazing day. It is a commonly held value in the
village that people do not throw things at other people and hit
them. That standard was pushed aside today and everyone was
throwing snowballs at everyone. Gender barriers broke down.
Some of the girls were among the most aggressive. As a matter
of fact, a lot of aggression was expressed, all in a good way.
There seems to be a psychological need to at times throw away
cultural rules and let loose. We sure did that today, and at the
same time did nothing immoral. Too often, when the rules are
temporarily abandoned, destructive behaviors ensue.

It was a special day for me as I related in a new way to
many of the people of the village. Today I told them I am not a
shabaab, but rather a young boy. I did act as a youngster. I felt
free. I forgot that I am sixty-eight years young.

I asked Juma if what I did at his house this morning was a
problem. He said no, it was fun and his children really appreciated it. He asked me to do it again. I will probably never know
the impact I made today on the lives of children. They need
some carefree fun in their lives now and then.

I asked a number of people if it had also snowed in the

Israeli settlements around At-Tuwani. They all said it had snowed there also. It is God who makes it snow on everyone whether they be Muslim, Jewish, or Christian. The important thing is whether we respond to God's gifts with joy and whether we allow those gifts to bring us together. To make exclusive claims on God is to deny the oneness of God. There was nothing exclusive about that snowstorm.

February 3, 2008, Sunday

As I was walking in Yatta yesterday, a boy informed me that he was in the car in which we saw the two camels. That was neat.

This morning the Doves went with the shepherds while I stayed alone at Khoruba in order to watch them down the valley and be on the lookout for soldiers and settlers. I also served as lookout for the shepherds in the Humra Valley to my left. I could see the whole panorama from where I was sitting. It was a strategic position and I enjoyed it, except there was a cold breeze from the northeast, blowing directly, I think, from Sulimania where Peggy is. It was a beautiful day. When soldiers arrived across the valley, the shepherds immediately retreated, and the soldiers left. Our main work now with the shepherds is to film and document what happens. The shepherds are not quite ready to push.

February 7, 2008, Thursday

After worship yesterday morning with the Hebron team, I headed out to the Beqa'a where I spent the day visiting friends, some of whom I had not seen in several years. I visited two families who have recently had their homes demolished. I learned another home and the new medical clinic may be demolished in the next few days and alerted the Hebron team.

This morning I headed back to At-Tuwani. The road was closed at al Fawwar so we had to walk across the road and get another van. Apparently this is collective punishment for the suicide bombing at Dimona, near Be'er Sheva a few days ago. I told the soldiers that what they were doing will not bring peace. Maybe I was wasting my time. It is clear to me that Israel does not want peace. The soldiers said they were just doing their duty. I thought of the nuclear weapons program at Dimona. I detest suicide bombings, but I also detest what Israel is doing.

Last evening the soldiers closed the road to Karmil from At-Tuwani, the first time this road has been closed for a year. They scooped up lots of topsoil from a wheat field to close the road and put huge concrete blocks across the road. We went through a field and found an opening where we easily crossed the settler road to get to At-Tuwani.

Eileen told me they had a talk with Gdalia today. He is really angry that CPTers visited Beit Ummar families related to the two cousins who went into Kfar Etzion settlement and were killed. He needed CPT to listen to him. He thinks we are hypocrites for visiting terrorists. I would like to tell him that I would be happy to visit the families of Baruch Goldstein or Ygal Amir, that I went to see Nati's family after he was killed, but that his friends threatened and drove me away. We want reconciliation, not to continue the hatred. We want peace with justice, not to support one side.

February 8, 2008, Friday

I stayed at Khoruba as a lookout again today. It was not long before soldiers came. The shepherds ran away. Ehud confronted two team members and said the soldiers are really angry at us for the video of soldiers taking down their pants. Those guys were his friends, and we ruined their careers in the military. He said we only cause trouble.

Ehud said some amazing things. He said that since Havot Ma'on is thirty years old and At-Tuwani is only ten years old and actually is a landfill, the settlers have the right to the land. Has he never seen the ancient stone houses in At-Tuwani? He said our team is bringing in children from other places for school patrol, using them, and trying to cause problems between them and the soldiers. "The settlers here are crazy," he said, "but the soldiers have to protect them, otherwise the Palestinians here would attack them." I have heard this before. "Unless the soldiers are harsh with the Palestinians, they will kill all the Jews." Ehud admitted there are no terrorists in At-Tuwani.

I went to bed exhausted. It is a wonderful feeling to go to bed ready to rest, feeling that you have given your all that day.

February 9, 2008, Saturday

We went up to be with the shepherds again this morning. At 11:30, two military jeeps and a police jeep arrived. The shepherds ran away with their sheep, down to the west. The jeeps parked across the valley from us. At 11:32, a settler dressed in white joined the police and soldiers. Another jeep arrived at 11:34.

Almost immediately, eleven soldiers and police started walking toward the Humra Valley where Juma's family had their sheep. I headed there and got there before the soldiers. At 11:45, another police jeep arrived. There were at least twenty heavily armed Israelis and four shepherds. It was the soldiers who seemed afraid.

The At-Tuwani shepherds did not move. The soldiers ordered the shepherds to leave the area. They moved a few steps but did not leave. They argued with the soldiers. Then a man from the DCO (He is new and speaks fairly good Arabic) came with maps in his hands, greeted the shepherds in Arabic in a respectful, friendly way and told them they could be there, just not up close to the trees. Apparently settlers called the soldiers and greatly exaggerated the situation, saying shepherds were close to the outpost. When the soldiers had ordered the shepherds to leave, they were simply following the orders of the settlers. The man from the DCO seemed to understand this and reconfirmed the right of the shepherds to be in the valley. The man from the DCO greeted Juma, who had joined us, and joked with him. Juma told them, "You brought lots of soldiers for a little problem."

At this point, a policeman walked up to Juma and in a joking, but clearly condescending way, gave Juma a light slap on his cheek. I later asked Juma about it. Juma told me the policeman said, "I came to help you." "No," Juma replied, "you came to help those settlers." Juma is a man of great spiritual depth and strength. Who was that policeman to say anything condescending to him?

I went back to Khoruba and watched. The soldiers seemed unconcerned about the shepherds down in Meshaha or on Khoruba hill and left at about half past one. In ten minutes, a jeep returned and parked across the valley from me. Two of the soldiers walked up to the settler shack. Joy and Sean joined me. After consulting with the settlers, the soldiers drove toward us. I headed toward them and was close to the jeep when it stopped. I greeted Ehud and the other two soldiers who jumped out of the jeep, but they ignored me. With guns drawn they ran toward a shepherd and his sheep as they ran away. Joy and Sean were right in front of them, videotaping them. They soon stopped and gave up the chase. I asked them if this was the peace of Shabbat, if they were proud of chasing shepherds. They said nothing.

These were the soldiers who expressed so much anger at CPT yesterday. I wonder what they were thinking today as they were the ones who were being videotaped. It is clear that they were taking orders from the settlers to drive those sheep away. I feel bad for those soldiers. They must know that what they are doing is wrong.

February 10, 2008, Sunday

I suggested I go to Tuba this afternoon to do school patrol and spend the night there. Teammates thought that was a good idea. Up at Khoruba, Joy told me there seemed to be a lot of settler activity and that I should be careful. In response to her concern, I changed my course and went farther down the valley before taking the middle way to Tuba. There were two places where I could briefly be seen from the outpost. As I went down the last valley before going around the big hill below and southeast of the chicken barns, I saw two settlers on horses take off from the trailer. That concerned me. I soon realized they were heading out the road above me.

Joy called and was very concerned. I altered my course farther east from the chicken barns and kept going. I then saw them behind me. I decided the best thing was to ignore them and keep walking. I was prepared to walk toward them, but unless they got closer, walking toward them did not feel right. They yelled at me a few times, but I pretended I did not hear them. I always had a valley between us, so I was not scared. When I heard horses above me, east of the chicken barns, I stopped and rested behind some rocks until I was sure the settlers had left the area.

It was great meeting the children at the chicken barns, even though I had to wait almost two hours because the soldiers were late. The children were excited about me visiting Tuba and all insisted I must visit them. Many of them wanted to hold my hand as we walked together on the rocky path. They said that last Thursday afternoon a group of settlers yelled at them and told them to go away. One settler gestured as though slitting their throats.

I visited the Ali Ibrahim Awwad family, a large extended family on the southwest side of Tuba, up on the side of a cliff. I had a delightful time. I started out watching them feed and milk their sheep, was invited into their tent where I was surrounded by children and women, and then went up on the side of the cliff and visited there, part of the time in their cave. It was good to connect with so many of them. Their living on the side of that cliff is amazing. I had to be careful to not slip and go tumbling down the mountain. They must have some goat genes in their family. But the view is gorgeous.

February 11, 2008, Monday

I spent the night in Ibrahim and Imtere's tent. They have no electricity, so it was a cozy evening with a lantern, talking about issues of faith, politics, and family. I told them watching television never gets this good. We woke up early, listened to the BBC, prayed, and ate breakfast, and then I walked with the children to the chicken barns. Today the soldiers were punctual and waiting.

I walked back to Tuba and visited with Omar and his family. We talked about Peggy spending two nights with them last July during a time of constant harassment from settlers. While she was here, Gdalia and some settlers tried to force Tuba shepherds off of their land, but the shepherds refused to leave. Soldiers came, and also representatives from the DCO, for yet another round of discussions of where the shepherds may or may not graze. The DCO reaffirmed the shepherds' right to be on their land and refused to bow to the settlers' demands that the shepherds be removed.

I noticed that all the bread I ate in Tuba was whole wheat. Apparently aid agencies have started giving out whole wheat instead of white flour. That's a wonderful way to improve the nutrition of the people here.

I then met a Tuba shepherd and his flock of goats. He said we would not go to Meshaha or Khoruba today. I sensed he was afraid. Their strategy seems to be to keep going back on the land, not concede the land to the settlers, but know when to back off. They are very wise. We slowly made our way on the very steep hillsides where there is no grass, only thorny shrubs that the goats seem to like. It felt safe. We were out of view. We slowly proceeded up the valley. We could not be seen from the outpost, but soldiers could have seen us from the tops of the mountains around us. The shepherd said if we see soldiers he will leave and I stay to talk with the soldiers.

Then, after a while, the shepherd seemed to grow braver. We started moving closer to the outpost, to where there was more grass, but where we could easily be seen. We saw two settlers in the outpost, but the shepherd seemed unconcerned. Then at about quarter of twelve, we saw three masked settlers with clubs coming toward us. He took off with the goats. I did a quick bit of videoing. The situation felt very threatening. I did not want to meet the masked settlers. I did not think it would be possible to talk with them. The shepherd and the goats headed down the valley and up the next mountain. I felt the need to be both in a position to videotape and escape. It seemed best to go around the mountain, staying at about the same altitude. The settlers could not see me, and I could see the shepherd and the goats.

After five or ten minutes the danger seemed to pass. I checked with the shepherd who invited me to go back to Tuba with him. I decided to head back to At-Tuwani. I needed time to recover from this frightening encounter.

February 16, 2008, Saturday

At a little before nine o'clock, Eileen, a Dove, and I went to Susiya for an action planned by Ta'ayush. We got to Susiya early and did a lot of visiting as people slowly started to arrive. There were about twenty Ta'ayush people, a van of Palestinian activists from Beit Ummar, and maybe fifty local Palestinians from villages in the area, including about ten women. At eleven o'clock, we marched on the Israeli only road to the roadblock between Susiya and Yatta, just below the military base. The purpose of the march was to demand that the road between Susiya and Yatta be open for Palestinians. The gate was open when we got there.

Soon five military jeeps arrived. The soldiers just watched us and did nothing to interfere. We milled around the road-block and listened to a few speeches. Then the group walked up the hill and all the way around the small military base. Shepherds had a flock of sheep up close to the base where the grass had probably not been grazed of years.

I walked over to Ehud and a group of soldiers that I recognized from encounters in At-Tuwani. They refused to talk with me. I greeted them, joked a bit, and then left. I thought of all the issues between us: The videotape, the confrontations with them, our preaching to them. I wanted to listen to their concerns.

At about half past twelve, we headed back to Susiya. After more visiting I caught a ride with Ezra to Hebron. We had a serious talk about strategy. He said today was a big victory. Three years ago the soldiers would not have allowed us to do what we did today. That may be because the Israeli military has essentially conceded the South Hebron hills to the Palestinians. That does not necessarily mean they will not continue to take orders from the settlers. It may be due to the increasing strength of the Palestinians. Ezra thinks we should be at that roadblock several days a week to keep it open.

A man from Tuba came to the house Saturday evening. He said he was hit in the face by a rock thrown by a settler from a very short distance. This happened between Tuba and Havot Ma'on. He was going to the hospital and to the police.

February 18, 2008, Monday

I went out on school patrol in Hebron this morning and saw about eight soldiers detaining one man. The soldiers had their guns drawn. I said to them, "You do not need to be afraid."

Jessica and I went to the Yatta Road checkpoint. Soldiers were taking their time letting anyone through. At least twenty children were waiting. Some of the children became impatient and started taunting the soldiers. One soldier became very aggressive. I asked him if he thought what he was doing will bring peace. He didn't respond. I said, "What you are doing makes no sense and prevents peace. Why can't you just let the children go to school?" Jessica handed him a copy of a court order in Hebrew, ordering soldiers not to interfere with children going to school. The soldier called his commander and within a minute or two the soldiers allowed all the children to bypass the metal detectors.

I stayed for worship. The focus was on loving our enemies. I needed that.

Back in At-Tuwani, Cassandra and I went over to the gate.

Most of the children were already there, and two soldiers were talking with the children. I talked just a bit in Russian to the one who knew no English. The other one was Ehud, who told me the Doves are good people, not like CPTers, who are very bad.

February 20, 2008, Wednesday

There was no school today because of continuing rain, so we did not go out on school patrol this morning. At about quarter of nine I noticed villagers walking up the hill toward the gate followed by a village tractor. A soldier jeep was stuck in the mud. Joy and I watched the tractor pull the jeep out of a deep rut. What a story. These were the same soldiers who have been driving the shepherds from their land. Ehud was there. Now the shepherds helped the soldiers. I am constantly amazed at the graciousness of these Palestinians. They understand the biblical concepts of turning the other cheek and giving a cup of cold water. It is interesting that the soldiers didn't get the settlers to help them. Last April a villager also used a tractor to pull a soldier jeep that got stuck.

I was surprised to see the school children there. They had not heard that there was no school today. After things settled down, two soldiers walked with the children back up the hill past the settlement.

February 21, 2008, Thursday

Both Hebron and At-Tuwani teams came to Bethlehem (Grande Hotel) for a two-day CPT strategic planning retreat. We started by sharing our expectations and hopes and then looked at our current mission statement. There seemed to be agreement that it was a wonderful statement but quite inadequate in saying what our mission is. We then worked at creating a new mission statement, starting with brainstorming what we think our mission should be. That went well and we seemed to have a lot of agreement, but it was long and laborious. We came up with this statement.

We are a faith-based organization that supports Palestinian-led nonviolent grassroots resistance to the Israeli Occupation, and the unjust structures that uphold it. By "getting in the way" of violence and educating in our home communities, we help create a space for justice and peace.

A significant change in wording is that we are no longer saying we are here to reduce violence. Sometimes, if we stand for justice, the overt violence may increase. If we seek to reduce violence while ignoring the injustice, our work is little more than pacification, or at best, making the Occupation a little less oppressive. But through our actions we may be able to lessen the cost of active nonviolent resistance, and reduce the violence directed toward those who work for change.

February 22, 2008, Friday

We had an intense day today. Yesterday we made a long list of the things both teams are currently doing. This morning we looked at that list and asked if those activities can fit into our mission statement. Are there things we should stop doing? How could we change what we are doing to make it fit better? Questions we asked included, "Are Palestinians asking us to do this and telling us how they want us to do it? Is this a form of resistance to the Occupation? Who are our partners? Are Palestinians leading the actions we participate in? Are we living where our partners think we should be living? Are we supporting nonviolent resistance, or making the Occupation more bearable?"

This afternoon we talked about how we could help build a movement against the Occupation in our home countries. I said I think we need to make a major shift in CPT in seeing the work of CPT not only in the field, but also at home. There are many people who support CPT through prayer and financial support, but for various reasons cannot come to Palestine. There are reservists who can be away from home for only short periods each year. We can find ways to include these people in the resistance movement. Maybe some of us have created an image of CPTers as super-heroic people who do things our supporters could never do, thus disempowering our supporters.

Suppose we created possibilities for people back home to join in our work through regional groups that could do educational work (including arranging speaking opportunities for CPTers returning from projects), organizing direct action events in their home communities, lobbying, recruiting for CPT, and supporting other groups working to end the Occupation. We were in agreement that CPT should explore this idea.

I enjoyed my time in Bethlehem, but it also was difficult. The meals were opulent. Much food was wasted. The hotel was too fancy for me. My heart the whole time was in At-Tuwani, with the people of the world that do not have the same privilege and power that we white Westerners do. I hope I will never forget my home in At-Tuwani.

Our level of consumption is a struggle for me. It feels condescending to me to help the poor and not identify with them. How can I work in At-Tuwani for a week and then go to Bethlehem and live on a level of consumption that would be impossible not only for the people of At-Tuwani, but for most of the world? Being a white North American gives me the special power to consume as much as I want, but it does not give me the right to take more than my fair share. Do we live on the same moral level as the Israeli soldiers who say, "We do it because we can"?

February 23, 2008, Saturday

At quarter past ten about thirty Ta'ayush people came. They soon left to do actions in Susiya and Tuba. I spent the whole time in At-Tuwani because villagers were concerned that the military might harass them today because of the Ta'ayush actions. Many of the villagers took their flocks up to Khoruba, along with shepherds from Tuba, Maghair al Abeed, and Mufakara. The other team members were there.

Military and police jeeps went up to Khoruba where a big confrontation developed between settlers, soldiers, and shepherds. At about half past twelve, five settlers went to Meshaha and kicked sheep and confronted shepherds, who stood up to the settlers. The soldiers stood and watched and did nothing. Actually, soldiers also attacked sheep. One soldier kicked a sheep in the mouth and broke two of its teeth. Why would someone kick an innocent sheep in the mouth? What is going on in the hearts of these soldiers? What is the Occupation doing to them?

At this point, five Ta'ayush people arrived, immediately jumped into the confrontation, and took over. The shepherds were upset that the Ta'ayush people did not ask what happened, didn't try to understand the situation, didn't listen, and didn't seek any direction from the shepherds. It then became a confrontation between Ta'ayush and the settlers. It is really important that we listen to and take our direction from the people who live here. We are their guests. We are here to serve, not direct them. They understand the situation much better than we do. We do not want to disempower them.

Twice Gdalia drove down toward the village. I so much wanted to talk with him, something I still have not done this winter.

February 24, 2008, Sunday

A group of soldiers, led by Ehud, came to the Humra Valley this morning, just up from the village and ordered all the shepherds to leave, even though the DCO has repeatedly said the shepherds could be there. The soldiers jumped out of their jeep and tried to drive away all the sheep. One of the shepherds tried to get in the way of the soldiers. Ehud got very angry and was going to arrest the shepherd, who then ran away. Three soldiers ran after him. Again the DCO came and yet again reaffirmed the right of the shepherds to be there. Ehud was still taking his orders from the settlers.

Cassandra and I stayed in the village in case the soldiers came looking for the shepherd. Later we walked over by the gate to wait for the children. We passed Tom Fox's olive tree that someone had broken off. I thought of Tom, and my wife, Peggy, in Iraq.

The soldiers arrived a half hour early just like us. Ehud walked toward me and wanted to talk. He was very angry. He said that Sean's behavior up with the shepherds this morning was totally disgusting. I pressed him to be specific about what Sean did but got no specific answer as to anything Sean might have done wrong. He said things like "Sean wanted me to do something bad so he could videotape me doing it." He clearly was upset about being videotaped. He mentioned his friends being punished because of our taping them. He said he could not take the abuse here any longer.

He expressed a lot of frustration with the Palestinians, with CPT, with the whole situation here. In fact, he said he is so frustrated that he asked to be transferred to the Syrian border, that this was his last day here. He apparently thinks it will be easier to deal with Hezbollah than the people of At-Tuwani. He may be right. This has been a difficult time for him, and we have played an important role in pushing him to this point of frustration. How many times have we confronted him and stopped him from removing the shepherds? The DCO and police did not back him up as he followed the orders of settlers. We are glad he is frustrated. He should be frustrated. He needs to come to terms with what he has been doing here.

He tried to justify himself. He repeated the myth of Israeli innocence. He said he never mistreated a Palestinian and that he always instructed his soldiers to be polite with Palestinians. I affirmed him as a person. He is a good person. With much emotion he said, "I look after these school children every day, and their parents are angry with me." He seemed incapable of understanding why the Palestinians would be angry with him. He has tried to be nice to the children. Actually Ehud did a better job of escorting the children than many other soldiers have done. He was usually on time and treated the children well. However, he could not grasp that he is an occupying soldier. Maybe it is difficult for him to face what he has done here and maintain any self-respect. He repeatedly drove shepherds from their land to please the settlers. This morning when he came to Humra, where there is no question of the shepherds being allowed to graze, Ehud immediately jumped out of the jeep and ran at the sheep. The Palestinians are not interested in his politeness or in his goodness. They experienced him as an oppressor.

He made it clear that he is not willing to give up Israeli control here. He could accept a Palestinian state, but it must be subservient to Israel. He is a good, kind man, but he cannot accept the Palestinians as equals, share power with them, or cooperatively work things out with them. Israelis must dominate and control.

I told him his perspective will never lead to peace. But sadly, I fear he has no vision for peace. So tomorrow he will go to the Syrian border prepared to kill anyone who might attack Israel. He gave chocolate milk to each of the children as they came from school. He is a good, kind man.

A group of about twenty European members of Jews for Justice came for a tour. I spoke a bit with them about our work here, and then Kiefah spoke with them about the vision of the women's cooperative that keeps growing. I expressed how grateful I am that Jews come here in friendship. A rabbi from Rabbis for Human Rights also came with two others this morning.

February 25, 2008, Monday

Two soldiers walked with the children this morning. They appeared to be a new group of soldiers. I greeted them in Hebrew, and they didn't seem to know how to respond. My guess is that they were given strict orders not to talk to us, and so did not know what to say. It is true that soldiers talking with us has created problems for the military. Our conversations have not helped military morale.

This afternoon I met the same soldiers and talked a little with them as we waited for the children. When they said they were new here, I told them this is the very best place they could be. They didn't seem convinced. They probably were told this is a difficult place for soldiers. I hope to have them trained and oriented in a few days. I kept thinking about Ehud.

February 28, 2008, Thursday

It was hard leaving At-Tuwani this morning, but I also knew it was time to go. On our way into Jerusalem we saw a vanload of Palestinians sitting on the ground, guarded by Israeli police. It looked like they were having their ID's checked. Were some of them in Jerusalem without proper permission? Or were they just being humiliated and reminded of who claims to be in control? It doesn't matter. What was happening was wrong. It was a snapshot of what the Occupation means.

February 29, 2008, Friday

While I was going through the tedious security procedures at the airport in Tel-Aviv this morning, procedures rooted in fear and desire to control, I was thinking about another world, about At-Tuwani, where, at the very same time, local villagers, Israelis, and internationals, Muslims, Jews, and Christians, about a hundred people, had gathered to reopen the road to Yatta that the Israeli military had closed on February 6.

The action began with women removing soil from the mound of earth blocking the road. Then the women and children moved a large concrete block from the road. With everyone helping, soon the road was reopened. The action ended with Friday noon prayers at the place where the road had been blocked.

I wished I could have stayed in At-Tuwani just one more day, but my heart was filled with gratitude for having had the privilige of living and working with the marvelous people of At-Tuwani and the South Hebron Hills, and all the Israeli and international peace activists who are working for a world of justice and peace.

Thank you God for this privilege. Thank you for the vision and hope those people have shared with me.

Afterword

The real goal of the Occupation, the torturing of the people of the South Hebron Hills, is to rid the region of its Palestinian inhabitants, part of a dangerous dream of creating a greater Israel, extending from the Nile to Baghdad, ethnically cleansed of Arabs, a racist home for Jews only in a purely Jewish state. For there to be peace, Israel must recognize and come to terms with both its history of ethnic cleansing and ongoing attempts to rid major portions of Israel/Palestine of its Palestinian inhabitants. Until Israel repents of its atrocities against the Palestinians, there is no hope for peace and reconciliation.

The path chosen by those currently in power in Israel, the path of domination and control, of humiliation, oppression and violence, and its goal of an ever-expanding Israel, is bound to fail. It is a path that runs counter to the Creator of the Universe, against the structures of reality, against nature. On that path, all sides lose.

There are Israelis who believe that the injustice, the sin of Israel, is so great that God will not allow the state of Israel to continue much longer. Israelis like Avraham Burg, former speaker of the Israeli Knesset, argue that to survive Israel must turn from its racist oppression. Otherwise, as Burg put it in *The Guardian*: "There is a real chance that ours will be the last Zionist generation. There may yet be a Jewish state here, but it will be a different sort, strange and ugly."[1]

I do know that God's judgment, the logical consequences of our actions, is already operative in destroying the soul of Israel. I see that in the arrogance, the callousness, the brutality, the hardness of heart so many soldiers and settlers display. The only hope for a strong and secure Israel in the future is a just settlement with the Palestinian people, a settlement that would give security and freedom to both peoples.

Everyone in the Middle East has been victimized by the oppression, by the fear, by the desire to dominate and control. But people in the Americas, in Europe, and in the Muslim world, also have been wounded by the tragic failure to find a way to peace in Israel/Palestine. Judaism, Islam, and Christianity have been brutalized and weakened by their followers' failure to live up to the best ideals of their respective religions, by subordinating faith in God to political expediency, by turning from faith to fear.

Neither side is going to disappear. The idea of an exclusive state for any one group evokes horrendous images of ethnic cleansing, violence, and turmoil into the distant future. The Palestinians are not fading away as many Israelis have hoped. They, like the people in At-Tuwani, are refusing to leave their land, refusing to give up their humanity, and instead, are claiming their dignity and rights.

The land of Israel/Palestine has been a multi-cultural and multi-religious society for thousands of years. Although there have always been Jews living here for the past three thousand years, never was Palestine exclusively Jewish. For there to be peace, it must continue to be pluralistic. Both older Israelis and Palestinians fondly remember not so long ago when Muslims, Christians, and Jews all lived in peace in the Holy Land. The vision, then, must be of building a tolerant, pluralistic, multi-religious society. That vision must be democratic, with equal rights for all, with each person having one vote. Each side will need to recognize the validity of the other side's experience, including both their pains and hopes. Whether that can best be accomplished through a one or a two state solution is not for me to say. For a thoughtful discussion of this issue, see Ali Abunimah's book, *One Country: A Bold Proposal to End the*

Israeli-Palestinian Impasse (New York, Metropolitan Books, 2006). Maybe the terms of the discussion need to be changed. We could ask how everyone can have equal rights and responsibilities. How can we ensure the legitimacy, the cultural and religious identities, and the rights of all people living in historic Palestine? There is a need to imagine alternative futures that move beyond fear, domination, separation and violence. Israelis and Palestinians need to envision a future that both sides can subscribe to. An important factor in the fall of apartheid in South Africa was when white people finally realized it was in their own best interest to build a multi-racial society as opposed to separation and domination. Both sides can win if they choose peace with justice. The simplest way to end the violence is to end the injustice.

Israelis have the power. The future is partly in their hands. If Israelis desire peace, they can move toward peace which I am certain will evoke a positive Palestinian response. For that to happen, Israel must stop its humiliation of Palestinians, the theft of Palestinian land, and the demolition of Palestinian homes. For there to be peace, Israelis will have to come to terms with their racism and accept Palestinians as fellow human beings and agree to live side by side with them.

Although it seems totally unfair, it is the oppressed people of the world who usually lead the way to peace and justice. It was the black people in South Africa, people like Nelson Mandela, who offered a way out for their oppressors, who led the way to freedom for both blacks and whites. Palestinians need to take the lead toward a new nonviolent future. That is already happening in At-Tuwani and throughout Palestine. That some Israelis are responding is a sign of hope. Reconciliation, rather than revenge, can lead to peace. The whole structure of fear and domination can be undermined by former enemies coming together to create a new reality, as illustrated by Combatants for Peace and Bereaved Families.

Is there hope? On a political level, I see little hope. The statements made by political leaders often seem unconnected with the real world on the ground. Vague promises mean little. Instead of governments taking concrete steps toward peace, the situation continues to deteriorate. Sadly, I have still not seen any evidence of either the Israeli or U.S. governments working toward peace. There was talk of disbanding settlement, but I have not seen this happening. The future is in God's hands.

The hills are turning green in At-Tuwani. The apricot trees are blooming. Life continues. There is hope.

1. *The Guardian*, September 15, 2003. Available at www.guardian.co.uk/world/2003/sep/15/comment.

Forming a Women's Cooperative

In the name of Allah, the most gracious, the most merciful. I was born in 1976, finished school in the eighth grade, and agreed to an arranged marriage. That meant moving from the city of Yatta with its conveniences to what I considered horrible conditions in the village of At-Tuwani, with no electricity, running water, school, or even a clinic. All that was very difficult for a sixteen-year-old girl. Now I am excited about life in At-Tuwani and all its possibilities.

The people in At-Tuwani and surrounding villages are very simple farmers and shepherds. They depend on their land and flocks, a life that, until recently, has been self-sufficient. Our land supported us and we felt secure. In 1982, there was an historical event that disturbed our secure conditions: the building of the Ma'on settlement on At-Tuwani land. That led to a series of aggressions against powerless people: the stealing of our lands, the blocking of our roads, and the attacks on our people. The result was the spread of poverty, fear, and insecurity.

I am interested in women's conditions and what effects these events have had on women directly. Women are suffering, not only from the occupation of our land, but also from traditional women's roles which have confined women to their homes, taking care of the children and helping in the farm work. Many of our women have been married under sixteen years of age, with no chance or legal right to education. Women have been suffering and voiceless.

With my simple education, I started to think of changing this condition, knowing that any activity of women to express their suffering and change conditions will face the opposition of tradition and the objections of men. In 2004, I began talking with a group of women about the possibility of forming a special women's cooperative to deal with the oppression of women. I also began to share my ideas with some of the men, including my husband, who was supportive. One man in particular in the village was especially helpful in convincing some of the village men that women also have rights and have an important role in the village. Some of these men gave their wives permission to join our newly formed women's cooperative.

Our first step was to collect the handiwork done by the women in the village and put them in an ancient stone house in the village. The goal was not only to preserve our heritage, but also to improve the economic base for women by making and selling our handicrafts.

Two months later, members of Christian Peacemaker Teams and Operation Dove arrived in the village and had a major impact on our way of life, not only in their support for women, but also in helping us get back some of the land stolen from us, being present during planting and harvest times, and helping make it possible for children to go to school.

Finally, I wish that peace will be present all over the world, and there will be a feeling of security for all people in the world. I hope women will be given all their rights in life. We give the praise to Allah.

Kiefah Adara
At-Tuwani
January 2007

GOLAN HEIGHTS

Sea of Galilee

Haifa

Nazareth

Mediterranean Sea

Jenin

Nablus

Jordan River

JORDAN

WEST BANK

Tel Aviv

Ramallah

Jericho

Jerusalem

Beit Jala

Bethlehem

ISRAEL

Gaza

Hebron

Dead Sea

At-Tuwani

GAZA STRIP

N
W   E
S

0   MILES   25

359

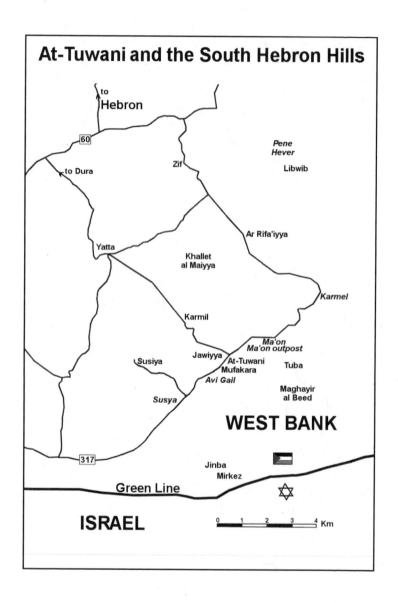

At-Tuwani and the South Hebron Hills

to
Hebron

60

to Dura

Zif

Pene
Hever

Libwib

Ar Rifa'iyya

Yatta

Khallet
al Maiyya

Karmel

Karmil

Ma'on
Ma'on outpost

Jawiyya

At-Tuwani
Mufakara

Tuba

Susiya

Avi Gail

Susya

Maghayir
al Beed

WEST BANK

317

Jinba
Mirkez

Green Line

ISRAEL

0   1   2   3   4 Km

Glossary

ACRI. The Association for Civil Rights in Israel. This Israeli human rights group has provided legal representation for the people of the South Hebron Hills.

Allah kareem. "God is generous." Muslims regularly repeat these words when something bad happens.

Civil Administration. This arm of the Israeli Military governs Palestinian life by being in charge of civilian affairs in the occupied territories.

Dibs. A molasses made from boiling down grape juice.

DCO. District Coordinating Office. Originally intended in the Oslo agreement for coordination between Palestinian police who were expected to take over police functions in areas placed under the Palestinian Authority and the Israeli military. These are the offices where the Israeli military administers the pass system. Palestinians must go to the DCO for travel permission, and they are taken to the DCO for questioning by Shabak.

Doves. Members of Operation Dove.

Eid al Adha. The feast of sacrifice. A feast to remember Abraham being willing to sacrifice his son, and the grace of God in saving his life. It takes place each year during the pilgrimage to Mecca.

Eid il Fitir. The feast at the end of the month of Ramadan.

ERM. Environmental Resource Management. A British aid group that helped pay for the clinic, cisterns, and toilets in the At-Tuwani area.

Fatah. The political party of Yassar Arafat.

Hajj. The Muslim pilgrimage to Mecca. Also a term of respect used for people who have made the pilgrimage.

Ha'aretz. One of the major Israeli newspapers.

Hamas. An Islamic resistance group that won the Palestinian election in January, 2006. The group runs a large humanitarian aid program. The military wing of Hamas has taken credit for some of the suicide bombings.

Haram. Forbidden, sinful.

IDF. Israeli Defense Forces. The Israeli military.

Ilhamdililah. The praise is to God. One of the most commonly used words in the Muslim world.

Insh'allah. If God wills. Muslims usually add these words when discussing anything in the future.

ISM. International Solidarity Movement. An organization that coordinates international volunteers for nonviolent action in support of the Palestinians.

IWPS. International Women's Peace Service. The group coordinates international women coming to stand in solidarity with Palestinian groups.

Machlube. A meat, rice, and vegetable dish. The word literally means "upside-down" because it is served on a big platter after the contents of a big pot are emptied upside-down on the platter.

Machsom. The Hebrew word for checkpoint or roadblock. The Palestinians sometimes use this Hebrew word when referring to roadblocks constructed by the Israeli military.

OCHA. The Office for the Coordination of Humanitarian Affairs, an arm of the United Nations which coordinates the humanitarian activities of various NGOs working in the occupied territories and monitors obstacles to humanitarian activities.

Operation Dove. An Italian Catholic organization similar to Christian Peacemaker Teams, sponsored by the Community of Pope John XXIII. The international peace team in At-Tuwani is a joint project of Operation Dove and CPT.

Ramadan. The Muslim month of fasting.

Refuseniks. Israelis who refuse to do military duty.

Taboon bread. A delicious bread baked on rocks heated with fire.

TIPH. Temporary International Presence in Hebron. The Hebron Accords provided for international observers in Hebron from Norway, Sweden, Denmark, Switzerland, Italy, and Turkey.

Salaam Alykum. Peace be unto you. A common Muslim greeting.

Shabak. Intelligence wing of the Israeli Army. Recruits Palestinian informers through threats and intimidation.

Shema. The Jewish confession of faith repeated in every Jewish worship service: "Hear O Israel, the Lord your God is one."

Shabbat. Saturday, the Jewish Sabbath.

Ta'ayush. One of the Israeli peace groups that we work with. Ta'ayush has a special commitment to the people of the South Hebron Hills.

The Author

Art Gish has been active in peace and social justice work for the past fifty years, beginning with work as a conscientious objector with Brethren Volunteer Service in Europe (1958-60). He worked in the Civil Rights Movement in the 1960s, and has actively opposed United States involvement in wars since his youth. He has been working with Christian Peacemaker Teams in the Middle East since 1995.

Born and raised on a farm in Lancaster County, Pennsylvania, Gish was reared in the Church of the Brethren. He and his wife, Peggy Faw Gish, are members of New Covenant Fellowship, a communal farm near Athens, Ohio.

Gish is the author of *The New Left and Christian Radicalism* (Eerdmans, 1970), *Beyond the Rat Race* (Herald Press, 1972), *Living in Christian Community* (Herald Press, 1979), and *Hebron Journal: Stories of Nonviolent Peacemaking* (Herald Press, 2001).